BALANCE

THE ECONOMICS OF GREAT POWERS FROM ANCIENT ROME TO MODERN AMERICA

GLENN HUBBARD
AND TIM KANE

SIMON & SCHUSTER

NEW YORK   LONDON   TORONTO   SYDNEY   NEW DELHI

Simon & Schuster
1230 Avenue of the Americas
New York, NY 10020

Copyright © 2013 by Glenn Hubbard and Tim Kane

All rights reserved, including the right to reproduce this book
or portions thereof in any form whatsoever. For information address
Simon & Schuster Subsidiary Rights Department,
1230 Avenue of the Americas, New York, NY 10020.

First Simon & Schuster hardcover edition May 2013

SIMON & SCHUSTER and colophon are
registered trademarks of Simon & Schuster, Inc.

For information about special discounts for bulk purchases, please contact
Simon & Schuster Special Sales at 1-866-506-1949
or business@simonandschuster.com.

The Simon & Schuster Speakers Bureau can bring authors to your live event.
For more information or to book an event, contact
the Simon & Schuster Speakers Bureau at 1-866-248-3049
or visit our website at www.simonspeakers.com.

Designed by Ruth Lee-Mui
Maps by Jeffrey L. Ward

Manufactured in the United States of America

1   3   5   7   9   10   8   6   4   2

Library of Congress Control No.: 2013003803

ISBN 978-1-4767-0025-0
ISBN 978-1-4767-0027-4 (ebook)

ACKNOWLEDGMENTS

I n preparing this book, we have received assistance from many quarters. Our agent, Andrew Wylie, was instrumental in encouraging us to imagine the book in the first place, and we were fortunate to have the team at Simon & Schuster, led by editor Ben Loehnen, help craft it. Our highest acknowledgment and thanks go to research assistance from Naoko Funatsu, Juliette Ginsberg, Emily Ordun, Tim Marr, Evelyn Smith, and Brad Strang. Wilhelmina Sanford made our collaboration work smoothly by coordinating conversations, meetings, and edits no matter how late in the day we asked for her help.

Dedicated to our families and our nation's future.

CONTENTS

BALANCE

1

INTRODUCTION

And on the pedestal these words appear:

> *"My name is Ozymandias, King of Kings:*
> *Look on my works, ye mighty, and despair!"*
> *Nothing beside remains. Round the decay*
> *Of that colossal wreck, boundless and bare,*
> *The lone and level sands stretch far away.*
>
> — Percy Bysshe Shelley, from "Ozymandias"

Human life one hundred years ago, on the eve of the First World War, was dramatically and measurably worse than it is now. The average annual income of a person in Western Europe was $3,077, and only a thousand dollars higher in England and America.[1] No one had televisions or antibiotics in 1913, let alone computers. A thousand years ago, life was more miserable still. The average annual income in any region of the world in A.D. 1000 is estimated to have been the equivalent of four hundred dollars, except in northeast Asia, where it was fifty dollars higher. Human life was generally "nasty, brutish, and short," as the philosophers said, perhaps more so in cities than in the state of nature. But two thousand years ago, human life was rich and happy in a civilization that had emerged like an island in the sea of historical misery. The emperor Caesar Augustus presided from his modest house on the Palatine hill over the marbled city of Rome and the interlinked empire of the same name. After four prosperous decades of rule by Augustus, which had followed a century of civil wars, A.D. 13 was the last full year Rome enjoyed before his death. Historians credit Augustus with carving a stable and prosperous empire in the marble of time, a Pax Romana that endured for centuries. Yet Rome did not, perhaps could not, last forever. Three centuries of Roman leaders after Augustus could not cure the relentless stagnation of Roman politics and erosion of its economic vitality. Why?

This book is not about *empire,* but about *economic* data and the hard facts of Great Powers in human history. We stand on the shoulders of historians who have perceived this subject matter as a narrative of great leaders, great armies, and great cultures. All were mortal. Thanks to countless scholars, our generation can understand this puzzle better than ever before. What our book aspires to add comes from our peculiar domain of economics, which by nature sees the world in a most unnatural way. We see "supply" and "demand" and "incentives" and "constraints" in markets not just for goods and services, but also markets for prestige, security, and political power.

A quarter century ago, the Yale historian Paul Kennedy penned an authoritative survey of the deeper forces shaping world affairs, in *The Rise and Fall of the Great Powers,* which introduced readers to the insight that *relative* economic strength was the main foundation for military and diplomatic forces that dominate most traditional narratives.[2] The explosion of unparalleled historical data in recent years gives us an opportunity to reexamine the Great Powers.

Consider imperial Rome, which many do now as a unipolar and intellectual forefather of Pax Americana in our time. The popular imagination sees Germanic tribes massed by the thousands on the far side of the Danube River, clanging their battle axes and shields, readying to invade. In the end, we have been told, Great Powers succumb to barbarian hordes. This image echoes through history, as far back as the three hundred Spartans fighting against the Persian armies at the "hot gates" of Thermopylae, to the noble British resisting the dark continent of fascism, even to our modern struggle against jihadi terrorists. This heroic image must be recognized as an irresistible illusion. Military defeat is, of course, a capstone on the decline of Great Powers, but history errs in confusing symptom with cause. Recoil at the idea that mundane currencies, debt notes, and productivity ratios determine the future. But, at the very least, agree that the truth about the fate of nations is not swords, not plowshares, but a combination of the two.

The Battle of Adrianople on August 9, A.D. 378, is just as good a date as any to mark the turning point in Rome's decline and fall. The invading Goths were cornered near the city of Adrianople (located near the modern city of Edirne, Turkey) by Roman forces led personally by Emperor Valens. He wanted to repel the foreigners once and for all. On that day, however, the Romans did more than lose the battle; they were routed. Emperor Valens was killed in battle along with most top officers, tribunes, and soldiers. Rome's vulnerability sparked a century of Germanic invasions that pushed further against the imperial border until the great city itself fell.

That account of the battle is more or less correct, but it misses the point. For one, Roman society had been rotting internally, not just for decades, but for *centuries,* before Valens died in battle. More importantly, that story mistakes why the Goths were fighting in the first place. They were rebelling against their Roman *allies,* not invading, and only because pillage was their only recourse to starvation. In the year 376, these Gothic tribes were fleeing the Huns and were allowed to settle south of Danube as new allies of the Roman army. But Valens inadequately supplied them with promised land and provisions, then sent them on a death march to a different city, where they were denied entry. It is no surprise the Goths rebelled, but their success proved how weak the empire had become. This chapter of history affirms that the decline of Rome, contra Kennedy, was caused not by imperial overstretch or any kind of external threat. It shows, as does history from ancient empires to modern Europe, that the existential threat to great civilizations is less barbarians at the gates than self-inflicted *economic* imbalance within.

Overcentralization of political power, for example, is a common factor in imperial decline, usually a century or more after the centralization is enacted. Many Westerners know the story of the seven epic voyages of Admiral Zheng He (Cheng Ho). A century before Christopher Columbus discovered the New World, the Ming empire could have dominated the world if it had not abruptly turned inward in the middle of the fifteenth century. Few realize how dramatic and economic in nature the story is. The Yongle emperor Zhu Di ruled from 1402 to 1424, and ordered the restrictive trade policies of the Confucian technocrats to be reversed. He opened trade missions with Japan, the Philippines, India, and beyond. He funded a strong navy that stamped out piracy. Then, thanks to centralization of authority, Zhu Di's successor closed off trade, which was reversed by the next emperor, then reversed again by the next. The great Ming treasure fleet was ultimately destroyed in harbor at the emperor's own command. To confirm the message that the act symbolized, imperial decrees made the construction of oceangoing ships punishable by death.

Empires and nations often lose their balance without understanding the tectonic economic forces in motion. On the other hand, rulers are often unable to adapt even when they understand those forces, an eerie and fascinating parallel to the Great Powers in our time. Imperial Spanish rulers went bankrupt again and again, even as shiploads of New World silver flooded Spain. They remained oblivious to the productivity revolution that empowered their rivals. Great Britain panicked in 1900, as European rivals caught up to its industrial might. Partially in denial of relative decline, Great Britain could not imagine expanding the level of potential engagement with its subject territories beyond free trade.

Indeed, if America's global economic power ends, it will almost surely be due to a loss of fiscal balance that forces it down the well-worn path of history's Great Powers. The cracks we hear—a minor credit warning from Moody's or acrimonious political fights over the debt ceiling—confirm that the only existential threat facing America is from America itself.

Once we look at history through the lens of economics, we can never look back. History becomes much more than a drama of personalities, revealing a surprising rhythm of policy choices that seem irrational with the benefit of hindsight. One theme in this book is that political institutions are often too slow to adapt to changing economic reality. The institutional focus of our theory of decline is neither original nor timely. Mancur Olson (1932–98) was a pioneer, particularly his *Rise and Decline of Nations,* published in 1982. The political scientist Francis Fukuyama, who rose to prominence with his prescient "The End of History" essay in 1989, has been leading scholarship in this area ever since.[3] And we are happy to find common cause with Daron Acemoglu's and James Robinson's *Why Nations Fail,* the 2012 book that made their decades of academic research on economic institutions publicly accessible. Their book powerfully explains how "inclusive" institutions trump "extractive" ones in generating long-term economic growth, and the political roots of vital institutions like the rule of law and property rights.

What our book adds is a new way to *measure* economic power, that vague notion so often expressed in daily discourse but never well defined. We also examine how once-vibrant societies become politically and economically stagnant, rather than how they grow in the first place. The bulk of the book studies the Great Power imbalance, invariably economic. Finally, we use those lessons to focus on the pending imbalance of the United States; we do so not just as scholars but as policy advisers.

AMERICA'S EXISTENTIAL THREAT IS FISCAL

America today faces a financial imbalance, threatening its world leadership as an economy and a power. The threat comes not from foreign enemies but from a breakdown in long-term fiscal discipline. In recent years, the budget deficit has grown to roughly $1 trillion every year, the mathematical result after $3 trillion in expenditures are matched by only $2 trillion in tax revenues, roughly. Readers are no doubt aware that what we are describing is a much bigger dilemma than the so-called fiscal cliff, the nickname of the political standoff that ended 2012 but was really just a minor chapter in story that has grown more dire over the past four decades.

Recent research by Harvard economists Carmen Reinhart and Kenneth Rogoff suggests that countries with a total debt to gross domestic product (GDP) ratio that exceeds 90 percent face a tipping point of decline.[4] And the United States, with annual deficits that now amount to 5–10 percent of annual GDP and a debt-to-GDP ratio of around 70 percent, is rapidly heading toward a critical level of imbalance. That is a consensus—of *economists*. The consensus of *politicians* is a rather different kind, a bipartisan unwillingness to take action, arguing that "deficits don't matter" and/or that deficits should be fixed . . . later (after the current recession/election/drought/insert-crisis-here has passed in a few years). Indeed, the United States has been getting away with runaway national debt at relatively low interest rates in recent years only because of the perverse contrast with European sovereign debts that are even more precarious. America is the debtor of last resort, the safe haven in a global glut of indebted sovereigns.

Where consensus is lacking among economists as well as politicians is how to bridge the fiscal gap. There are countless plans to fix the budget, coming from various blue-ribbon panels, notably the Bowles-Simpson commission, created in 2010 by President Obama. There have been hundreds of similar plans proposed ever since Ronald Reagan spotlighted the issue during the 1980 presidential election. And while we could proffer another solution, it is no longer credible to believe that even the best economic plan will be a solution. It is not just the economy that is imbalanced. Runaway budget deficits are not a math problem. They are a process problem, a *political* problem.

Many plans to fix the U.S. federal budget would work in a technical sense, but none can be enacted. Our political institutions cannot accommodate them. Dealing with this threat requires a change in Washington. The stagnancy of U.S. *politics* is the focus of *It's Even Worse Than It Looks: How the American Constitutional System Collided with the New Politics of Extremism,* by political scientists Thomas E. Mann and Norman J. Ornstein. Mann and Ornstein finger political polarization as the core dilemma, although we disagree with their blaming one party more than the other, but they seem unaware that the field of institutional economics has chronicled historical patterns of stagnation since long before the American political parties existed.

Institutions are the "rules of the game" that guide our aggregate behavior. One example of an economic institution is the patent, which a government issues to an inventor to protect her idea from being copied by anyone without her permission. Think of a patent as a property right over something intangible. The more fundamental institutions are political, such as the idea of "checks and balances" between government executives who administer and enforce the law and the legislators who make it. Sometimes a behavior emerges that is not well checked by existing rules, and this rule-bending can usually only be stopped by new rules.

A useful analogy to the dilemma of rule-bending comes from

professional sports. Some sports, notably soccer and baseball, tend to be conservative, allowing few rule changes. In contrast, American football and basketball have been much more open to revising their rules. The evolution of play in those games has made them popular—and economically successful.

Football players have long known that injuring an opposing quarterback can ruin the opposing team's chance of winning. In response, the National Football League (NFL) has tweaked its rules to protect the players. "Roughing the passer" after the ball has left the quarterback's hands became a penalty in 1938. Helmets became mandatory in the NFL in 1943. Low "chop" blocks have been barred with incessant new rules over the decades. But as the blocking behavior evolved, the rules evolved as well. Recently, a rash of helmet-to-helmet and concussive hits has proved hard to stamp out by existing rules. The NFL is working to update its rulebook and may even require new kinds of helmets.[5]

The same behavior-rule-behavior dance happens with nations and economies. This interaction of economics and politics can be viewed as a story of trial and error, with governments competing over time to find the right balance of laws and behaviors that will yield maximum prosperity with minimum instability. Unfortunately, the consequences of new behaviors (price inflation, for example, from debasing one's coinage) are often not well understood until it is too late. Acemoglu and Robinson don't agree with what they call the "ignorance theory"—that leaders simply don't understand adverse consequences of policies—but the authors limited that critique to modern development.[6] International aid agencies have missions based on the assumption that foreign rulers are ignorant rather than malicious. That assumption is naïve and counterproductive, we agree. But it has little application to Rome in A.D. 301.

Even when ignorance is not a factor, perverse incentives are. Presidents and legislators often know good policy from bad, but their incentives are short-term reelection rather than long-term national growth, a specific problem for representative democracies. Trade policy offers a useful lesson. When nations agree to open their borders with "free" trade agreements by lowering tariffs, many industries lobby for nontariff barriers (for restrictions on imported beef in Japan or genetically modified crops in Europe). Even though economists since Adam Smith have argued that mercantilism is unproductive, the lure of managed trade is a siren song during election season. The policy may be irrational economically while perfectly rational politically.

That economic-political tension in a democracy is normal, and usually not economically life-threatening. Statesmanship can counterbalance selfish politics. Even when politics overwhelms good policy, international competition tends to tip the balance for the better. (Which nation makes it easiest to open a new business in the fewest days and with the lightest paperwork? Which nations welcome innovative and entrepreneurial immigrants?) But something about the modern welfare state, the so-called entitlement state, has corrupted the balance between good economics and bad politics.

THE ENTITLEMENT STATE

A new behavior of modern nations has emerged in the past few decades, unchecked by wise leadership or by international competition. Its symptom is the rising fiscal imbalance in nearly every advanced industrial economy, meaning annual deficits that accumulate into a pool of debt. The lowest recent level of U.S. debt held by the public relative to the size of the economy was 23.9 percent of GDP in 1974, which in real dollars was $344 billion. Today, the level is around 75 percent of GDP, or $11,578 billion (note: this figure does not include debt held in government accounts).[7] By contrast, the European Central Bank reports that 2010 debt among member countries ranged from 119 percent of GDP in Italy to 143 percent in Greece and 6.6 percent in Estonia.[8] Interest payment on higher debt levels is a major expenditure category that crowds out normal government functions if interest rates rise. That is, higher interest payments reduce governments' ability to fund defense research or education.

The U.S. debt level is alarming today because the pattern of ballooning budget deficits is occurring during *peacetime* (although two wars are winding down), an unprecedented departure from historical norms. Figure 1 shows the debt-to-GDP ratio over the course of constitutional history. Until the 1970s, the ratio generally declined during peacetime and spiked only during wartime. Five episodes of spiking debt established the norm—the Revolutionary War debt, Civil War debt, World

War I debt, Great Depression debt, and World War II debt. Although the Great Depression debt spike was not caused by war, as the other episodes were, the pattern was similar—a sudden increase in annual fiscal deficits that approached 10 percent of GDP per year, followed by a gradual decline in total debt. Debt reduction occurred not because debt principal was paid down but rather because growth in the economy outpaced the debt. The outlier in America's debt episodes is the sixth one, in play since the middle of the 1970s. This episode is different in its features, neither sudden nor caused by a military crisis. We are not ignoring the wars in the Middle East during this era, but their total cost is a fraction of previous major wars. Besides, annual U.S. defense spending fell from 10 percent of GDP in the 1950s and 1960s to 6 percent in the 1970s and 1980s to 4 percent or less ever since.

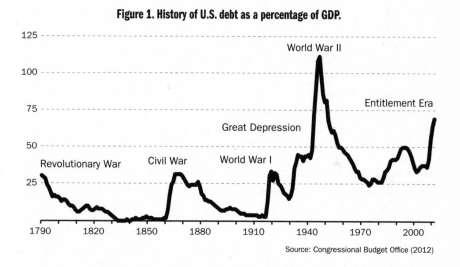

Figure 1. History of U.S. debt as a percentage of GDP.

Source: Congressional Budget Office (2012)

What changed? Entitlement spending. In 1971, annual spending on Medicare and Medicaid was $11 billion, which was 1 percent of GDP. In 2010, those two programs cost $793 billion, or 5.5 percent of GDP. Add in Social Security and today these big three entitlements equal more than 10 percent of the nation's economic output. According to the Congressional Budget Office's (CBO) June 2011 Long-Term Budget Outlook,[9] entitlement spending will grow to 15 percent of GDP over the next two decades. This spending along with interest payments on the debt and entitlement spending will absorb all expected tax revenue under current tax policy. It wouldn't be wrong to call this scenario the entitlement bubble.

Entitlement implies a form of government spending to which all common citizens are guaranteed depending on circumstances, unlike discretionary spending, which can be lowered more easily (such as dollars budgeted for defense, highways, or space exploration). Table 1 shows how entitlement expenditures have grown in contrast to declining spending on defense. According to official records, two times more federal funds were spent on physical resources (energy and transportation) in 1943 and 1944 than on human resources (education, health, welfare, and all entitlement programs), a 2:1 ratio. In 1970, the ratio had reversed to 1:5. In 2000, the ratio had shifted further to 1:15, and in 2010 it was 1:27. Projections of how this ratio will crowd out infrastructure investments are easy to imagine.

TABLE 1. FEDERAL EXPENDITURES AS A PERCENTAGE OF GDP

	National defense	Social Security	Medicare	Health (Medicaid)	Income security
1940s	17.0	0.1		0.1	1.1
1950s	10.4	1.1		0.1	1.3
1960s	8.7	2.6	0.4	0.3	1.5
1970s	5.9	3.8	0.8	0.8	2.6
1980s	5.8	4.6	1.5	0.9	3.1
1990s	4.0	4.2	1.9	1.3	2.7
2000s	3.8	4.4	2.4	1.9	2.9
2010s (est.)	4.2	4.6	3.0	2.5	3.4

Source: Office of Management and Budget, 2013 budget, Table 3.1.

The larger question then: *How* did this happen? The introduction of Medicare in 1965 and structural reforms to Social Security in 1972 made binding and growing expenditure commitments into the long-term future, beyond the horizon of political consequences. These entitlement promises, we can see clearly in retrospect, expanded beyond the obligations assumed by the creators of these programs. Promises of escalating future entitlements as the benefits were tweaked and excesses left in place have yielded obvious political payoffs as the years have gone by. Even now, after the results of the 2012 election are in, some of the first interviews of elected officials center on promises not to change the growth rates in entitlement programs. We are not talking about cuts. We are talking about slowing the growth of programs with technical adjustments, but this policy discussion is, to put it mildly, politically charged.

Unfortunately, the economy cannot outpace the entitlement problem through faster growth in the economy. As the CBO makes clear, "Without significant changes in government policy, [entitlement growth and medical cost inflation] will boost federal outlays sharply relative to GDP in coming decades under any plausible assumptions." [10] Higher tax rates could be tried, but many Republicans and most Democrats misunderstand the limits of more taxation, which the CBO hints would likely create disincentives that have not been included in their forecasts. Despite the political dilemma, it is rare for any president or legislator to offer real, here-and-now cuts, let alone structural changes. The political process has neutered the legislative process in reacting to economic forces.

THE DEMOCRACY PARADOX

If the fiscal dilemma the United States has worked itself into is easy to trace to its policy origins, a solution should also be easy to pinpoint, no? The symptoms and even proximate causes of the debt crises for nearly every Western nation are well known, yet solutions are elusive. Proposing plans to fix the programs themselves are almost irrelevant, or worse, are excuses for inaction. It is the political structures that enable and defend the entitlement bubble that need attention and reform. The rules of the political game must change.

Many rule changes are controversial when first recommended, but become widely acclaimed and later taken for granted. In the game of American football, the forward pass was illegal until 1906, when none other than Theodore Roosevelt urged reform.[11] Eighteen players had died and another 159 were maimed in the previous year. Likewise, the three-point shot in basketball was controversial when first used in a game between Fordham and Columbia in 1945, but it opened the game and leveled the playing field.

In the United States, the Constitution is the ultimate institution—the hierarchy of rules. For centuries its political-fiscal structure worked well. New economic challenges are historically not well understood by the existing politics—inflation in imperial Rome, technological regress in Ming China, mercantilism in eighteenth-century Spain, as we explain later in this book. In each case of Great Power decline, the historical record shows that rulers did what seemed to make sense in the short term but were often hostile to long-term growth. Modern legislators, we believe, are ignorant of the nature of debt risk. It is perhaps a willful ignorance, but the small-percentage risk of a catastrophic bubble collapse makes one by definition impossible to foresee. What we need to blame are the political rules, not the political rulers.

Fortunately for the United States, the Founding Fathers anticipated the unanticipated, and crafted a Constitution that could be amended to defend the nation against future threats. Even during the ratification of the document in 1787, the states decided to amend the document with no fewer than ten additions, which we know as the Bill of Rights. The people have amended the Constitution seventeen times since then, about once every fifteen years. The last amendment was in 1992.

The founders recognized that having rulers for long terms could breed tyranny, but too short a term in office could hinder competence and patience. Their remedy was terms of varying lengths, of two, four, and six years for the House of Representatives, presidency, and Senate, respectively, but crucially with no limit on the number of terms that could be served. A norm developed for individuals to serve no more than two presidential terms—a tradition established by George Washington. The two-term norm held for a century and a half, until Franklin Roosevelt shattered it. Many Americans voted for President Roosevelt during the critical years of the Great Depression. He was elected to his fourth term in 1944, a few months after the Allied invasion at Normandy during World War II. Later, a formal rule was proposed to require a de jure two-term limit on future presidents. It was adopted in 1951 as the Twenty-Second Amendment, less than six years after President Roosevelt died.

The entitlement dilemma mirrors Roosevelt's breaking of the two-term presidential norm. Budget balance during peacetime was the American norm for almost two centuries. The existing political institutions supported this outcome. But the fiscal consequences of entitlement expenditures were larger and longer than the politicians who created those programs realized. Understandably, early efforts to fix entitlements misdiagnosed the problem, but now we know that the institutions of American democracy have proven inadequate at self-correction.

America could change the rules of the budgetary game, leaving no room for entitlements to balloon because of legislative passivity. One way to do so is through the passage of a fiscal amendment to the U.S. Constitution. Indeed, 70 percent of voters favor the idea of a balanced budget amendment,[12] though few economists have supported the specific ideas proposed in the 1980s, in 1995, and as recently as 2011. Although every serious analyst acknowledges the U.S. fiscal situation is unsustainable, a genuine threat to America's long-term economic vitality and power, this fix seems too draconian. It's as if we were Greek voters, expressing a strong preference for staying in the euro and also a strong preference against the austerity necessary to stay in the euro. Voters everywhere want to eat their cake and have it, too. This paradox defines a Great Power democracy in decline.

The peculiar stagnation of Western democracies, at first glance, is categorically different than the collapse of history's empires. Comparisons of A.D. 13 Rome and A.D. 2013 America are interesting but not taken all too seriously. Rome was an empire, after all. Our reading of history suggests this overconfidence of "modern" differentness is just another symptom in common. Great Power decline almost always follows a template: denying the internal nature of stagnation, centralizing power, and shortchanging the future to overspend on the present.

ROAD MAP

Before turning to the case studies, the next two chapters describe our theory of Great Power decline. Chapter 2 presents our novel approach to measuring power, which we think is an approach superior to the normal, vague language one finds in this literature. Rather than present a truckload of varied statistics, we put forward an algorithm that computes economic power in a hard but understandable way. It builds on a history of economic measurement of national power that stretches from modern theories of growth to pioneers of economic measurement in England a full century before Adam Smith published his *Inquiry into the Wealth of Nations*. Chapter 3 shifts from the hard data about power to consider the relatively new field of behavioral economics. We apply the theories of individual behaviors of patience and loss aversion to collective national action and the behavioral impact of rules on the largest scale.

The case studies were a challenge. Which Great Powers should we select for a book of economic challenges such as this one? Rome was essential, and it is the subject of Chapter 2. Ming China was also essential, and though some readers may be familiar with the stories of Zheng He's treasure ships, digging into China's economic history gives us the opportunity to present some counterintuitive observations that should challenge the preconceptions of even the best-read readers. We wanted to pick case studies that challenged our theory, as well as those cases that were unavoidable. Imperial Spain is fascinating. Its repeated bankruptcies and failed effort to dominate Europe embody the triumph of militaristic thinking over settling for mere prosperity. The history of Ottoman Turkey is unknown to many Americans, but Chapter 7 may have more lessons for America than any other Great Power. In Chapter 8 we retell Japan's trajectory since the Meiji Restoration of 1868, which is essential in understanding the model of how many developing countries have developed ever since. Chapters 9 and 10 together cover Europe. Chapter 9 is about Great Britain, which we argue never really declined, but did fumble its potential, and not once, but twice. Chapter 10 covers the Eurozone; we also discuss the new science of measuring institutional quality. Our last case study is an odd duck: the state of California. At once richer and more powerful (per capita) than the United States as a whole, it has all of America's strengths and weakness, only more so—the polarization, the entitlements, the debt. The Golden State is a golden example.

We draw on each of the seven case studies when we turn to America in the final two chapters. We start Chapter 12 by looking at the polarization of politics, and we also dig much deeper into the political roots of the entitlement crisis. We have been surprised at the consensus of opinion that thinks political polarization can only be fixed by curbing free speech rights. Newspaper editorials—presumably the strongest free speech advocates—parrot the message of "campaign finance reform" while seemingly unaware of the control such reform surrenders to the two political parties (that is, monopolies). Polarization is a measurable phenomenon, and even a casual study finds that it started getting worse exactly when the courts restricted political speech rights in the 1970s. This timing coincides with the year we identify as America's turning point, institutionally, toward Great Power decline. Finally, Chapter 13 offers a plan to reform America's institutions, built on a careful study of the Constitution as well as democracy itself.

All nations fall, as the great economic historian and Nobel laureate Douglass North reminds us, when political institutions reveal their "inherent instability." Such thoughts can be needlessly fatalistic, though. Most nations are born and sustained by overcoming crises. Rome might have fallen one, three, or five centuries before it ultimately did. That lesson should not be lost on modern nations. Sweden showed the way large European welfare states can succeed with reforms. By contrast, Greece today seems determined to show how reform can fail. What has been lingering in Japan for two decades, haunting Europe in recent years, and now loose in the United States is the beginning, not the end, of a global fiscal storm.

Discussions of economic power are often loose, as if economic power is something that represents a yardstick against which the players are reshuffled every decade or so. Will China surpass America? Will Europe fall behind? Will Brazil always be the nation of tomorrow? We hope to show that the economic crisis at the beginning of the twenty-first century is a much bigger storm than most people realize. And slower, making it more dangerous. The whole world system is brittle, with demographics and debt compounding the risks. We should all recognize that when Great Powers of the past declined, rarely were they replaced by challengers. Rome fell, and the world went dark for a thousand years. The big question facing America and the Great Powers of our generation is whether we can learn from a newer, richer, more economic history in time to amend our broken ways.

2

THE ECONOMICS
OF GREAT POWER

Wealth, as Mr. Hobbes says, is power.

— Adam Smith

n 1992, Lester Thurow, then dean of the Massachusetts Institute of Technology's Sloan School of Management, warned in
his book *Head to Head* that the red-hot Japanese economy had
overtaken the United States. Compared to the postwar American
average GDP growth of 3 percent per year, Thurow and many others
pointed with alarm at Japan, which was growing almost twice as fast.
Its gross national product (GNP) per capita was "technically 22 percent
above the United States," he warned. Who could deny that America had
fallen behind? He cited the alarming numbers, from the trade imbalance
to the undersized research-and-development investments in America. In
a *Washington Post* op-ed, Thurow described the advantage of Japanese
companies: "In head-to-head competition with European or American
companies, its companies have been impossible to beat. Japan's market
share goes up, the rest of the world's goes down . . . no one is investing
more to secure future economic success." [1]

American newspaper editorialists and pundits worried that the economic model of the United States—whatever it was—had been incontrovertibly proven inferior to the Japanese model of managed capitalism, sometimes called Japan Inc. Yet almost before the ink was dry on the pages of Thurow's book, the Japanese economy stalled. Its recession was severe, led by the collapse of a massive Tokyo property bubble and followed by what Nobel laureate Paul Krugman called Japan's "lost decade." That decade has now become two.

Japanophobia was the 1980s version of *declinism,* the tendency of the public to see rivals abroad and failure within, even if both are illusions. This phenomenon has a long pedigree. Robert Kagan recently observed: "In every single decade since the end of World War II, Americans have worried about their declining influence and looked nervously as other powers seemed to be rising at their expense."[2] During most years of the Cold War, from 1945 to 1989, Americans feared that Soviet growth would propel the communist East past the capitalist West. Editorial pages around the country fretted that our morally superior system would fall behind the Soviet's relentless focus on materialist power. What an illusion it all turned out to be.

In what we might call the declinist genre, most books have a deservedly short shelf life. But one from the 1980s stood out and remains popular because it put some bite in with its bark. One might even say that Paul Kennedy changed the popular conception of history itself with his 1987 book, *The Rise and Fall of the Great Powers.* It had its warnings, to be sure, but it was much more than a declinist manifesto. Kennedy encouraged readers to think about history in economic terms. The book began with a careful explanation of the rise of the Western world, diverting to a lengthy description about Ming China on the second page, then long sections about the powerful Muslim world of the 1500s, before shifting back to the roots of the European "miracle"—meaning the relentless march of material progress that came along with the Renaissance, Reformation, and industrial revolution(s). Kennedy's greatest contribution may have been his emphasis on long-term, relative economic power:

> Similarly, the historical record suggests that there is a very clear connection *in the long run* between an individual Great Power's economic rise

and fall and its growth and decline as an important military power (or world empire). This, too, is hardly surprising, since it flows from two related facts. The first is that economic resources are necessary to support a large-scale military establishment. The second is that, so far as the international system is concerned, both wealth and power are always *relative* and should be seen as such.[3] (emphasis in original)

The cover art used for Kennedy's book tells a story in its own right. The original hardcover edition, published by Random House in 1987, shows three figures striding up and down the globe. In front is John Bull, personification of British power, descending from the globe. Mid-stride atop the globe is Uncle Sam, followed by an ascendant Japanese salaryman. The paperback version, first published in 1989, shows a different image, with five figures wearing national flag placards—Japan, Great Britain, China, America, and the Soviet Union—reaching for a floating or bouncing earth globe.

Kennedy's book made an impact, perhaps greater in the long term than in merely tempering the hysteria of the times. Soon after its publication, Moscow's empire dissolved and Tokyo's export engine imploded. "I got that wrong," Kennedy remarked during a 2010 interview with PBS when asked about the cover art.

Today the world focuses on the biggest version of the declinist threat. The new bogeyman is China. Its population is eight times that of Japan, and though its per capita income level starts from a far lower base, its growth rate seems even hotter. No time in history ever experienced an economic boom that compares to China at the dawn of the twenty-first century. Many see China's rise as an inevitable threat to American supremacy, but nobody knows for certain how the new rivalry will play out.

Economists tend to see the likely outcome differently than military strategists and historians. Modern consensus theories of economic growth suggest that the miracle economies of Asia (Japan after 1950, Korea after 1960, the Southeast Asian tigers after 1970, and China after 1980) *should be the norm*. The nondeveloping economies of Africa and Latin America are the puzzle. Because ideas flow freely, any economy should in theory be able to adopt existing technologies without paying for their initial discovery. The assembly line. The limited liability corporation. The law of supply and demand. It's all free. Any economy can adopt these freely and should then converge to the per capita income frontier. Because the frontier—what economists technically call the production possibilities frontier—has been defined more or less by the U.S. economy for more than a century, every other country in the world has the potential to grow much faster than the United States can. Economists call this claim the theory of convergence.

Bradford DeLong, an economist at the University of California, Berkeley, was one of the first scholars to debunk convergence theory, doing so in a 1988 journal article that pointed out that most countries had not seen their income levels move toward the path of convergence. Quite the contrary. While the richest countries have converged toward a higher income level, the majority of poorer countries have stagnated and diverged relative to the top, particularly in Africa and South America. A case can be made that convergence is happening over a longer time frame—through regional clubs, perhaps, or if the theory is assessed in terms of populations instead of countries (with populous China weighted with more people itself than the nearly five dozen nations of Africa). Nevertheless, the most that can be said is that the theory of convergence remains an unresolved and troubling puzzle for scholars, policymakers, and anyone concerned about poverty.

One part of the theory hasn't been debunked—the one concerning the growth trajectory of converging countries. Here the theory predicts that follower nations will *approach but not surpass* the leader, or the frontier. Many countries have approached the income per capita frontier defined by the United States, but none has surpassed it. This growth ceiling describes Japan's experience, where it seemed like its income would accelerate past the U.S. level but instead settled into a steady-state growth rate on par with that of the United States. Korea is following a similar path, roughly four decades behind Japan. We should anticipate that the experience of China will be the same as well—approach, not surpass. Economic development is ever faster in a wired world, that's true, but even the fastest-growing country will need a full generation to raise the quality of its human capital to the world standard.

Perhaps our prediction of China's not-so-scary growth trajectory lacks drama, though its economic fundamentalism may offend many observers. We might be wrong. History has yet to be written, after all. And in fairness, this narrative has gotten ahead of itself. Thinking carefully about the course of modern power relations requires a deeper examination than most popular accounts have made, and deeper in two ways. One, we should look deeper in time. The lessons of great power, particularly of hegemonic powers, have a small sample size and should be taken as broadly as historically possible. Second, we should look deeper analytically into the conception and measurement of economic power. For better or worse, *economists* are the protagonists in this story.

WHAT IS THE WEALTH OF A NATION?

What did Adam Smith, the great Scottish moral philosopher who is remembered as the first economist, mean when he wrote of "wealth" in his famous 1776 book, *An Inquiry into the Nature and Causes of the Wealth of Nations*? Common sense says that wealth is a stock of riches. A country with a large population and a large landmass, thick with natural resources of minerals, timber, and navigable rivers seems intuitively richer than its peers. It's hard to disagree that the country with the most gold and silver is the wealthiest of all.

Adam Smith disagreed. While the royal families of Europe compared their wealth in terms of gold, gems, and land, and while all their subjects dreamed of harvesting some sliver of relative wealth, a few eccentric philosophers wondered if the engine of civilization was something different. Adam Smith may have been the most eccentric—and most insightful—but he was not the first to think this way.

A century before Smith published his great work, another Englishman was pioneering the idea of measuring a nation with numbers rather than words. His name was William Petty. In the service of Oliver Cromwell, England's Lord Protector during the 1650s, Petty was responsible for assessing and mapping all of Ireland in what was called the Down Survey, used partly to confiscate lands to pay for the conquering British army. As a founding member of the Royal Society, Petty applied his quantitative mindset to science, entrepreneurship, and accounting on behalf of English power. In 1665, Petty published *Verbum Sapienti* (Word to the Wise), which presented his estimates of English and

Welsh population, income, expenditure, land, and other assets in one integrated account. His posthumously published *Political Arithmetick* (written in 1676, but published in 1690) endeavored to use "numbers, weights, and measure" as the basis of social science to prove that his home country was not suffering from economic decline, as many then feared.[4] As he explains in the book's preface:

> The method I take to do this is not yet very usual; for instead of using only comparative and superlative words and intellectual arguments, I have taken the course to express myself in terms of numbers, weight, and measure; to use only arguments of sense, and to consider only such causes as have visible foundations in nature; leaving those that depend upon the mutable minds, opinions, appetites, and passions of particular men to the consideration of others: really professing myself as unable to speak satisfactorily upon those grounds (if they may be called grounds) as to foretell the cast of a die.[5]

The theme of *Political Arithmetick* is simple. It is an argument that the Netherlands during that era was more powerful than France. Even though the French population was ten times larger, its merchant fleet was nine times smaller. Petty also noted Dutch superiority in foreign trade (both imports and exports), foreign assets, labor specialization, urbanization, and more. The only economic metric smaller in the Netherlands was its rate of interest on capital, which was then half that of France, a sign of the deeper financial markets in Amsterdam.

Adam Smith combined Petty's lessons about quantitative precision with insights of the French "physiocrats" that the important aspect of power is economic production during a given time. Smith opens his *Wealth of Nations* with the observation that the "annual labour of every nation" (an interesting concept) is the basis of that nation's annual consumption. Observing that one aggregate measure on a national scale will always equal another, known mathematically as an identity, is a profound insight. His interpretation, which celebrates the factors of production, represented a departure from the traditional mercantilist perspective, which viewed wealth as an accumulated fund. Smith recognized that the mercantilist view of wealth, measured as a stock rather than a flow, was not a comprehensive picture of a nation's power, let alone of its potential for growth. Spain may have more gold and raw materials than France in a given year, yet be far less powerful. How so? The stronger nation is the one that can produce more weapons and soldiers, not the one that has more gold to hire mercenaries. Eventually, that stock of gold will empty.

Imagine two neighboring farmers, Fred and George, who receive equally sized plots of land from their father. George has little grain stored (and little money on hand), while Fred's granaries are overflowing and he has a stash of gold coins as well. George, however, has more land under cultivation for the coming year, enhanced by an irrigation system. Rather than save, George has sold his excess grain and invested all his cash, even purchasing fertilizers and a new tractor. Which farmer is richer? Economists today would say that Fred's stock of wealth creates an illusion of greater prosperity, and that the stronger farm has more investment and thereby potential for a much higher flow of grain production in future harvests. George wins. Or as Sir William Petty wrote: "A small country and few people may be equivalent in wealth and strength to a far greater people and territory."

During the two centuries after Petty's groundbreaking work, other philosophers and bureaucrats continued to advance the measurement of national productivity. The hunger of English sovereigns for tax revenue drove much of the interest, though that effort was often clouded by the government's desire for secrecy. The economist Angus Maddison relayed an anecdote about a "pioneer of macromeasurement," Gregory King (1648–1712), who composed exquisitely detailed accounts of British fiscal numbers unlike anything previously assembled. Because these metrics were new and sensitive, considered practically state secrets, King refused to take the risk of publishing them.[6]

Odd as it may seem to readers, the very idea of "GDP" was unknown in Adam Smith's day and would remain so for generations afterward. Progress toward such a comprehensive measure did not occur until well into the twentieth century. It was spurred by the emergence of an international economic crisis unlike anything before. Technological transformation from rail, automobiles, and telephony created a genuine boom in prosperity across the Western world. But the newly linked societies were as vulnerable as ever to excess debt, financial bubbles, and panics. The Great Depression in the 1930s blindsided political leaders, who realized only in hindsight how blind they were. They needed a sharper way to see their own economies.

At the time, indicators of national economic health consisted of rudimentary measures such as stock price indexes and freight car loads, and those were clearly inadequate. Even today, our sense of the unemployment rate during the Great Depression (the often-cited 25 percent) is based on speculative data. As the 1929 shock wave rippled through the banking sector in the United States, federal government officials began seeking a more detailed, dependable account of the whole society. Simon Kuznets, an economist at Harvard University, provided a pioneering model in a report to Congress in 1934. His model segregated the economy into its component parts, including labor, capital, and industry. Within the industrial sector, Kuznets provided further distinctions among branches of industry, including agriculture, transportation, and manufacturing. By analyzing changes in incomes that occurred in each of these sectors from 1929 to 1932, he gauged the complex impact the Great Depression had on the American economy. Kuznets's methodology allowed for a then-unprecedented degree of nuance in the government's ability to monitor and respond to economic fluctuations.[7] Washington's increased reliance upon centralized economic planning during World War II led to its demand for expenditure and product estimates alongside income accounts. By the close of the 1940s, Kuznets's model had evolved into the formal measure he called Gross National Product, or GNP,[8] the value of final goods and services produced by residents of a country during the course of a year. Kuznets later was awarded the Nobel Prize in Economics for this contribution.

No country had anything like Kuznets's GNP, but the idea spread quickly and freely to other capitals. Ten years after Kuznets made his report to the U.S. Congress, the approach was given a boost during the famous Bretton Woods Conference of 1944. At Bretton Woods, New Hampshire, the nascent United Nations convened and established institutions such as the International Monetary Fund (IMF) and the International Bank of Reconstruction and Development. As the IMF and the World Bank worked to stabilize the postwar international economy, they relied on GNP measures to monitor their efforts.[9] Additionally, the emergence of new third-world nations in the aftermath of the war encouraged the comparative study of economies, and Kuznets once again proved an innovator among his peers. In 1948, he developed a proposal for a quantitative framework, derived from national income accounts, that could be used to compare national economies. His framework served as both a resource and a check upon theoretical models of economic reform.[10]

The textbook[11] definition of GNP is much more sophisticated than many non-economists realize. GNP is the market value of all final goods and services produced by the citizens of a country during a given time, typically one year. "Value" is a tricky concept in itself, but in practice it means the transacted price. The key phrase in the definition of GNP is "final goods," which includes all new Ford Mustangs sold to customers, but does not include the value of the suppliers' parts sold to Ford (tires, engines, leather seats), nor does it include any used cars sold during the year. Neither used goods nor intermediate goods count as final. In 1991, the United States officially modified its main accounting measure from GNP to gross domestic product (GDP), the main difference being that GDP measures economic activity within a country's border, including products made by foreign-owned factories, but it does not include products from American-owned factories located abroad. The Honda plant in Ohio counts in GDP, for example, but not GNP.

Despite the revolutionary impact of GNP on our understanding of economic activity, it is still natural for people and even great leaders to fall back into the lazy definition of wealth in mercantilist terms, that is, as a stock of assets rather than as a flow of productivity. One school of thought in economics, known as the Austrian School, disparages the notion that any quantitative metrics can represent most aspects of the quality of life. And to be fair, measuring quality is a constant challenge for the professionals in government service who compose the GDP accounts (the Bureau of Economic Analysis in the United States). How do you measure the quality improvement of an iPhone 4S compared to an iPhone5, for instance? Other critics dislike that GDP is necessarily blind to non-economic values: human rights, environmental pollution, or human anxiety. Some people believe that the so-called slowdown in

GDP growth during the 1970s was caused largely by the implementation of environmental rules that made America's air and water so much cleaner.

MICROSCOPES AND TELESCOPES

If we think of the idea of gross domestic product as an economic microscope—offering a profoundly detailed view of living, breathing economies—what then is the telescope that lets us look back in time? The very idea of history, perhaps. People have always had narratives of the "way things were" to contrast with the "way things are." Benjamin Franklin, one of America's oldest and wisest Founding Fathers, often remarked how useful science was in changing the lives of common people for the better. But merely observing the march of progress is not what we mean by an economic telescope.

History is also filled with observations of the ebb and flow of economic prosperity and panic. Price inflations and deflations cut across all goods. These short-term ups and downs in the economy are understood as the *business cycle*, a cycle that has been a part of human history forever. In the nineteenth century, business cycles were more frequent and sharper than in modern times. They were also regionally focused, as economies were only lightly integrated by trade. Cycles happen for a variety of reasons—financial leverage, natural disasters, mass panics, or small technological disruptions in the circular flow of economic activity. The field of economics has been incrementally improving its understanding of the business cycle, but where economics failed for years was in its analysis of macro trends, especially before the invention of GDP. Making a distinction between a business cycle and long-term growth is difficult enough with good data, and all but impossible with shoddy data. A sudden decline in rail freight could represent a widespread recession or it could be consequence of some other new transportation system (the automobile, for example).

Simply looking back over centuries at all the new inventions mankind has made is a useful way to think about economic growth, but observing broad trends is not seeing economic growth in the modern sense. An economic telescope begins to be possible with accurate whole-nation measures of GDP *per year*. Take the nation's GDP in one year and compare it to the previous year, and a growth rate can be calculated. With that rate calculation, you can telescope change over decades. The final piece that clarifies the single-country telescope image is a correction for fluctuating prices, or inflation. Price inflation distorts the comparison of one year's economy to the next, but once economists control for prices across a large basket of goods, they can calculate what is technically called *real* economic growth. Apply that capacity across multiple years, especially when you smooth out the cyclical fluctuations within a decade, and a powerful image of long-term change comes into focus.

In recent decades, the growth rate became an important target for policymakers in its own right, regardless of the actual GDP level. Britain, for example, might be able to claim a superior economic policy model if its growth rate were double that of France's, while France could claim superiority so long as its overall level remained the highest in Europe.

Cross-country comparisons highlight a different problem: while it is simple enough to compare the U.S. dollar to the Japanese yen at any point in time, the exchange rate between currencies is highly unstable over time. That instability complicates GDP comparisons between countries over a decade, a year, or even an hour. Exchange rate fluctuations are so wild that international economic comparisons based on them are notoriously inaccurate.

In 1968, a team of economists at the University of Pennsylvania, working closely with the United Nations' International Comparison Program (ICP), began to formulate a methodology that would allow for comparisons across borders that transcend the volatile currency market. By 1982, this team, led by Robert Summers, Irving Kravis, and Alan Heston, had formulated a systematic method of benchmark comparisons that relied upon indexes of purchasing power parity (PPP). This PPP method uses a standardized basket of goods—housing, food items, clothing, computers, and so on—to adjust GDP per capita with respect to the cost of living within each nation. "The U.S. looks good by comparison when the International Monetary Fund adjusts for purchasing-power parity," says Harvard economist Edward Glaeser, "because American entrepreneurs from Sam Walton to Jeff Bezos have made our nation a bargain hunter's haven." [12] Thanks to PPP, the telescope can see across different countries as well as backward in time.

This Summers-Heston methodology (Kravis was less involved in its expansion over the following decades) gave birth to the Penn World Table (PWT), an enormous database of benchmark comparisons. The PWT is now on version 7.1, which includes data on 189 countries and territories across six decades [13] up to the year 2010. Since its inception, the PWT have provided an astounding degree of detail on comparative global development, which has, in turn, facilitated the emergence of landmark studies of macroeconomic history.

Consider the two charts showing different "telescope" views using PWT data. The first, Figure 2, shows absolute GDP per capita values for a handful of countries from 1950 to 2010 using 2005 dollars. [14] The second, Figure 3, shows the same data in percentage terms relative to the frontier established by the global productivity leader, which is the United States.

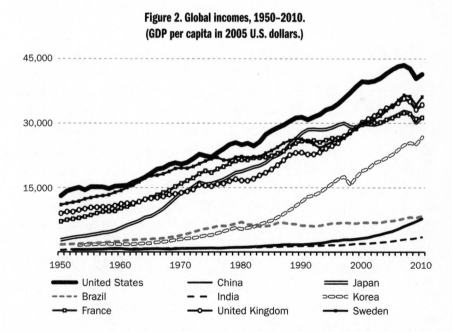

Figure 2. Global incomes, 1950–2010.
(GDP per capita in 2005 U.S. dollars.)

Source: Penn World Table, Mark 7.1

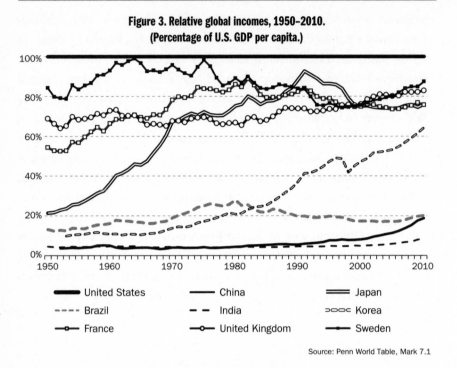

Figure 3. Relative global incomes, 1950–2010.
(Percentage of U.S. GDP per capita.)

Legend:
— United States   — China   ═══ Japan
---- Brazil   – – India   ᴐᴏᴏᴄ Korea
—□— France   —○— United Kingdom   —▪— Sweden

Source: Penn World Table, Mark 7.1

The PWT data enable us to generate pictures worth a thousand words. We can learn more from carefully studying these two pictures than from a truckload of punditry about the world economy. What stands out? First, the United States has a dominant position in terms of GDP per capita, whether in absolute or relative contexts. Second, the major European economies are bunched together. Third, Korea stands out as the single country making a transition to the upper tier of economies in this period. Fourth, China and India are much poorer than many realize, though China seems to be fast leaving India behind. And fifth, the Latin American economies appear stuck at 20–30 percent of top productivity.

What fascinates us in these charts is how quickly some countries approach the U.S. level, only to settle into a steady 75–80 percent range relative to the United States, a level at which major European economies have hovered for decades. This trend is remarkable, and it tells us something important about how the world economy works.

Growth in a poor economy is no miracle. Edward Prescott, another Nobel laureate in economics, once said that the Asia's growth is not at all surprising or miraculous. The tragedy is that other nations are not growing as fast as Korea and China. They should be, according to the theory of *convergence* discussed earlier, right? Why aren't they? Think of it this way: Leading economies such as the United States, Canada, France, and Germany can make progress only by slowly advancing through the thick forest of scientific ignorance, but other economies can run across the open field of established science and technology. For that matter, no Asian county needed to rediscover the laws of economics, accounting, or stock options.

Even so, catch-up growth only gets a country so far, as we can see by Japan's arrival in the "Eurozone" plateau. Rising above that 80 percent ceiling seems to require a different kind of economy, based on entrepreneurship instead of centrally managed capitalism. The puzzle is why so few economies are galloping across the 10–70 percent range. Why is convergence struggling?

Curiosity about this and similar questions motivated other economists to expand macroeconomic measures farther back in time. The PWT figures are based on near real-time measures of goods, prices, and output. It is much harder to come up with such details for the U.S. or British economy in 1930, let alone making estimates for 1800 or beyond. The challenge is even greater for non-industrial economies. Lucky for us all, historical accounting of this kind was the passion of British economist Angus Maddison. His book *The World Economy,* volumes 1 and 2 (2006), extends the comparative technique as far back as year A.D. 0 and includes an astoundingly detailed account of population dynamics, trade, GDP per capita, and more variables across two millennia.[15] Here in Table 2, for example, is an abridged reproduction of his Table 2-30, which compares the United Kingdom and India:

TABLE 2. COMPARATIVE ECONOMIC PERFORMANCE OF INDIA AND BRITAIN, 1600–1947 [16]

Per Capita GDP (1990 International Dollars)

	1600	1857	1947
India	550	520	618
United Kingdom	974	2,717	6,361

GDP (Million 1990 International Dollars)

	1600	1857	1947
India	74,250	118,040	255,852
United Kingdom	6,007	76,584	314,969

Today Maddison's exhaustive work is respected and admired. His data, published by the Organisation for Economic Co-operation and Development (OECD), stands alongside PWT as the other great economic telescope of our times. Developing the telescopes was a quiet twentieth-century revolution, largely unappreciated outside the world of scholarship. Before the existence of the Summers-Heston and Maddison telescopes, historians and journalists had to rely on ad hoc micro-data and anecdotes.

Twenty-five years after Paul Kennedy's *Rise and Fall of the Great Powers* was published, readers can see the world with a clarity that few could in 1987. Leaders in previous centuries could scarcely imagine this clear view, let alone have it. Thanks to the heroes of macromeasurement, the world will never be the same. Although the concepts of GNP, then GDP, then GDP per person, and growth have become so popular as to be ubiquitous, the progress of macromeasurement remains incomplete. The downside of *better* data is that they can be thought to be perfect data. In a dangerous world, mildly faulty data may seem like a nuisance rather than a threat, but bad data can cause phantom menaces.

KEEP FEAR ALIVE

Declinism has "emerged as the time's chic intellectual pose," says Daniel Gross, a well known contrarian thinker and former senior editor of *Newsweek*.[17] A quick glance at the nonfiction bestsellers list since the financial crisis of 2007–2009 confirms it. And declinism is the one reliable area of consensus in Washington, D.C. Pundits, politicians, and journalists from all along the political spectrum have been clamoring about the decline of American power in the twenty-first century. Thomas Friedman, the *New York Times'* insightful editorialist, laments that the United States has "[fallen] behind in the world it invented."[18] Fareed Zakaria makes similar predictions in his bestselling *Post-American World*. Meanwhile, the archconservative Patrick Buchanan wonders whether or not the nation can even "survive to 2025."[19] Comedy television star Stephen Colbert caught the nation's attention in 2010 when he organized a march on the National Mall to "Keep Fear Alive." Colbert, as usual, had a great sense of the national zeitgeist, a pessimism hardly in short supply (or demand) even after the Great Recession had technically ended. But Colbert would be the first to note that pessimism, declinism, and national fear-mongering have been around since long before the present.

As we described earlier, the declinist narrative always includes an antagonist, some exotic foreign power poised to overtake our nation's lagging economy. After the United States had defeated Nazi Germany and imperial Japan, the antagonist role fell to Joseph Stalin's Soviet Union, which loomed large and dangerous. The contrast of Soviet communism to American capitalism gave the declinist story an ideological edge, a specifically economic edge. Soviet acquisition of nuclear power in 1949, coupled with the fall of China to communism in that same year, and the launch of Sputnik in 1957, fanned American fears that this totalitarian economic ideology was leaving our military, our technology, our economy, and even our free and open democracy in the dust. Following on the heels of the Sputnik launch, President Dwight Eisenhower's science advisory committee warned that U.S. military expenditures and capabilities were set to fall far behind those of the Soviet Union. Specifically, the committee's Gaither Report said Russia's economy was "increasing half again as fast" as America's. Further, it warned that by 1980, the Soviets would have an economy more than half the size of ours, and it would continue to expand.[20]

Hindsight is twenty-twenty, as they say. As we all know now, Russia by 1980 posed no *economic* threat of the sort it had seemed to pose in the 1950s. Dire warnings about rapid Soviet growth rates, including the educated guesses emanating from the Central Intelligence Agency, proved to be inflated. According to Angus Maddison's data, growth of Soviet GDP during 1950–73 did indeed exceed U.S. growth average, 3.4 percent to 2.5 percent, but collapsed soon after. The Soviets grew by exhausting their physical resources and giving little concern to industrial pollution, worker rights, or investments in technology or workers' skills. In the end, Soviet leaders struggled to feed their growing population, which contracted as per capita incomes fell from $6,059 in 1973 to $4,626 in 2001. Those numbers from Maddison refer poignantly to the *former* Soviet Union. That Great Power, which George F. Kennan had wisely warned[21] Americans not to demonize, collapsed in 1991, just as the Berlin Wall had fallen in November 1989—barely thirty years after Eisenhower's advisers were sounding the alarm.[22]

As Russia fell from power, Japan rose to take its place as America's bogeyman. From 1970 to 1990, the United States ran trade deficits with Japan in nearly every advanced industry, including automobiles. Japan maintained these favorable trade balances even as the value of the yen doubled relative to the dollar and as Japanese goods became more expensive for Americans to consume. Japanese GDP per capita climbed ever closer to the U.S. benchmark, and Japanese annual growth rates soared to as high as 8 percent.[23] PWT estimates now indicate that Japan's postwar growth rate was above ten percent. Unlike the CIA's make-believe estimates of Soviet growth, the Japanese data were rock solid.

Then, as now, a flurry of academics and pundits warned of America's decline relative to this emerging superpower. Their criticisms not only disparaged American performance relative to Japan, but also questioned the basic assumptions underpinning the capitalist system. Lester Thurow's *Head to Head* boldly declared that "one hundred years from now, historians looking back are most apt to say that [this] century belonged to Japan." Thurow grounded his assertion in the belief that Japanese-style "producer economics," which emphasizes investment over consumption and a tight relationship between government and industry, had "major advantages" over American "consumer economics." But he also envisioned a heated economic battle with European powers, asserting that American market fundamentalism would prove inferior to the managed capitalism of the other advanced economies. James Fallows,

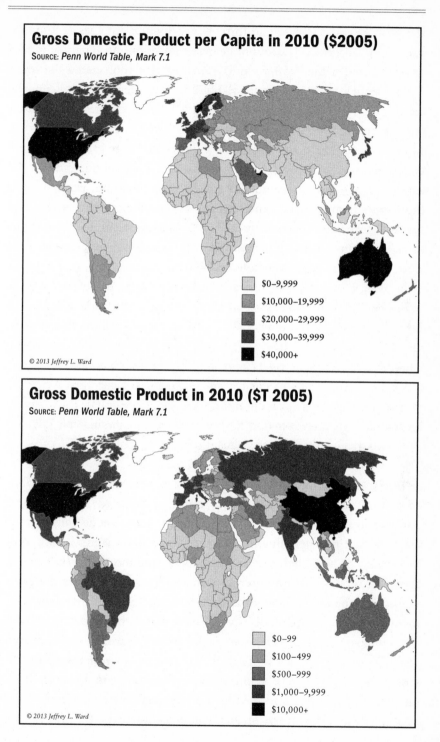

Gross Domestic Product per Capita in 2010 ($2005)

Source: *Penn World Table, Mark 7.1*

$0–9,999
$10,000–19,999
$20,000–29,999
$30,000–39,999
$40,000+

© 2013 Jeffrey L. Ward

Gross Domestic Product in 2010 ($T 2005)

Source: *Penn World Table, Mark 7.1*

$0–99
$100–499
$500–999
$1,000–9,999
$10,000+

© 2013 Jeffrey L. Ward

the great liberal observer and former speechwriter for President Jimmy Carter, joined Lester Thurow in heaping praise on the Japanese model. In an article for the *Atlantic* in 1993, when few appreciated the severity of Japan's burst real estate bubble, Fallows kept up the drumbeat touting its Asian system of capitalism. "When the American industry was doing everything right according to American economic theory, it began to collapse,"[24] he concluded. Fallows thundered that the American model—emphasizing efficiency among its competing firms—was inferior to the Japanese model of government guidance, which selected industrial champions in coordination with its cooperative keiretsu network of firms. The keiretsu firms had a ruthless desire to "win at any cost," he argued without irony, and win they did in industry after industry. American producers and economists were baffled, said Fallows. How was it that Japan had improved capitalism and left the United States behind? Fallows expanded his "Looking at the Sun" essay into a bestselling book of the same name in 1994. An excerpt worth noting:

> Because the Asian system as a whole will almost certainly be the main source of worldwide economic energy for the next generation, Western economies should make every effort to remain involved in it. The expansion of Western economies is likely to remain slow through the 1990s; East Asia's growth will be the main offsetting force.[25]

Within a year or two, the Fallows thesis was irrelevant, though it took until the end of the 1990s for everyone to realize it. In 1994, in America, which had supposedly lost its technological edge, the commercialization of this new thing called the World Wide Web was erupting. Netscape was born that year, as was Yahoo!, and the Microsoft browser as well. Skeptics said the Internet was a fad, but meanwhile the gritty reality of Japan's problems was becoming impossible to describe as a mere business cycle. The severity of Tokyo's asset bubble was no fluke. The collapse of the Nikkei stock index soon followed, and it remains roughly 80 percent below its peak value some two decades on. The American declinists were wrong again, with the supposed virtues of the alternative model revealed as vices. Keiretsu networks, now understood as a fancy name for cronyism, lock bad debts up in zombie firms.

To be fair, Fallows himself noted the fickle media interpretations of what was happening in Japan. The story was much bigger than a business cycle, he insisted. He was right on that point, and deserves credit for the strength of his convictions even after Japan had fallen into recession. Nonetheless, Fallows's long view of the clash of economic models was wrong. The best case is that he had the wrong models in mind. The worst case is that Fallows, like thousands of similarly smart thinkers, did not know how to measure economic power correctly.

CONFUSION AND CONSENSUS (A NECESSARY PRIMER ON GROWTH)

"Nobody Knows Where Economic Growth Comes From" is the title of a ten-sentence article published in the summer of 2012 in *Slate* by Matt Yglesias, a journalist who tends to make provocative claims laced with pithy insights.[26] Of course, Yglesias is right, but probably not in the way he intended. Saying that economists in the early twenty-first century do not understand what causes growth is like saying that doctors do not understand cancer, that meteorologists do not understand the weather, or that evolution is just a theory. While there are limits to our knowledge, let us not confuse humility with ignorance.

Unfortunately, economists use this rhetorical device as much as anyone else. Elhanan Helpman, a highly regarded Harvard economist, titled his 2004 book *The Mystery of Economic Growth*. William Easterly's book *The Elusive Quest for Growth* is another case in point. Taking their cue, the media describe growth in reverent tones as a "mystery" or worse, a "miracle." In contrast, Easterly's point is that so-called development experts at the World Bank too often try to force data correlations into policy causations, and fail tragically. Once national data became available, scholars confirmed a correlation between capital investment and growth rates, as Adam Smith and others had described. However, more nuanced recent research shows that the investment in capital doesn't lead to growth. Rather, it is growth that starts first, and investment follows.[27] If that seems confusing, consider the historical examples of communist Russia and China. Industrial investment was their obsession, yet growth was weak.

The kind of GDP *accounting* economists can now do has affirmed and debunked some theories, while generating new ones. The progress we've made in peeling the onion can be measured by two papers that laid down the half-dozen cutting-edge facts of growth. Nicholas Kaldor published a paper in 1957 that established six "stylized" facts about relationships among capital, labor, and output and became famous within the profession. These observations were known to be generally true, but not why they were true, effectively laying out a research agenda for the profession. It was a challenge met, contra Yglesias's statement. A half century later, Stanford economists Charles Jones and Paul Romer published an updated list of new Kaldor facts. While Kaldor's original facts were about tangible inputs such as labor and capital, and their relative ratios, the new Kaldor facts are about intangibles—scale of markets, long-term accelerations, institutional diversity, and human capital.

The great insight of growth economics in the late twentieth century is that most growth in national income cannot be accounted for by increases in measured physical inputs like capital and labor. The logic that twice the amount of steel in a bridge makes it twice as strong does not have an economic parallel. Twice as many workers plus twice as much capital in a nation might easily yield three times the output. The famous Solow equation used a term to account for the unexplained residual of growth. It is still called "technology" in most textbooks, but that word was really a euphemism for the measure of our ignorance. That's what Yglesias was getting at, but it's fair to say that we've started to understand more about how technology gets created in a macro sense than was known in the late 1960s. The brain gives birth to scientific ideas— hence the importance of human capital, education, and health, not to mention the social capital that celebrates intelligence and the organizational capital that enhances collaboration. The busy hands of ambitious entrepreneurs give birth to technology.

It's easy to understand why some commentators call growth mysterious: The phenomenon is overdefined. There are so many potential causal variables that lead to growth, and so few case studies with matching data, that it is mathematically difficult to identify the ultimate cause. Yet more and more scholars are confident about what is at the center of this onion. In their book *Why Nations Fail*, Daron Acemoglu and James Robinson explain that the foundation for all of the various variables is *institutions*, as we noted earlier. As Acemoglu joked in an interview, the title should be *Why Nations Grow,* but that isn't a sexy enough title for a bestseller. Their book is the synthesis of decades of highly acclaimed scholarly research. It can be read as another popular summary of failed states, but *catch-up* growth is only part of its story. The primacy of institutions also explains growth at the frontier. That is, growth by leading economies, also known as Great Powers.

When we, and Acemoglu and Robinson, claim that institutions are the foundation for growth, we are making a claim that is both big and small. It is small in the sense that this isn't all that controversial. Everyone agrees that a society's economic institutions—property rights, work rules, market freedom—are *one of* the main factors that define relative prosperity and growth. Our claim is big, however, in saying it is 100 percent of the explanation. Jared Diamond, author of the famous *Guns, Germs, and Steel,* disagrees and offers that institutions explain perhaps 50 percent of the international differences today.[28] The small claim is a consensus. The big one is why we are writing.

There are different kinds of growth. The first type of growth is commercial expansion such as a new trade route. The resulting specialization of labor is known as *Smithian* growth, named after Adam Smith in the typology of economic historian Joel Mokyr. Mokyr defines another type as growth that comes from scale effects, but this type is similar enough to Smithian growth that we need not distinguish it here. The second type is investment, or *Solovian* growth (after Robert Solow), which is the diversion of income away from consumption and toward durable equipment that enhances output. Innovative growth, which some call technology proper and others simply call "ideas," is the easiest to explain. Build a better plow and farm yields increase. This third type is called *Schumpeterian* growth, after Joseph Schumpeter.

For most of human history, growth of all kinds was immeasurably slow and practically invisible in real time. Progress was so slow that productivity gains were absorbed by population growth, leaving average incomes unchanged over the centuries. For thousands of years, humanity was stuck at an average individual daily income of three dollars per day (as valued in today's U.S. dollars). When an innovation such as, say, crop rotation came along that was copied widely enough to raise farm yields and prosperity, the extra produce went not into higher average incomes but into a larger population. A 10 percent increase in output was caught in the Malthusian trap of a 10 percent increase in population. The advantages of scale were marginalized by more mouths to feed until the marginal gains faded to nothing. And given mass illiteracy, increased manpower did not generally increase brainpower.

As the centuries passed, all three growth processes ground away. Meanwhile, states emerged from tribes, with each successive state trying out a slightly different set of institutions. Some states thrived and conquered, for a while. The others were absorbed. The institutions in those states often blocked the three growth processes, but they sometimes enhanced them.

Critics will say that the institutional theory fails because other explanatory variables such as geography are even more primal. Others refuse to believe that politics explains human progress more than science does. We'll address these objections in turn, but notice how they come from diametrically opposed positions. The science theory is fundamentally heroic: but for Isaac Newton, there would be no theory of gravity. In contrast, the geography theory is fundamentally antiheroic: but for warm rain and navigable rivers, there would be no food or trade here.

The geography theory is a valid explanation of growth differences, or at least it was until the industrial revolution. For more than two centuries since then, it has become much less relevant. Also, the effect of geography on growth is essentially transnational. All of Eurasia had advantages from more domesticated animal species and varieties of grains that other continents lacked, but this difference doesn't explain why Rome—not Greece, Egypt, or Israel—conquered the whole Mediterranean.

As for technology proper, it does indeed stand as a key cause of growth, though we assert it stands on the foundation of institutions. First, consider the fact that invention is common while innovation is rare. The Chinese were the first to invent paper, gunpowder, clocks, and the printing press, but those technologies were more successfully enhanced and utilized after spreading to Europe. Second, most discoveries are not unique. It is known that the wheel and the windmill were invented many times, then forgotten, until finally one society had the institutional framework to implement them widely and pass them on permanently. Their successful exploitation commercially and subsequent diffusion make all the difference economically. Institutions explain innovation.

Another reason that the technological explanation is inferior is that invention itself relies on institutional ingredients. Brains and incentives are two of them. A free, policed market to sell an innovative product, a legal system to defend intellectual property, and a stable currency provide the necessary environment for worthwhile invention. Sure, some may explore science for its own sake, but the promise of a stock offering for successful start-up companies is an undeniable amplifier for technological curiosity. More fundamentally, smart brains don't grow on trees. Isaac Newton stood on the shoulders of giants, giants who happened to reside in unburned books in unburned libraries and colleges.

Our model of growth has three pillars—Smithian scale, Solovian investment, and Schumpeterian innovation—resting on a foundation of institutions. Rome's growth came largely from the benefits of scale inside its well-supplied cities and scale through trade networks as well, but those were only possible through its institutions of a secure border, respect for law, and public works. When the institutional development stagnated, so did the growth.

THE RELATIVISM OF PAUL KENNEDY

Paul Kennedy's *Rise and Fall of the Great Powers* pushed readers to think about *relative* economic strength as the foundation of "great" power. For economists today, this approach seems obvious, but for historians and the general public, Kennedy's in-depth scrutiny of relative economics was a watershed. We consider Kennedy's ideas in many ways the launching point of our own work here. Economic power *is* the foundation of military power. Despite agreeing with Kennedy's premises, we disagree with many of his conclusions. To begin with, we are suspicious of the prediction concerning a new equilibrium, or what is often called a balance of power among nations. Multipolarity is possible as an aftermath of the unipolar status quo when a single nation dominates all the rest, but there are other, less benign possibilities. When Roman civilization fell, it was superseded not by a rival but by a dark age. More fundamentally, we disagree with Kennedy's core conclusion that America's military expenditures come at the expense of economic vitality. This conclusion, the overstretch hypothesis, assumes a zero-sum pie of resources that a nation distributes between investment and protection.

"[T]he implications of defense expenditure for economic growth are far more ambiguous than Kennedy suggests," wrote Charles Kupchan in a 1989 review of the book in the influential journal *International Security*.[29] He offered a number of counterexamples that "appear to confound Kennedy's persistent allusion to the negative relationship that exists between defense spending and economic performance." Instead, Kupchan pointed to imperial myopia, something Kennedy himself described as existing in Hapsburg Spain, and which historian Aaron Friedberg identified as central to British decline during the turn of the last century. "While British elites were all too aware of the rapid growth of German power, they lacked the analytic skills and *methods of measurement* needed to come to terms with the long-term implications of relative decline," wrote Kupchan (emphasis added). President John F. Kennedy's economic adviser, W. W. "Walt" Rostow, had a similar reaction to the book, which he reviewed in *Foreign Affairs* in early 1988.

[A] relative reduction in military outlays does not automatically translate into a higher growth rate, nor is a relatively high rate of growth incompatible with a relatively high rate of military expenditures. For example, the burden of U.K. military expenditures declined in the years down to 1978, while the economy continued to deteriorate. Something of the same could be said of the American economy in the 1970s, when military expenditures declined to a trough of just under five percent of GNP in 1979. On the other hand, Taiwan, with 20 percent of U.S. GNP per capita and a proportionate military outlay higher than the United States, enjoys a per capita rate of growth almost four times higher.[30]

This last critique obscures Rostow's deeper understanding of the patterns of economic growth. Rostow was well-known for developing one of the classic theories of development, the "stages of growth," which described an S-shaped pattern: slow during the takeoff, followed by a rapid ascent, concluding with a slow-growing, modern consumption-based economy. Rostow knew that Taiwan's fast growth was a feature of its takeoff stage.

It may be unfair to applaud a historian for highlighting the centrality of economics and then criticize him for failing to understand every dimension of economics, but the success of Kennedy's book made such scrutiny inevitable. Near the end of *Rise and Fall*'s chapter about the latter part of the twentieth century, the author observes that "an increasing proportion of the American population was moving from industry to services," which is correct, but then he wrongly asserts: "that is, into low-productivity fields." [31] This mistake is common, a stereotype that service jobs are predominantly low-skill work in fields such as retail and transportation, not in high-skill fields such as medicine, research, architecture, software, and engineering. Alan Ingham leveled a powerful critique in the last issue of the *Economic Journal* in 1989: "One longs for a model, or at least some stated assumptions of how economies develop, and some semblance of an integrated set of data. The stories told are very convincing taken one by one, but whether they all add up is another matter." [32]

A final review of the book caught our eye, written by Immanuel Wallerstein in the *British Journal of Sociology* in June 1989. "I have no quarrel with the list [Kennedy] makes, although we are never quite clear how exactly we know if a given power is a Great Power." [33] Wallerstein is saying that the account is exactly that, a historical accounting exercise. While the book is hailed as a "marvelous synthesis," it does not try to explain the rise and fall with a rigorous model that can interpret the clash of institutions, civilizations, and cultures that underpins the clash of militaries. Kennedy deserves credit for pointing us all in this direction, and it's long past time to take up the challenge. The Penn World Table gives us all the raw data we need to think about power more carefully.

BUT CHINA IS DIFFERENT!

During the past third of a century, the *communist* Chinese government has converted a poor mega-state of one billion people into a fast-growing capitalist miracle. China has maintained growth rates of around 10 percent for almost a decade, and its GDP per capita is almost 26 times higher now than it was three decades ago. Not only that, but Beijing owns more than $1 trillion in U.S. debt. India, too, has attracted global attention. Its real GDP growth rate surpassed the 10 percent benchmark in 2010, while its GDP per capita has doubled over the past decade. By contrast, the United States seems stuck with slow growth rates (often below 2 percent), rising unemployment, and accelerating sovereign debt levels. In light of such numbers, who can deny that the United States, for real this time, is losing status relative to the economic powerhouses of the East?

Maybe *this time is different*—a worldview highlighted (skeptically) in the book of the same name by Carmen Reinhart and Kenneth Rogoff about financial crises. China represents a different quality of challenge. Even so, Sinophiles should remember that the deep narrative of history is tethered to economic forces, for all countries. There is no German physics distinct from French physics, just as there is no Chinese economics that will make its rise fundamentally different from those of Russia and Japan. A large, poor country growing quickly will soon approach the productivity frontier. For that reason, we reject the image that America has much to learn from another rising giant, cast as a bogeyman, no matter how big its population or fast its growth. But America has very much to learn from the fallen empires of the past.

In that latter context, we realize how easily some will interpret this book as declinist in its own right, or as hypocritical about declinism. We hope to convince you that our viewpoint is nuanced rather than hypocritical, or balanced, if you will forgive the pun. True, we disagree with the crude declinism one finds in Paul Krugman's populist essays, which express, as libertarian scholar Brink Lindsey writes, "not subtlety or insight or analytical ingenuity, but the Manichean worldview of the true believer: one mass political movement, defined by its noble intentions, accomplishes unalloyed good, while a rival mass political movement, motivated by base and selfish values, works to undo that good."[34] Political polarization is an unhelpful guide to America's economic dilemmas and may be making those dilemmas even harder to solve.

Our view of America's situation in the world today is that the nation risks drifting toward decline even as it enjoys the momentum of innovation-fueled economic growth. As the economist Tyler Cowen says, the United States is still enjoying the benefits of growth based on the low-hanging fruit of the previous century, but what will propel us forward in this century? It must be understood that there are economic forces pushing in both directions. Moreover, it is just as foolish to note only one side of the forces as it is to declare that the outcome is certain. One might imagine probabilities in the game of Great Powers, but anything more is deterministic nonsense.

THE PROBLEM WITH GROWTH

Media commentary about China is dominated by growth rates, which have become the shorthand measure of economic vitality, with scant attention to other relevant statistics. Most recent articles fail to contextualize growth rates with any mention of the overall size of China's economy, either in terms of total GDP or the more relevant GDP per capita. Suspicious that this shorthand was too common, we scrutinized a random sample of recent newspaper articles about China's economy. As a simple initial look, we chose the first ten non-editorial articles that appeared in a Google search of, for example, "Washington Post Chinese economy." Each article was scored for any kind of mention of the GDP growth rate, the relative size or GDP of the Chinese economy, and GDP per capita (or any other absolute or relative measure of productivity). Articles by the *Washington Post* and the *New York Times* often referred merely to the relative size of the Chinese GDP, not actual figures, but we counted that. We gave credit for throwaway phrases such as "the world's second largest economy." Figure 4 shows the results.

Figure 4. Quality of reporting on China's economy.
Percentage of articles that mention key economic measures.

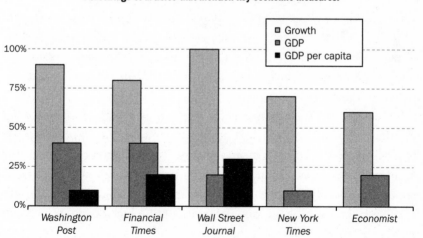

Source: Tim Kane and Glenn Hubbard

As expected, nearly all articles surveyed mention China's GDP growth rate. However, the GDP *level* was mentioned in just 13 of the 50 articles. As for productivity, coverage was weak—a mere 6 of 50 articles. Three were published in the *Wall Street Journal,* two in Britain's *Financial Times,* one in the *Washington Post.* Clearly, GDP per capita and GDP are important indicators, yet newspapers tend to focus on growth figures in isolation. Is this because growth rates fuel more captivating tales of decline and triumph? If you agree with *Washington Post* columnist Robert Samuelson's warning to "keep matters in perspective," beware the next time you see a China piece in the news that neglects to mentions that its GDP per capita is one-fifth of the U.S. level.

We wondered if economic commentators would fare better, so we randomly looked at twelve articles by writers such as such as Robert Samuelson, Paul Krugman, Thomas Friedman, David Smith, and Niall Ferguson. Would their coverage of the Chinese economy provide more context? *Yes,* in fact. Eight of the eleven expert op-eds reference GDP growth, six mention GDP, and five refer to productivity in some fashion. Ferguson mentions all three variables in his *Newsweek* essay,[35] as does Samuelson in one of three essays.[36] Krugman mentions growth in all three essays, GDP twice, but never productivity. In two essays about the Chinese economy, Friedman mentioned none of the variables at all.[37] This tendency to gloss over concrete figures is common. Krugman wrote in one piece that "China is still a poor country, it's growing fast, and given its sheer size it's well on the way to matching America as an economic superpower," which touches on the three concepts without giving them real substance.[38]

We understand that growth is the modern yardstick of international economics, and a good yardstick to be sure, but it needs to be combined with other metrics to have meaning. Russia's GDP growth boomed for decades, as did Japan's. But both were misunderstood, and the misunderstanding deeply affected foreign policy. Our public dialogue would be enhanced if the global economic conversation included GDP, productivity, and growth.

HOW TO MEASURE ECONOMIC POWER

A measure of *economic power* is easy to imagine, and here we will endeavor to actually design and apply such a measure to international data over the past six decades. The measure of one country's economic power at a moment in time should be a combination of its GDP, GDP growth, and GDP per capita (which reflects technological prowess). All three variables can be viewed on a single chart, using two axes to measure two variables and a circle whose size represents the third variable. Figures 5 through 7 show a progression of the world's biggest economies using this three-variable framework with GDP growth (ten-year average) on the *y*-axis, GDP per capita on the *x*-axis (using 2005 dollars), and GDP scaled to the area of each circle. In 1970, shown in Figure 5, the United States had the highest productivity with just over $20,000 per person, but "Europe"—an aggregate of seventeen nations in Western Europe—had the largest overall GDP and was growing twice as fast (8 percent versus 4 percent), while Japan had the fastest growth rate of all at 10.6 percent. China in 1970 had the lowest productivity level, and slowest GDP growth.

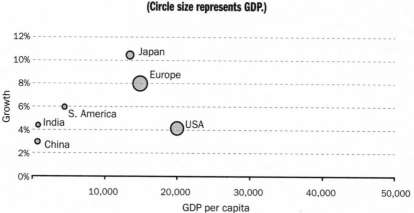

Figure 5. Global economic power, 1970.
(Circle size represents GDP.)

Source: Penn World Table 7.1

By 1990, the situation was dramatically different.[39] Neither Europe nor Japan caught up to the United States level of GDP per capita, and the growth rates of both economies fell dramatically. China, meanwhile, remained extremely poor but had a high and rising growth rate. Notice how the overall size of Europe's GDP was larger than America's in 1990, $9.1 trillion versus $7.8 trillion (in 2005 dollars). Two decades later, America's GDP grew to $12.8 trillion versus Europe's $12.9 trillion. However, Western Europe has a combined population of 402 million people compared to 310 million in the United States, which means that the United States has a 25 percent ($10,000) higher average income level per person. Meanwhile, by 2009, China had a $10.3 trillion economy overall, double-digit economic growth rates, and had doubled its productivity level.

Figure 6. Global economic power, 1990.
(Circle size represents GDP.)

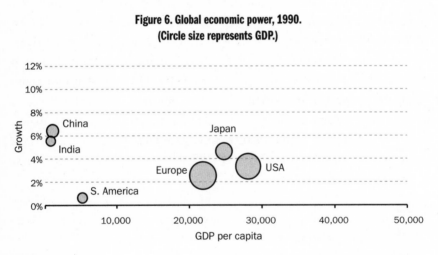

Source: Penn World Table 7.1

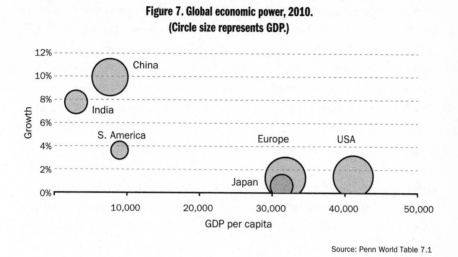

Figure 7. Global economic power, 2010.
(Circle size represents GDP.)

Source: Penn World Table 7.1

As interesting as these charts are, it is difficult for many observers to keep track of the three dimensions and how they interact. Our first instinct was to combine them in a single variable by the simplest means possible: multiplication. When this simple measure treatment (Power = GDP × Productivity × Growth) is used to calculate U.S. economic power in 1970, Japan had a relative power measure equal to 20 percent of the American level, Europe had a 69 (not including Germany), and China had a measure of 1.

While this multiplication method is one approximation of economic power, there are two problems with its simplicity. First, what does a negative growth rate imply for power? Negative growth rates occur more often than one might realize, but common sense suggests that describing any country with negative power is ridiculous, let alone zero power. The problem doesn't resolve by using long-term growth averages, not ten years or even twenty years. Even a wounded giant (like the Soviet Union in the 1980s) has might that is self-evident. One way to address this problem is to set a lower minimum bound for the growth factor (for example, using a rate of +0.2 percent for all countries with growth less than that). But the linear approach has a second problem. Does it make sense for a country with 10 percent growth to have twice the power of an equivalent peer with 5 percent growth? Imagine two equal powers in Europe during the 1700s with identical populations and output levels, with the only difference being that the northern country experiences a temporary growth spurt when it discovers huge silver deposits. Would it make sense to say the northern country is three times as powerful just because its growth rate averages three times higher during that decade?

Our goal in developing a power metric is to produce an equation that will be easy to understand but also agreeable to scholars. We tried a number of nonlinear conversions of the growth rate to address the problems described above, and assessed it by examining theoretical extremes as well as historical data. For example, we tried converting the growth rate using a square root, a natural logarithm, and more complicated formulas. The nonlinear approach proved to be a much better treatment of historical data, notably during the early twentieth century when major wars played havoc with income levels, both national and personal. We'll leave the longer description for the endnote,[40] but in short this is the equation we came up with for calculating a country's economic power:

$$\text{Economic Power} = \text{GDP} \times \text{Productivity} \times \text{Growth}^{1/2}$$

Ultimately, the simplest approach of using the square root of the growth rate worked just fine. For instance, two countries with growth rates of 9 and 4 would have those numbers converted to growth metrics of 3 and 2, respectively, in our economic power formula. The following figure shows six examples of how the power equation can make six very different economies comparable with one metric. Seventeen major countries of Western Europe, including Eurozone members Germany and Spain as well as nonmembers Sweden and the UK, had a combined level of GDP equal to the United States, growth that was slightly slower, and average GDP per person of $32,000 versus $41,000. When those variables are computed to generate a measure of economic power, Europe had a score of 456, and the United States had 623. By contrast, China had a 2010 economic power score of 251, slightly more than half of Europe's. Although China's growth rate was 9.9 percent, its power level was relatively low because of its weak productivity (measured by GDP per capita). Table 3 has the complete results, showing that in relative terms compared to the United States, Europe's economic power in 2010 was 73 percent, China's was 40 percent, Japan's was 15 percent, and India's was six percent. The three leading of economies of South America (Argentina, Brazil, and Chile) combined for a power score that was 7 percent of the U.S. level.

Figure 8 shows graphically what we think is the best way to imagine economic power of six major economies in 2010, except here power is measured relative to the United States at its peak in the year 2000. The United States itself has a larger GDP and higher productivity than ten years ago, but its long-term growth rate has slowed by half. As a result, American economic power is just three-quarters of its 2000 peak.

TABLE 3. CALCULATING ECONOMIC POWER IN 2010

	United States	Europe	China	Japan	South America	India
GDP per capita ($)	41,365	32,004	7,746	31,447	9,236	3,477
Growth	1.4%	1.2%	9.9%	0.5%	3.6%	7.7%
GDP ($T)	12,833	12,875	10,303	3,988	2,394	4,079
Economic Power	623	456	251	93	42	39
... relative to the U.S.	100%	73%	40%	15%	7%	6%

Source: Calculations by Hubbard and Kane, data from Penn World Table, Mark 7.1.

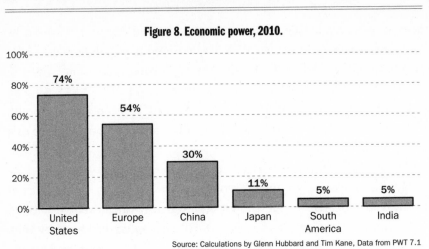

Figure 8. Economic power, 2010.

Source: Calculations by Glenn Hubbard and Tim Kane, Data from PWT 7.1

This comparison of economic power is extended across six decades in Figure 9. Despite the setback in recent years, the trend is very positive for American economic power, which has increased by 700 percent. Japan's power increased more dramatically, up from 1 percent in 1970 to its peak of 24 percent in 1990, but it then dwindled to 11 percent recently. China, meanwhile, should be understood as inheriting the Asian "miracle" model from Japan and Korea, but its economic power has only risen to the level of 30 percent so far.

Figure 9. Growth of economic power, 1970–2009.

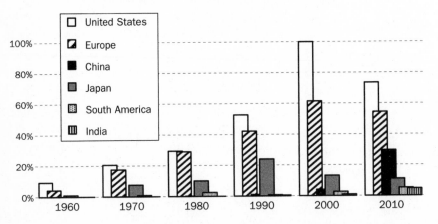

Source: Calculations by Glenn Hubbard and Tim Kane, Data from PWT 7.1

When we look at the world through these "economic goggles," stories about America's antagonist look very different. Europe is a shadow of what it should be and what its proponents assert. And while China's growth rate and overall size are impressive, its low average productivity levels mean that on balance, Beijing is still weak. No doubt that will not be the case in thirty years, but even given that, there is no reason to assert that America will decline. China's GDP will be larger but its growth rate will shrink dramatically, yielding a power level that will probably not surpass America's. Our impression of these hard data on economic power is that the primary threat to America, as we wrote earlier, is America itself.

AN ECONOMIC POWER WORLDVIEW

In 1961, during a difficult moment in the wake of the Bay of Pigs crisis, President John F. Kennedy expressed his appreciation for a quantitative view of American exceptionalism. Kennedy said to his trusted adviser Walt Rostow: "We can't afford a nervous breakdown. We're forty percent [of the free world's power], and there's no one to cover for us." Kennedy was ahead of his time in thinking about power as a measurable quantity.

Here we continue the intellectual journey of measuring economic power—two economists applying their worldview to grand strategy—to show that the challenge of relative great power is not rising adversaries competing over scarce resources. Nor is the danger that the leading power overstretches itself, or misallocates its energies between military expenditure and economic investment. We reject those ideas. History shows instead that Great Powers lose their leadership role when they stop pushing at the technological frontier.

We take as given that the fundamental Paul Kennedy theses are correct, namely: 1) that a state's military power derives from its economic productivity; and 2) that economic power is important relative to contemporary nations.

Our contribution can be understood in two parts. Our first thesis is a stylized fact—something generally true with rare exceptions—that Great Power decline is fundamentally *economic* in nature. Second, economic decline is a consequence of stagnant institutions, primarily a political system biased into status quo inaction.

On the first thesis, we disagree with Paul Kennedy's extended claim of imperial overstretch as a cause of decline, which is rooted in his belief that states face a trade-off between security expenditures and economic investment. Economies become unbalanced in many ways, excessive military expenditure being one, but there are too many counterexamples of thriving economies coincident with war-fighting and large militaries for that to be fingered as a cause, whole or partial.

Our second thesis is that economic imbalance occurs because states stagnate politically. This explanation is an institutional one that has been well developed by economists such as Mancur Olson, and by Nobel laureates Douglass North and Elinor Ostrom. We take our cue from these scholars in viewing politics through the lens of economics, in which political agents act with the same kind of self-interest—in seeking office, passing legislation, and managing bureaucracies—that everyone else has. To seek profit as one would seek reelection is a natural, amoral act in itself. But a society needs good rules to govern human passions in all its markets.

We do not believe that Great Power imbalance, by which we mean institutional stagnation within a single nation, is inevitable. Historians have a tendency to declare some theories determinist just because they are overtly quantitative, a common and wrong-headed complaint Paul Kennedy faced as well. To be sure, our approach is quantitative, recommending a new metric of great power, but the rhyme of history that we observe, a parade of decline, should not be seen as the inevitable destiny of America. Although the ominous pattern of Great Power imbalance follows from institutional decline, it must also be said that many, many times in history empires and nations did reform their institutions. Rome underwent numerous progressive reforms under many emperors and, some would argue, during the transformative rule of Julius and Augustus. And while modern history notes numerous institutional quagmires such as Peronist Argentina, postcrash Japan, and California, we can just as easily point to successes such as Sweden, Estonia, and Chile. But those stories will have to wait.

THE BEHAVIORAL EXPLANATION FOR DECLINISM

We close this chapter where we began. Why does the topic of declinism fascinate so many Americans? One might as well ask why the nightly news is filled with rare but sensational murders, baby kidnappings, and horrible mass accidents. "If it bleeds, it leads," say the editors. That may explain the popularity of declinism in some superficial way, but there is something more going on here as well. It is something that grand strategy needs to consider.

Rich nations generally have an overdeveloped fear about losing *their* status. On an individual level, we know that people worry about their demise, even while their circumstances improve. Gregg Easterbrook captured the zeitgeist in his 2003 book, *The Progress Paradox: How Life Gets Better While People Feel Worse:*

> For essentially all of human history until the last few generations, the typical person's lot has been unceasing toil, meager living circumstances, uncertainty about food, rudimentary health care, limited education, little travel or entertainment; all followed by early death.... Only by the 1970's did living standards, life expectancy, health care, education, and personal freedom [in the United States] begin to approximate today's.[41]

We look back at false alarms of past decades with some humor—global cooling in the 1970s before the more legitimate global warming concerns of the today, pollution-truncated life expectancy before over-population alarms, food shortages and mass starvation followed by an obesity epidemic, and so on. The cycle continues. Easterbrook argues that the peculiar American addiction to the declinist narrative may stem from a biological instinct. In the same ways new parents become sensitive to risks to their child, this protective instinct is mirrored in the way we collectively ponder our wealth. The irrational fear of loss is probably amplified by uncertainty. Does America deserve to be this rich? Was it luck?

These feelings have not been part of orthodox economics, but the study of behavioral economics has started to fill that gap. One of the more famous insights of the field is called "loss aversion," an individual mindset that guides choices in a way that looks a lot like declinism on the larger scale.

The ancients understood the heart and the mind to be in conflict, and so it's not a slander to call our collective paranoia an irrational perspective. Irrational doesn't always mean wrong—love can be irrational, faith can be irrational—but let's not pretend irrationality has no effect on the economy. Irrationality has benefits—and costs.

Oversensitive parents tend to keep their children alive. But overprotective parents can also stunt the development of their children, making them less aware of the world outside, less creative, and less confident than their peers. Risk aversion can be unhealthy. In his 2010 book, *The Rational Optimist,* Matt Ridley sounds this warning in relation to the current debate over the environment. His main argument is that there is a powerful, undeniable path of progress in the human condition, a trend that has a high probability of continuing in the century ahead. Ridley counters the pessimists with logical arguments, but he also observes that progress has enemies. He points out that some extreme environmentalists believe not only that the world is in great danger from human technology, but also that the only way to halt this danger is to stop economic growth and development altogether. Environmental extremists fantasize about human extinction. Lesser radicals call for an end to economic growth. Ridley describes the implications of such an approach:

> This means not just that growing your company's sales would be a crime, but failing to shrink them; not just that travelling further than your ration of miles would be an offence, but failing to travel fewer miles each year; not just inventing a new gadget would be illegal, but failing to abandon existing technologies; not just that growing more food per acre would be a felony, but failing to grow less—because these are the things that constitute growth.[42]

In the next chapter, we'll take a deeper look at behavior and attitudes. Those things have just as much an impact on the imbalance of nations as hard accounting of power does. Maybe more.

3

ECONOMIC BEHAVIOR
AND INSTITUTIONS

*In Europe and America, there's a growing feeling
of hysteria....
We share the same biology, regardless of ideology.*

— Sting, "Russians"

A common criticism of economics is that it is too simple, a weakness that distorts not only how personal behavior is modeled, but also how national behavior is understood. Is the national economy really well described as a mathematical identity with four parts—consumption, investment, government, and net exports? Can you assume every person is a self-interested, risk-neutral optimizer? And on that note, should we assume that national motivations are invariably self-interested? One of the main motivations in approaching this book, as we scan world history with economic goggles, is how behavioral factors on an aggregate level seem to cause the imbalance of nations. This approach to history isn't exactly new, nor are the mechanics settled, but we think the consideration of social factors is just as important as the application of raw power metrics.

First, let us admit how sterile our profession—the economics profession—can appear. When economists construct models of the world, we make a number of assumptions about the way people and things behave. The neoclassical model assumes that each human "agent" maximizes personal utility (that is, happiness), that all humans in the model have perfect knowledge, that preferences are stable, that decisions are immune from context, and that everything happens in a dimensionless point in space. Historians and philosophers may be forgiven for mocking us for our rational delusion.

The counterpoint is that a heart surgeon operates in a mental space that is also rationally ignorant. She assumes the human brain doesn't exist, nor the immune system, nor locomotives, dolphins, Jupiter, or Broadway. Those are irrelevant parts of reality for the purposes of the surgery at her fingertips. Her mental model isn't wrong, nor is the economist's. Simplifying assumptions are vital because they allow doctors and economists and all kinds of scientists to craft models and general theories that would otherwise be impossibly complex.

But with all due respect, simple theoretical models have their drawbacks and blind spots as well. Economic models are to the real world what theoretical physics is to engineering. An engineer might design a car or a bridge that is benchmarked to idealistic laws of gravity, momentum, and energy, but has to factor in practical complexities of friction and resistance, too. The friction and resistance in economics are the messy, emotional behaviors of human beings.

Consider the economic ideal of perfect competition, a world where all firms price their goods perfectly so that the market clears, and profits don't exist because firms perfectly balance costs with revenues. This ideal world has tremendous explanatory power, but it is also unrealistic if applied to any specific realistic situation. Perfect competition requires that all information be free and fully diffused, that humans be fully rational and self-interested, and finally that we be particularly good at obtaining what we want if we can get it. Marketing and sales conferences do not exist under perfect competition, because all knowledge is known by all. "Models of rational decision making in economics, cognitive science, biology, and other fields . . . treat the mind as a Laplacean superintelligence equipped with unlimited resources of time, information, and computational might," says renowned psychologist Gerd Gigerenzer, director of the Max Planck Institute for Human Development, in Berlin.[1]

Sophisticated objections to the theory of perfect competition started perhaps with the invention of game theory in 1950. Two economists working at the RAND Corporation, Merrill Flood and Melvin Dresher, developed the earliest version of a game called the prisoners' dilemma. Flood and Dresher's model was instrumental in proving that self-motivated agents could generate outcomes that were harmful to the market *and to individuals themselves*. The classical principles of economics assumed that rational people would also enhance well-being in a free market, so the Flood and Drescher concept was a surprise. Perfect competition remained an essential building block in economic instruction, but microeconomics would never be the same. Meanwhile, game theory proved invaluable in the development of nuclear strategy, international finance, and public policy, not just high academic theory.[2]

Microeconomics wasn't the only field guilty of too much simplification. An oversimplified macroeconomic model known as Keynesianism became the dominant paradigm among economists and policymakers in the 1960s and 1970s but was discredited by empirical experiences with inflation in the United States and elsewhere. The model is named after British economist John Maynard Keynes, who was justly famous during the 1940s and 1950s for writings that inspired a novel economic role for the government. When private sector consumption declined during a recession, Keynes argued, the government should compensate using fiscal expenditures in excess of revenues.

Keynesian theory meshed well with the development of GNP accounts. All types of private consumption—toys, food, clothing, furniture—were represented by a single, large number labeled "C" for consumption. All private investment—residential housing, new factory equipment, software—was summed up and labeled "I." All government spending was labeled "G," while the net of exports minus imports was labeled "NX." The sum of these expenditures is mathematically equal to the sum of incomes across the nation. According to Keynes, when C or I slips, the government should respond by raising G. In practice, Keynesianism is used to justify fiscal deficits in pursuit of smoothing aggregate demand but it morphed into a permanent stimulus: seemingly affordable in good times, essential in bad.

The economies of the Western world grew steadily for twenty years following World War II, which validated Keynesianism in the eyes of many. Unfortunately, the simplifying assumptions of the Keynesian model did not anticipate stagflation—high inflation coupled with shrinking GDP—which hit the United States in the 1970s. Nor did the model offer any way out of that mess. Stagflation stymied most economists, and dumbfounded politicians. In response, President Richard Nixon infamously implemented price controls (over protests of many of his advisers), President Gerald Ford promised to "Whip Inflation Now (WIN!)," and President Jimmy Carter saw inflation rise more than 10 percent per year during his single term in the White House.

Orthodox economists warned that a cure to inflation would cause a recession as bad as the Great Depression, but Paul Volcker's bold actions as Federal Reserve chairman from 1979 to 1987 challenged this consensus. He radically tightened money supply growth. The ensuing decline in output and increase in unemployment were not as long lasting as the conventional Keynesian theory anticipated. In 1980, Volcker not only raised the Fed's target interest rate from around 10 percent up to 20 percent, but he also promised to hold fast until the public's expectations of higher inflation settled down, which they did in the long run. Economic expectations, a kind of macro behavior, were the key to Volcker's success, though they were nowhere to be found in even the simplest Keynesian model. University of Chicago economist Robert Lucas developed a hypothesis in response to this revelation, emphasizing the role of expectations in economic outcomes. Such ideas eventually earned Lucas a Nobel Prize, and its manifestation in the Volcker "experiment" earned the U.S. central bank the American public's trust. In the decades that followed, the nation developed its own expectation that the Fed's wise monetary policy would unfailingly keep the economy strong, if not entirely recession-free.

Despite this history, Keynesian theory remained the mainstream paradigm for most politicians. It has been more than three decades since the Volcker shock allowed the U.S. economy to return to rapid, real growth. In that time, superficial Keynesianism has regained its popularity, giving intellectual cover for politicians to push spending and deficits higher, perhaps expecting the Fed to bail them out. We can only hope this latest Great Recession will open everyone's eyes. Recent failures to manage aggregate demand responsibly, coupled with the current fiscal crisis in Europe, should, at a minimum, call for a thoughtful reassessment of our political trajectory.

The good news is that both game theory in microeconomics and expectations theory in macroeconomics represented a fundamental shift in how economists think. No longer is an elegant theory with mathematical neatness credible on its own. The behavior of the real world, measured using empirical data, is essential to any policy. As any football or basketball coach can tell you, players learn more in five minutes of a real game than from an hour of chalk talk.

HOW DO PEOPLE REALLY BEHAVE?

The Nobel Memorial Prize in Economic Sciences has been awarded increasingly to behavioralists in recent years, including Herbert Simon (1978), Maurice Allais (1988), Gary Becker (1992), Vernon Smith and Daniel Kahneman (2002), and Elinor Ostrom (2009).[3] A leading textbook described behavioral economics as "the study of situations in which people make choices that do not appear to be economically rational."[4] Many others paved the way for the behavioral revolution, notably game theorists such as John Nash and Reinhard Selten (awarded in 1994), and Robert Aumann and Thomas Schelling (2005).

How much cash do you have with you right now? No matter how much it is, we can we be sure how much it isn't: infinite. Conventional economics assumes that agents in the market have limited physical resources. Bounded rationality, a theory developed by Herbert Simon in 1955, holds that people also have a limited endowment of intangibles such as time, information, and brainpower. However, Simon argued that individuals, despite their bounded rationality, tend to make choices that are good enough. Often, real humans aren't trying to maximize outcomes at all, even within the scope of their constraints. From the perspective of behavioral economics, humans will happily settle for what is *good,* not necessarily what is *best.*

Consider this example: You arrive at the supermarket. You're shopping for breakfast cereal. In the orthodox perfect world, you would know how each cereal tasted relative to the others. You would also have perfect knowledge of your own preferences—say, the monetary value you would assign to each spoonful's sweetness, freshness, and crunch. You would possess complete awareness of your marshmallow value vis-à-vis raisins, granola, chocolate, and so on. In the orthodox world, your mind would compare this comprehensive evaluation to the stated market price both here and at competing local groceries. In the end, perfect you walks away with the best cereal, content with your choice. Ridiculous? Of course. Then again, the physics of frictionless surfaces is a ridiculous simplification, but useful when designing airplanes.

Simon's critique is that the orthodox map of economic behavior was so simple that it was misleading. Thinking takes time, and thinking about everything is impossible. Simon explained that humans operate with "bounded rationality." Even if shopping for cereal in the real world yields what seem like suboptimal outcomes (say you bought Frosted Flakes for $3, not realizing that a favored box of Cheerios was available across the street for just $2), Simon observed that satisficing—selecting a choice that is good enough within the constraints of time and place— leaves most real-world humans happy with their chosen outcomes.

Bounded rationality also encourages "herding," which is the tendency of individuals to follow the crowd when they do not have time enough to consider a decision thoughtfully. Popular deference to "bad" emperors is the ultimate example of herding in human civilization. That happens in democracies as well, for example when newly elected (or reelected) presidents see their approval ratings jump by 5 or 10 percentage points after winning an election.

Another insight of behavioral research is called the endowment effect. This describes the way individuals assign significant additional value to goods and ideas the moment they claim possession over them. A toy in the store might be worth five dollars, but worth even more after you own it for a few days. Hapsburg Spain's far-flung claims, especially their effort to dominate the Netherlands, come to mind as a political manifestation of the endowment effect.

The way constrained brains think has forced humans to use what are known as *heuristics,* or logical, decision-making shortcuts that make efficient use of neural time. A young child's heuristic is to obey the advice of their parents because so much of the world is dangerous and unknown to them. A politician's heuristic is to follow the advice of the party elders rather than think through the nuances of legislation. General heuristic shortcuts include looking to past experience, modeling the behaviors and decisions of our peers, and relying on gut reactions and emotion to inform our choices. None of these options represents what a classical economist would consider a wise economic calculation. Emotions, the past, and peer environments are, after all, assumed to have no effect on the typical economic agent.

What does this matter for Great Powers in world history? Kings are satisficers, too. Bounded rationality takes on new significance when viewed from the perspective of voters, politicians, and nations at large. When a legislator is expected to lead on literally hundreds of issues, she will be overwhelmed, but she is also bound by something else entirely. What is the legislator optimizing? Odds are the objective for most legislators is not maximizing economic growth in the long term but maximizing reelection in the short term. Even when those two goals coincide, the legislator is often unaware of what the best policy choice might be. They are as rationally ignorant as the heart surgeon and the hungry shopper.

Despite popular jokes to the contrary, the average legislator is both incredibly smart and incredibly busy. These men and women are expected to be policy experts on topics as diverse as farming, trade, telecommunications, health care, industrial regulation, and taxes. In addition, they must be experts in the profession of politics, which includes media, rhetoric, and coalition-building, not to mention fund-raising and office management. Imagine this legislator's brain as it considers an innovative proposal for revising unemployment insurance. Odds are high that it will transform this complicated decision into an easier one, using the same heuristics and shortcuts we use when shopping for cereal at the grocery store. First heuristic: vote along party lines or in a manner similar to how you have voted in the past. This legislator simply hasn't time enough to make a fully informed choice. The end result is not likely to be an innovative policy. And that's why stagnation sets in.

Now consider a constituent in this representative's district. November has arrived, and it is time to vote. Not only does the voter have a more constrained understanding of policy nuances than his or her incumbent representative; democracy, too, adds another challenge. As the great economist Gordon Tullock, one of the fathers of the field of public choice, explains: "in the case of politics the information problem is much worse than it is in the market."[5] The outcome of an election may have a large effect on a voter's personal finances, but the voter has a vanishingly small effect on that outcome. If 300 million people vote on what you eat for dinner tonight, you may care what they decide and also rationally doubt your vote will make much difference. Many citizens make the sad but theoretically rational decision to pay only superficial attention to politics. This so-called political information problem leads to another layer of political heuristics: political parties, or brands, evolve as important framing devices fit for our limited mental capacity.

The lesson of bounded rationality most relevant to Great Power history is simply that economic truth is never fully revealed. We operate within a scientific paradigm that approximates the truth of how the world works—physically, chemically, biologically, as well as economically—and which is only as good as the state of contemporary knowledge. Policymaking, then, is a much trickier endeavor than the choice of goods at the grocery store. Emperors, mighty as they may be, cannot know the unknown. We should shudder for the degree of economic ignorance that clouded the paradigms of the Europeans of the fifteenth century, let alone the ancients. Not only did those Europeans lack macro data, theories of labor specialization and comparative advantage, inflationary expectations, entrepreneurial innovation, and econometrics for most of recorded history—they also lacked Arabic numerals. The profound boundaries of economic rationality afflict every Great Power in the face of decline for the simple reason that they rarely know what truly ails their economy. Ignorance is the ultimate bind.

NATIONAL VISION AND DIVISION

For more than a thousand years, the people of Ireland appeared to be less, shall we say, "civilized" in the eyes of their British betters. Racism among the ethnicities of Europe was intense, and stereotypes were often rooted in long-term economic disparities. In this world of nasty stereotypes, for example, the Poles were dumb, the Jews greedy, the Irish drunk, and so on.

For centuries, average incomes in Ireland lagged far behind average incomes in Britain. The poverty of the Irish people concerned Sir William Petty in 1676 so much that he devoted his later life to the hunt for a solution. It eluded him, and it eluded others for four more centuries. For many, the persistent income gap evolved into a heuristic that Ireland would always be economically inferior to Britain.

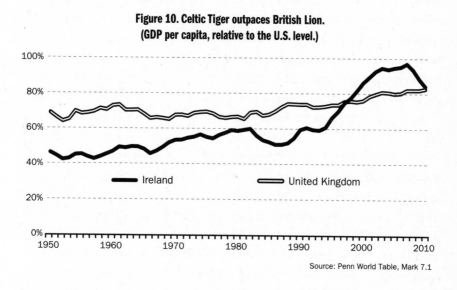

Figure 10. Celtic Tiger outpaces British Lion.
(GDP per capita, relative to the U.S. level.)

Source: Penn World Table, Mark 7.1

You can imagine the reaction, then, to the sudden productivity miracle in Ireland in the 1990s and 2000s. In the span of a single generation, the average Irish income rose significantly. A 2002 essay in the *New Statesman* surveyed the 11.5 percent GDP growth rate and 3.7 unemployment rate and proclaimed: "Such statistics make a joke out of all those old Irish jokes. Ireland today equals success. On this side of the Irish Sea, we have become so enamored of the emerald isle that, according to an ICM Research poll of March 2001, one in four Britons claims to have Irish roots."[6]

The narrative of the Celtic Tiger not only knocked over the false heuristic of inferiority, but also may have established a new heuristic. Now more than ever, global elites appreciate that no nation is guaranteed its relative status in the world. No nation can be presumed to be either permanently backward or permanently advanced. Rather, every nation must mind its institutions if it hopes to develop. This new heuristic, what we might call the "law of equal national opportunity," is a healthy development.

All this talk of nations begs an interesting question for behavioral economics: What is a nation? The formal definition may be clear, but let's think about the question in terms of national passion. Why are people patriotic? Why do some go crazy with enthusiasm during the Olympic Games and World Cup soccer matches, while their fellow citizens remain apathetic? Why would two Irishmen cheer side by side in the evening when their national soccer team scores a winning goal over the French, then bad-mouth each other's religions the next day at their respective Catholic and Anglican churches? Passion in each case derives from our group *identity*. According to many economists, such passion is utterly irrational.

In 2010, Nobel laureate George Akerlof and economist Rachel Kranton published *Identity Economics,* a book that Bloomberg ranked among its top thirty of the year. Their main point is that the decisions that shape your life often hinge on your perceived place in society, not solely on a calculation of financial costs and benefits. The child raised in a home where the television constantly plays the nightly news, where mom always cooks and cleans, and where children are expected to succeed in school or face a grounding will learn much different habits of expected behavior, or norms, than the child raised in home in which everyone plays classical instruments and eating is a self-serve free-for-all. No matter how similar they are in other ways, these two children will grow to live differently on account of the norms they inherited.

Akerlof and Kranton say that "norms are powerful sources of motivation. Norms effect fine-grain decisions of the moment—decisions as trivial as which t-shirt to wear to go jogging. Norms drive life-changing decisions as well—on matters as important as whether to quit school, whether and who to marry, whether to work, save, invest, retire, and fight wars." [7]

Identity can help explain a wealth of counterintuitive economic behaviors. Consider, for example, tax compliance—the rate at which individuals in a nation pay their taxes in full. In the framework of conventional economics, people decide whether or not to pay their taxes by weighing the potential benefits of a lower tax burden against the likelihood that they will be caught and punished for not complying. In many nations, however, there is "voluntary overcompliance"—tax participation rates above and beyond what conventional models would predict. One proposed factor motivating these high participation rates is tax morale, an intrinsic desire to pay taxes that is shaped, in part, by cultural norms such as fairness, reciprocity, and patriotism.

A recent international study conducted at the University of Texas at Dallas expanded upon these determinants, finding that membership in a majority ethnic group within a nation has an effect on tax compliance. Members of the ethnic majority are more likely to comply. More homogeneous nations have higher tax compliance rates on the whole as compared to more diverse states. Feeling as though your attitudes, values, and broader cultural identity fall in line with your country's values and culture makes paying up at the end of the year easier to bear, while feelings of isolation can have precisely the opposite effect.[8]

The reason that identity behavior is relevant to the rise and fall of Great Powers is twofold. The broadest-reaching social identity we hold is our nationality. The nation-state may be a relatively recent concept in the scope of history, but we will use the term here flexibly to encompass the largest contemporary sociopolitical unit, whether that was an ancient empire or an ethnic culture. In addition, our class, faction, religion, and creed affect our identity. Such groups often harden within states, especially democracies, into *political* identities that become ideologically rigid. Rigid political identities stymie consensual progress so that institutional reform, short of revolution, becomes impossible.

National identity is powerful and diverse, establishing unique and durable norms for each society. As Francis Fukuyama explains: "The propensity of human beings to endow rules with intrinsic value helps to explain the enormous conservatism of societies. Rules may evolve as useful adaptations to a particular set of environmental conditions, but societies cling to them long after these conditions have changed and the rules have become irrelevant or even dysfunctional."[9] The strength of norms has benefits for the rise and continuance of social order, but it can also serve as a barrier to economic progress.

This observation leads to this question: What marks the American identity? Americans are known throughout the world as a culture that values individual liberty. Free speech. Freedom of assembly. The right to own property. The right to bear arms. And, of course, our economic culture is celebrated for its entrepreneurial capitalism with high appetites for risk, tolerance of failure, and light regulation. Although some of us don't think of our federal government as particularly limited in its power to regulate or legislate, the American brand is recognized internationally for emphasizing limited central power. That identity may still feel genuine, even if the underlying reality is eroding.

Most observers would agree that America's political and economic institutions have generated a high-performing model of capitalism. As the Penn World Table showed, the American economy has defined the technological frontier for roughly a century. But will those institutions be the sharpest at the growing frontier in this coming century? More importantly, will the next leap in capitalism, or whatever better system may come, happen in the United States? The Fukuyama critique suggests not, and political identity will make such an innovation even harder.

A BIRD IN THE HAND

An age-old proverb says that a bird in the hand is worth two in the bush. Although it originally meant that the value of a trained falcon was superior to two wild prey, the common interpretation today is that a sure bet is superior to a potential two-for-one return, and that taking a risk is foolish. This advice is not sound for an economy that needs inventors and entrepreneurs to fuel economic growth. Nor, it turns out, is the proverb good guidance for personal success.

A 1960s experiment by Walter Mischel at Stanford University tested the ability of preschoolers to delay gratification. The study observed children, aged four to six, on the campus of the Bing Nursery School. Each child was led into a room where a treat of some kind (Oreo cookie, marshmallow, or pretzel stick) lay waiting for them on a table. They were told that they could eat their preferred treat as soon as they were left alone. However, if the children waited for fifteen minutes until the researcher returned, they would get an additional second helping. Of the six hundred children in the study, only a third resisted temptation for the full fifteen minutes. A minority ate the marshmallow immediately, but most resisted for a few minutes before giving in to temptation. Mischel observed that some children would "cover their eyes with their hands or turn around so that they can't see the tray, others start kicking the desk, or tug on their pigtails, or stroke the marshmallow as if it were a tiny stuffed animal." However, the experiment became more revealing when Mischel tracked down the children decades later. He discovered a strong correlation between the children's impulse control and their later academic success. In his follow-up academic paper, he wrote:

> Delay behavior predicted a set of cognitive and social competencies and stress tolerance consistent with experimental analyses of the process underlying effective delay in the preschool delay situation. Specifically, children who were able to wait longer at age 4 or 5 became adolescents whose parents rated them as more academically and socially competent, verbally fluent, rational, attentive, planful, and able to deal well with frustration and stress.[10]

The discovery is fascinating in its own right, but try reading that summary again with the idea that instead of talking about *children,* Mischel is also talking about *nations.* Nations that build strong economies orient themselves toward long-term payoffs, even if this process requires some short-term pain. Economics distinguishes between consumption and investment for precisely this purpose. The canonical models of economic growth, in particular the Solow-Swan model, identify a sweet spot where the ratio of investment capital to labor in an economy will ideally balance consumption and investment to maximize the welfare of the citizens. Nations in the real world fall short of their rational ideals, just like individuals.

The marshmallow experiment hints at another behavior, known as *loss aversion.* Not only do people tend to overvalue currently held assets, they also feel extraordinarily badly about losing an asset compared to the potential happiness of doubling its value. A purely rational, risk-neutral person would value the loss of one dollar as twice as bad as losing a half-dollar. The pioneers of behavioral economics, however, have discovered a range of irrational instincts.

Daniel Kahneman and Amos Tversky pioneered this approach to economics. They were inspired to collaborate during a seminar at the Hebrew University of Jerusalem, at which Kahneman had asked Tversky to make a presentation about whether or not humans are statistically intuitive (that is, naturally numerate). "We already knew that people are good intuitive grammarians: at age four, a child effortlessly conforms to rules of grammar as she speaks, although she has no idea that such rules exist." [11] This query led to long and fruitful collaboration based on their shared belief that the answer was no. Humans are not the statistically intuitive rational agents of high theory.

Sadly, Tversky died a few years before his collaborator Kahneman won the Nobel Prize in Economics (which they would surely have shared, but the prize is never given posthumously). Kahneman recently popularized their research in the celebrated 2011 book *Thinking, Fast and Slow,* which pays homage to Tversky's genius.

The duo mapped the cognitive aspects of economic behavior in what is now known as *prospect theory,* which encompasses loss aversion. "The humans described by prospect theory are guided by the immediate emotional impact of gains and losses," Kahneman writes, "not by long-term prospects of wealth and global utility." [12] Another discovery was that real people do not value the potential loss or gain of a single dollar equally. His three summary points of the theory are paraphrased here:

1. People have *reference points*. Outcomes better than the reference point are gains, while those worse than the reference point are losses.
2. Behavior follows a principle of diminishing sensitivity. We think in terms of relative and not absolute values. As our reference endowment increases (that is, as we move from $100 to $1,000,000), the prospect of losing or gaining another $100 diminishes in importance.
3. People have loss aversion. Equivalent losses loom larger than gains.

Figure 11 reproduces an abstract model of prospect theory. The chart represents the "value" a real person feels when experiencing material gains and losses relative to their starting point at the origin. Notice how important that initial reference point is. A small gain along the x-axis is experienced as high-value, but the feeling declines as the gain increases.

Figure 11. Prospect theory in the abstract.

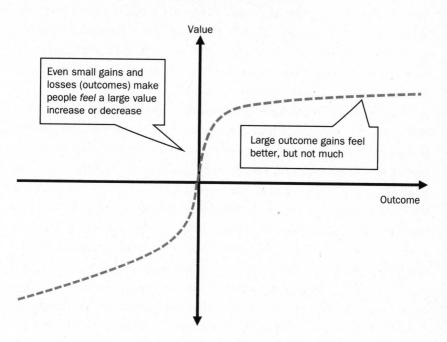

Loss aversion is not the same as risk aversion. A person, or national political institution, may prefer a riskier gamble over a safer gamble (risk-loving) while at the same time prefer not gambling at all (loss-averse). The application to Great Power behavior is this: a collective sense of loss aversion makes countries hesitant to change their economies, even when they see trading partners and perceived competitor nations growing and changing. Maybe this is why Americans are nostalgic for industrial jobs that are disappearing as the economy becomes more automated and service-oriented, even though average incomes have grown higher. We suspect most readers are uncomfortable with this fact, but here it is: America has already lost about half of the 20 million jobs in manufacturing at the peak level set in the 1980s, but overall industrial production is higher than ever because of robotic assembly lines. We are richer for it, but doubt lingers.

Politically, campaigns target loss aversion by shirking from fundamental reforms, especially detailed reform proposals. Instead, voters are offered vague promises of "hope and change," or other slogans that do not trigger a loss-averse reaction. Every time a specific Social Security reform is proposed, it gets easily tarred as a risky "scheme." Replacing unemployment insurance with individual accounts and enhanced training support is a nonstarter because the uncertainty of its effects makes the vote a political loser.

Our inability to weigh choices rationally across time also occurs in the aggregate. When critics objected to Keynes's then-unorthodox theories that called for short-term deficit spending to counterbalance depressed private sector consumption, he famously quipped: "in the long run, we're all dead." [13] Indeed, his line is a good one, and he surely did not intend for his policies to open the floodgates of persistent deficits even in a healthy economic climate. He assumed that officials can discipline their behaviors—stimulating in bad times while saving in good times. Unfortunately, politicians are not so rational. Short-term election cycles bracket legislators' time preferences, and their discounting of longer horizons is arguably total. It is only fair to note that our politicians' short-termism is a reflection of and response to voter time preferences. The voters are ultimately to blame for preferring gains today and pains tomorrow.

Change is hard. National institutions are the key to a balanced economy, but a tour of the latest thinking in behavioral economics suggests that there exist sociopolitical barriers to long-term prosperity.

THE TALL MAN PROBLEM

Michael Jordan might never have achieved greatness or fame on the basketball court if it weren't for Howard Hobson, a man that you, and Jordan, have probably never heard of. Jordan led the Chicago Bulls to six NBA championships. At six foot, six inches tall, the hypercompetitive, super-athletic "small forward" is generally acclaimed as the greatest basketball player of all time. Sports fans may remember that Jordan had a moment like Alexander the Great, who supposedly wept because there no more worlds to conquer. Jordan retired after leading the Bulls to three consecutive championships, in 1991, 1992, and 1993. After two seasons failing to find equivalent success in professional baseball, Jordan returned to the Bulls and led them to another three-peat in 1996, 1997, and 1998. The differences between the games can surely explain why Jordan was not nearly as successful in baseball as in basketball, but this proposition also implies that the rules of basketball as they had evolved in the 1990s made that particular game the perfect environment for his skills. If Jordan had played basketball in a different era, he might not have achieved so much.

Howard Hobson learned the game of basketball early in the twentieth century, leading his high school team in Portland, Oregon, to a state championship in 1921. How different the game was then! When James Naismith invented the sport at a Springfield, Massachusetts, YMCA in 1891, there were nine players on a team, a bucket instead of a rope net, and no such thing as "out of bounds." Goaltending was not illegal, which meant tall players could block shots as they headed down toward the basket. Although it seems hard to imagine playing the game this way, until the 1930s, a jump ball was held after every made shot. Under these odd rules, Hobson went on to play for Oregon, then to coach in the Ivy League. Ultimately, he returned to Oregon, where he led the team to fame in the first-ever NCAA tournament, on March 27, 1939. Hobson was more than a visionary coach, however. He was also an active advocate for rule changes to improve the game. Hobson's biggest contribution was a thirteen-year study of basketball that took the form of a doctoral thesis at Columbia University in 1944. That study, published in 1949 as the book *Scientific Basketball*, called for revolutionary rule changes that helped foster the environment in which Michael Jordan excelled.

Chapter 11 in Hobson's book describes a particularly vexing issue that distorted the game. Taller and taller players were dominating play, monopolizing both offense and defense by standing near the basket. They could also slow the game to a halt by holding the ball high out of the reach of the other players. Back then, there was no shot clock. An arms race of tallness was killing the game. There were even serious discussions about banning tall people from the game at some arbitrary height. "What shall we do with the tall man in basketball?" asked Hobson. "This has been a leading question in the game for many years." He went on to observe that the 1936–38 reforms, which eliminated the jump ball in most circumstances and instituted a three-second lane violation (in a three-foot-wide lane), had only resulted in "still more tall men." George Mikan, the giant six-foot-nine Lakers center, ruled the NBA through a combination of height and athleticism. "The entire problem reached a climax in 1944 and 1945 when seven-foot Bob Kurland almost singled-handedly led Oklahoma A&M to two national championships,"[14] Hobson noted.

Armed with his dissertation from Columbia University, Coach Hobson organized an experimental game between Fordham and Columbia on February 7, 1945. The court was modified, first by widening the key from six to twelve feet wide. This change made it difficult for tall men to clog the lane to the hoop. Second, Hobson added a strange new line to the court, which he described as necessary for his area-method of scoring. Shots outside this arc line, which measured twenty-one feet from the basket, would count for three points. Among the journalists invited to watch, the game was a sensation. Even the referees enjoyed the new format, though they had a new burden: determining whether a shooter's feet were inside or outside the arc.

It was not until the 1979–80 season that the National Basketball Association added the three-point shot, though the rival American Basketball Association had adopted it as early as 1967. Some college conferences allowed three-point shots beginning in 1980, but there was no uniform distance adopted until the NCAA established a standard arc in 1985. This was one year after Jordan had left the University of North Carolina and was selected, famously, as number two in the draft. To get a sense of how new the three-point shot is, go find a YouTube video of the final seconds of the 1982 NCAA championship game, in which Jordan, the freshman phenomenon, hits the final jump shot with fifteen seconds remaining. There is no three-point arc on the floor.

The three-point shot was an exciting addition, but it was not widely used by players or coaches during the first five seasons after its institution. Even the most aggressive shooters in the entire league attempted an average of one long shot per game. Jordan himself was slow to make the long ball part of his game, but he made a conscious effort to incorporate it in 1990. By midseason, he had scored more three-point shots than in the previous three seasons combined. "It wasn't a planned thing, it just happened," he said. "It makes guys have to play me farther from the basket. If they get up on me, I can go around them. If they don't, I can take the shot."[15] In one game during the 1992 Finals, Jordan scored 39 points, including six three-pointers. Not only did the arc change his game mid-career, it changed the sport. According to the *NBA Encyclopedia,* "basketball became more of a wide open affair as defenses were forced to spread out and respect the threat of the three-pointer, thus opening up lanes for slashing and driving to the hoop."[16] As Justin Kubatko reported in a 2011 story, no team averages fewer than a dozen three-point attempts per game these days, and guard Ray Allen holds the record with more than 2,700 completed three-point shots and a 40 percent shooting average beyond the arc.[17]

The tall man problem was solved. It was Hobson's new rule, not outright discrimination, that leveled the playing field. It also led to a league whose television contracts run in the billions of dollars. A method of change this successful bears scrutiny. Coach Hobson emphasized a cautious approach to institutional change that applies to both the rules of a game and the rules of a nation. The coach concluded his dissertation's recommendation by saying: "Major changes should never be made without sufficient evidence of their worth and must come through research and experimentation."[18]

ECONOMIC AND POLITICAL INSTITUTIONS

Modern debates over economic policy that take place on op-ed pages and cable TV tend to treat all topics as the clash of two simple theories: laissez-faire market fundamentalism versus big-government socialism. Less heated referees and participants use labels such as "neoclassical" and "Keynesian," but the point is that the diverse, nuanced world of economic understanding and consensus is lost when we simplify issues into a one-dimensional frame of reference.

A key distortion of the twenty-four-hour news cycle is a loss of *long-term* perspective. Regardless of your opinion on Keynesian stimulus spending as a form of *macroeconomic* potential, virtually no one thinks it has any bearing on a nation's long-term growth policy. Indeed, when it comes to growth policy, a consensus exists among academics and policy scholars—widespread agreement that a nation's economic *institutions* are ultimately what determine higher productivity levels and growth rates.

Institutions are constraints that structure economic behavior. These constraints include legal protection, markets, government regulation, government structure, social norms, and religious beliefs. Traditional economics tended to assume that institutions are structured so as to maximize efficiency and utility. More recent scholarship is more skeptical of this claim, as are we. Economists have been drawn to the importance of economic institutions because of their significant role in underpinning economic growth. As Nobel laureate Douglass North writes in *Structure and Change in Economic History:* "Institutions are in effect the filter between individuals and the capital stock . . . and between the capital stock and the output of goods and services and the distribution of income." [19]

And their significance can hardly be understated. From roughly the period of the Roman Empire until the end of the eighteenth century, the average standard of living of human beings increased little. In short, a peasant toiling on a farm in East Anglia in 1300 wasn't much better off than his Druid ancestors were. Conditions did not change much until an industrial revolution was sparked in England in the mid-eighteenth century.

Research by economists on institutions has aimed at the following questions: Why did the industrial revolution begin there and then, and not 1650 or even around the year 50, about the time Hero of Alexandria had developed a steam engine? And why England and not in China or the Roman Empire, states brimming with technical genius? Why did Hero's contemporaries not use steam engines to power instruments of production, instead of using them to wow tourists with magical toys?

Again, from economists: *institutions.* The economic revolution finally happened in England, in about 1750, because of institutions. As a consequence of the Glorious Revolution of 1688, the British government was able to commit to upholding private property rights, protecting wealth, and eliminating arbitrary increases in taxes. These institutional changes gave entrepreneurs the incentives to make investments necessary to make the most of technological inventions—the spinning jenny and the water frame, for example. Though a sophisticated economy at the same time, China, by contrast, lacked the institutions to allow entrepreneurship to flourish.

So why isn't the whole world rich? Do some countries just fail to comprehend the link between good institutions and growth? Perhaps—but the story is more complicated. There are rarely hundred-dollar bills on the sidewalk just waiting to be scooped up.

Raghuram Rajan and Luigi Zingales[20] confront the basic question of why economies might pursue anti-growth strategies in the first place. Their conclusion, as well as those of other authors, highlights the importance of *political* as well as economic institutions. They have described a development trap as an initial allocation of endowments such that constituencies created by those endowments support bad policies that reproduce those initial constituencies over time. In this case, sequencing reforms in favor of growth should create coalitions to overrule interests of a privileged elite. Such ideas are akin to those of Douglass North, John Wallis, and Barry Weingast in *Violence and Social Order* (2009), that static economies are dominated by rent-seeking coalitions that limit access both to political and economic institutions.

Rent-seeking is an awkward term, but it means that a group of people have the power to make money by manipulating the rules of government to their advantage. Economist Anne Krueger coined the term in describing the behavior of third-world bureaucrats who were technically corrupt—selling business licenses to applicants who preferred to skip the regulatory waiting period.[21] The existence of long waiting periods for licenses is usually a sign of rent-seeking. In modern economies, special interests often seek rents in the tax code by lobbying legislators. Monopolistic firms are natural rent-seekers, as are labor unions and guilds that expend their resources to limit competition.

This line of inquiry recognizes that explaining the emergence of growth requires a theory as to why some nations prosper while others fail to do so. Institutional explanations have centered on historical foundations—such as the rule of law, an independent judiciary, and property rights. Daron Acemoglu and James Robinson argue that a good theory must also point out factors that stimulate or check prosperity. They emphasize the connection between what they call *inclusive* economic and political institutions and economic prosperity. As with all traditional analyses of institutions as initial conditions for growth, they identify the historical foundations mentioned above as the keys to growth. By contrast, *extractive* institutions fail to protect property rights and do reward incumbent firms and interest groups. At the same time, political institutions can be inclusive, with broadly shared political power, or extractive, with concentrated political power.[22]

These insights offer a useful complement to the rich historical institutional approach. But we view them as incomplete for our purposes. Great Power decline reflects the inability of political institutions to adapt to changing economic realities. The runaway U.S. fiscal crisis of our time is taking place in an economy *with* inclusive economic and political institutions.

Perhaps the way to think about this paradox is that there is no perfect set of economic rules that guarantee growth. The rules of capitalism circa 1820 were great for promoting growth in 1820, but were insufficient for 1920 industrial capitalism and certainly for 2020 techno-capitalism. The idea of a corporation giving equity shares to workers is a recent phenomenon, an innovation beyond the imagination (and institutions) of early America because it blurs the distinction between labor and capital. Likewise, labor regulations instituted in the 1930s that were useful in giving collective voice to workers for decades have turned out to limit workplace flexibility in the twenty-first century. During the 1940s, one in three private workers was a union member, compared to one in fifteen today. If the rules governing collective bargaining in the United States are not reformed to make those industries globally competitive, that model is likely to go extinct.

It is well understood that a nation's transportation infrastructure creates broad growth benefits by lowering transaction costs and enabling the specialization of labor. The United States got a tremendous boost from Eisenhower's Interstate Highway System, just as Rome benefited from the famous Appian Way. But there is no equivalent public benefit from building a second interstate highway. Instead, to keep growing, the society must keep modernizing its physical and intellectual infrastructure. Better asphalt, for example, or Wi-Fi nodes that enable driverless vehicles. The same need for relentless modernization applies to institutions.

One pragmatic approach to measuring institutional quality is the Index of Economic Freedom, published annually by the Heritage

Foundation and *Wall Street Journal,* and which compares institutions across hundreds of countries from 1995 to the present. The index is a composite of ten distinct institutions, including openness to trade, income tax rates, and corruption. Added to the index equation in 2007 is business freedom, a measure pioneered by the World Bank that describes how easy it is to start a new company in terms of licensing fees, bureaucratic forms, and time delays. As you might expect, countries with higher levels of economic freedom tend to have much higher GDP per capita. The five freest economies of Europe in 2012 had an average GDP per capita of $46,593, compared to the average of $13,595 for the five least free European states.

Globally, the average index score has risen from 57.1 (where 100 equals perfect freedom) in 1996 to 59.5 in 2012, a 2.4 point increase. Countries are increasingly aware of how they compare to their peers, and much credit goes to the World Bank's efforts promoting a similar institutional measure known as the Doing Business index. Even though the freedom scores for most countries of the world are increasing, allowing nations to catch up to the successful institutional models of the West, particularly the United States, many leading economies are backsliding. Ghana's score went from 55.6 in 1995 to 60.7 in 2012, a five-point increase, compared to Greece's score, which dropped over the same time from 61.2 to 55.4. India's economic freedom rose by 9.5 points, while the United States gained four points from 1995 to 2007, after which it lost all those gains. Even though America has a relatively high institutional score of 76.3 on the freedom index, it needs to keep evolving its laws to keep its economy growing.

These institutional measures affirm a basic template for prosperity that is well understood. To be sure, there will never be a perfect institutional model, as economies are still testing new rules in the "arms race" of economic growth. However, many countries have fallen into the trap of thinking their laws are optimized. Most of the countries of Western Europe, for example, stopped trying to reform their individual economies and instead turned to "harmonizing" regulations within the Eurozone. And this tendency points to the real challenge: political institutions that become stagnant, making economic evolution impossible.

TEMPLATE FOR GREAT POWER IMBALANCE

The remainder of this book examines eight case studies of Great Power imbalance. Of course, we can't take a comprehensive look at all powers throughout history. However, we endeavored to be fair in our examination of a consensus group of the most important powers in history: Rome, China, the Ottoman Empire, the Spanish empire, modern Japan, the United Kingdom (reluctantly), modern Europe, and, finally, the curious case of California. We then look at the imbalance of the United States today.

This chapter has established a *template of Great Power imbalance,* which we will refer to while presenting each case study. Not every imbalance in history will exhibit all of these behaviors, but we expect most to be present in every case.

We mean for this book to be much more than a litany of failure. Within many cases of imbalance over the long term, there are examples of balance maintained despite the odds. Leaders found ways to overcome the pull of the template. Rome, for instance, survived for centuries that included tremendous internal challenges and transformations, most notably the Caesarian revolution. Every decade that a Great Power can maintain balance is a triumph because the pressures to fall are natural, powerful, and constant. Modern Sweden offers another example of a nation overcoming the template of behaviors and engineering a successful institutional overhaul. That said, here are the key factors to watch for:

- *Bounded rationality* means that rulers are limited in their ability to choose the ideal economic policies. Ignorance is the ultimate bind, especially for nations that struggled with economic crises before the discovery of the laws of economics. Further, the public choice of leaders is bounded by available candidates, as well as the veil of ignorance concerning their policies.
- National *identity* makes for strong cultural, political, and economic institutions, which are essential for growth and power, but that strength also implies a conservatism in the sense of resistance to structural change. Political identity is a key factor in polarization and gridlock.
- With *loss aversion,* leaders rarely innovate, since they are averse to losing their status as leaders. In a dynamic world, economic change is often happening

faster than political change, but loss aversion makes leading economies reluctant to reform.

- *Time preference* matters, too. Even when officials are cognizant of the need for reform, they defer necessary changes for another day or year. Voters, too, habitually discount the future value of higher prosperity tomorrow and avoid making painful choices in the present.

4

THE RUIN OF ROME

An empire remains powerful so long as its subjects rejoice in it.

— Livy

The New Testament tells the story of a man named Jesus of Nazareth, a leading prophet of his people who chafed against the local order. Jesus was crucified on the orders of Pontius Pilate, the local Roman governor in Jerusalem. For many who hear this story for the first time, it's hard not to imagine that the Roman Empire was evil. In the opinion of historical scholars, Rome at that moment had just transformed from a republic to an empire, but its story is much more complicated than these labels imply. Jesus lived in a remote corner of Rome, a Mediterranean-spanning civilization with its capital 1,500 miles away from Jerusalem. It is unlikely that Tiberius, the emperor, was even aware of the martyr or his crucifixion.

The scale of the Roman Empire was the central feature of its rise to power, and perhaps also its fall from power. That scale owes much to the rule of Augustus, who was the ruler of Rome when Jesus was still a boy. The ascent of Augustus, regarded as one of the greatest strategic and administrative geniuses in history, is an amazing drama. Though living far from Rome, the teenage boy, then named Octavian, learned that Julius Caesar had been assassinated by treasonous senators on the Ides of March in 44 B.C. On the day the messenger brought that news, Augustus was also told that he had been adopted by Caesar as heir.

The die of fate had been placed in the young man's hands. Should he hide among the local troops or sail for Italy? He sailed. After a half decade of civil wars among rival claimants to power, including Mark Antony and Cleopatra, Augustus emerged triumphant and declared himself *princeps* (first citizen). Romans prayed for an end to the century of strife and civil wars. The boy emperor secured the pax.

Augustus ruled from 27 B.C. to A.D. 14, four decades of prosperous expansion that set the stage for two full centuries of Pax Romana, a time of unparalleled prosperity. To put the era in context, no other civilization before or since Rome ruled the entire area surrounding the Mediterranean Sea. Not Spain. Not Britain. And no society approached its degree of technological sophistication for nearly two thousand years. "The Rome of 100 A.D. had better paved streets, sewage disposal, water supply, and fire protection than the capitals of civilized Europe in 1800," writes the economic historian Joel Mokyr.[1] The city of Rome reached a population of one million, a mark not rivaled anywhere else until London in the nineteenth century.

A century after the reign of Augustus, Rome stopped growing. Four and half centuries after the death of Augustus—and Jesus—the city of Rome and the western half of the empire that bore its name had fallen. But when, precisely? Was it A.D. 410, when foreign invaders sacked the city of Rome, a city that had not been marred in eight hundred years? Or was it the violent migration of Germanic tribes across the Rhine and Danube that led Emperor Aurelian in A.D. 271 to begin constructing defensive walls around interior cities? Was it instead when the last emperor, Romulus Augustus, was sent packing from the great city in A.D. 476 by the conquering barbarian Odoacer? Or was the fall of Rome less a moment in time than it was a centuries-long disintegration of the economy?

Rome, as a historical object, is difficult to discuss because it was so long-lived. The Roman society, economy, and polity of Augustus in the

year A.D. 0 are different than in Trajan's Rome in A.D. 117 or Caracalla's Rome in A.D. 217 or Constantine's Rome in A.D. 317. Imagine
our challenge in dissecting the fall of Rome as that of an historian two
thousand years in the future, after a third millennium of dark ages has
ravaged most evidence. Will they speak of the American troops of Pe-
traeus and Eisenhower as if they were the same army? Will they smear
together the rule of George Washington and George W. Bush and some
other President George circa 2180 as if they were roughly the same executives? No, to understand the military weakness of Rome in the fifth
century and its cultural weakness in the fourth century, we must look to
the economic seeds planted hundreds of years before. The rise of Rome
and the fall of Rome have the same roots.

A SKETCH OF THE ROMAN ECONOMY

With ample caveats about a paucity of data, the economist Angus Maddison[2] estimates the gross domestic product of Rome to be $25 billion
(in 1990 dollars), which is equivalent to the economy of the modern-
day state of North Dakota. Maddison also estimates the population
of Western Europe (Roman and non-Roman) at 24.7 million people in
A.D. 0, growing to 27.6 million in A.D. 200, but declining to 22.9 million and then 18.6 million over the next two-hundred-year increment.
The population in Europe did not recover to the level of the imperial
Roman peak until the eleventh or twelfth century A.D.

Before we get too far into the fall of the Roman Empire, it might help
to understand its rise. The birth of the *empire* was not a violent moment
when a happy republic transformed suddenly into a dictatorship of
Caesars. The "republic" during the century before Julius Caesar had devolved into an undemocratic, corrupt, and brutal society. It was a republic in name only, granting citizenship only to elites in the inner provinces
of Italy. Stability after the Social War and the intrigues that followed
was not established until the dictatorship of Sulla (138–78 B.C.), who
twice marched on Rome by force with legions from his wars in Greece.
This action provided young Julius a role model for how to respond to
a corrupt and antagonistic Senate. Nor was Sulla the first dictator to
usurp the Senate's authority and purge the elites on the wrong side of
a policy disagreement. In 133 B.C., the Senate had the tribune Tiberius

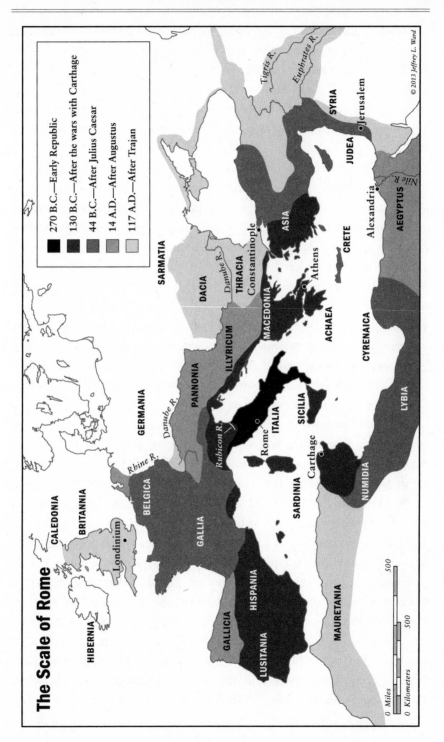

The Scale of Rome

270 B.C.—Early Republic
130 B.C.—After the wars with Carthage
44 B.C.—After Julius Caesar
14 A.D.—After Augustus
117 A.D.—After Trajan

© 2013 Jeffrey L. Ward

HIBERNIA

CALEDONIA

BRITANNIA

Londinium

GERMANIA

Rhine R.

BELGICA

GALLIA

GALLICIA

LUSITANIA

HISPANIA

MAURETANIA

SARDINIA

ITALIA

Rome

Rubicon R.

PANNONIA

Danube R.

ILLYRICUM

SARMATIA

DACIA

Danube R.

THRACIA

Constantinople

MACEDONIA

ACHAEA

Athens

ASIA

CRETE

CYRENAICA

LYBIA

NUMIDIA

Carthage

SICILIA

Alexandria

AEGYPTUS

Nile R.

SYRIA

JUDEA

Jerusalem

Tigris R.

Euphrates R.

0 Miles   500

0 Kilometers   500

Gracchus assassinated for suggesting popular land reforms—the equivalent of a public murder of a chief justice of the U.S. Supreme Court. For the whole century before Caesar's dictatorship, the aristocracy went to war with itself. We would argue that the imperial rule of Julius saved Rome, particularly his populist expansion of citizenship to foreign subjects, and that Augustus did even more to cement the power of Rome.

The agricultural economy prospered as the benefits of trade on Rome's roads and in an ever-expanding interior grew. And grew they did, thanks to the Roman legions. After the successful military conquests of Gaul by Julius Caesar—he was the first Roman general to cross the English Channel and the first to cross the Rhine River—the Senate in 49 B.C. ordered him to return alone to Rome. Whether one believes the paranoid Senate would have killed Julius or not, he decided to lead his army across the Rubicon and conquer Rome itself. But that act was not, to use Winston Churchill's phrase, the beginning of the end of Rome's greatness, as Daron Acemoglu and James Robinson assert, but rather merely the end of the beginning. Those authors finger Julius Caesar's dictatorship and the subsequent empire as the downward turning point in Roman history, which seems two centuries premature.

We should think of imperial Rome not as one era but two, historians tell us. The *Principate,* initiated by Augustus, lasted from 27 B.C.–A.D. 235, and technically includes the Crisis of the Third Century, through A.D. 284. That era was followed by the latter period, known as the *Dominate,* which lasted until A.D. 476; this period was marked by nearly constant war, civil and foreign conflict being almost indistinct. The evidence suggests that the economic peak was not at the beginning of the Principate but its end. This timing is critical.

Institutional change enables economic growth, but only up to a new level, or what the economist Walt Rostow called a "stage" of development. That means we can credit Principate institutions and technologies for fueling economic growth for nearly two hundred years, which then tapered off at that higher level. A few key institutions were the army; labor specialization, thanks to the scale of trade; and urbanization. The Roman roads enhanced all three. Roman markets, laws, taxes, and bureaucratic efficiency also helped. An absence of new technologies or further institutional development suggests that by the early third century, Malthusian pressures were likely eroding average incomes.

The economy itself was predominantly rural and agricultural. The famous orator Cicero declared that "of all the occupations by which gain is secured, none is better than agriculture, none more profitable, none more delightful, none more becoming to a free man." The majority of Romans lived in the countryside and the simple virtues of country living were celebrated by the elites as well. Wheat was the dominant crop, and bread was a staple of nearly every meal. Taxes paid to Rome, the *annona,* were usually paid in kind with grain. Yet it was the city that marked Roman civilization as different from tribes, the city that enabled specialized trade and services. Scholars currently estimate that 40 percent of Roman Italy was urbanized, or 25 percent if we do not count Rome itself.[3] We might wonder if Cicero's words may have been intentionally patronizing, or nostalgic, or if Romans themselves were unaware how economically relevant urbanization was to growth. From our modern perch, we know that urbanization was made possible by the uniquely Roman invention of concrete (*opus caementicium*) in the late Republic, as well as by advances in architecture and engineering. Nevertheless, land ownership remained the bank of every man. Even among the senatorial and equestrian (knight) classes, land was the dominant store of wealth.

CAESARIAN SEEDS

The interesting story of Roman civilization is not the dramatic narrative of one dictator succeeding another and another, but the economic logic of geographic expansion, assimilation, and growth. The expansion of Rome's economic scale, which lasted an astounding seven hundred years from 500 B.C. to A.D. 200, was exceptional in size but typical of the transformation of tribal human villages into larger city-states and then nation-states. Kin and clan networks gradually gave way to the emergence of impersonal rules of law, a transformation driven by the economic benefits of larger political units, which not coincidentally yielded military advantages. This process happened all over the world, but the little tribe on the Palatine Hill near the Tiber River in central Italy was the most successful of all. Rome's unique mix of institutions allowed it to dominate neighboring regions until it formed the strongest power in all of Italy, then in all of Europe, then the known world.

The ancient historian Cassius Dio explained the subtlety of institutional assimilation this way:

> The barbarians were adapting themselves to Roman ways, *were becoming accustomed to hold markets,* and were meeting in peaceful assemblages. They had not, however, forgotten their ancestral habits, their native manners, their old life of independence. . . . They were becoming different without knowing it.[4] (emphasis added)

Rome's geographic reach is one of the few things we know with some exactness. There were forty or so provinces at Rome's fullest extent, depending on how the lines were drawn at any given time. Sicily was the first Roman province, won from Carthage in 241 B.C. After the third and final Punic War in 149–146 B.C., Carthage (Tunisia) was destroyed and its lands taken by Rome. Illyricum (the eastern Balkans), Macedonia, Greece, and eastern Asia (Turkey) became provinces during the second century B.C. Parts of the Iberian Peninsula were annexed in waves from 220 to 19 B.C. Pompey annexed Syria as a province in 64 B.C. Nearby Judea became a client kingdom at the same time until parts were converted into a province decades later. Julius conquered Gaul in the bloody decade of 58–50 B.C. Egypt was an independent state until its queen Cleopatra VII was deposed along with her lover Mark Antony by their rival, the future emperor Augustus in 30 B.C. Augustus was also aggressive in expanding the frontiers within central Europe, conquering Raetia (Switzerland) and Dacia (the western Balkans) and pushing farther east into Asia. Northwestern Africa was the location of a handful of colonies and client states until A.D. 40, when Rome divided it into two provinces. Britannia was invaded in A.D. 43. Thrace (Bulgaria) became a province in A.D. 46. Emperor Trajan pushed Rome to its largest territorial limits during his reign from A.D. 98 until 117, conquering Dacia (Hungary) and even Mesopotamia (Iraq).

Credit goes to the army for the rapid expansion, itself one of ancient Rome's institutional advantages. Augustus made two wise reforms. The first was to use fifteen-year voluntary enlistments rather than conscription to create a professional army. The second was to establish a Praetorian unit in Rome to protect the city from rebellious generals (like his father). While they did protect the emperor from attack, an unintended consequence of the Praetorian guard is that they became the kingmakers as later emperors undercut the power of the Senate.

Flavius Josephus, a Jewish aristocrat in Jerusalem who participated in a rebellion but later befriended the emperor Vespasian, describes the unique nature of the Roman military:

> If you study carefully the organization of the Roman army, you will realize that they possess their great empire as a reward for valor, not as a gift of fortune. For the Romans, the wielding of arms does not begin with the outbreak of war, nor do they sit idly in peacetime and move their hands only during times of need. Quite the opposite! As if born for the sole purpose of wielding arms, they never take a break from training, never wait for a situation requiring arms. Their practice sessions are no less strenuous than real battles. Each soldier trains every day with all his energy as if in war. And therefore they bear the stress of battle with the greatest ease.[5]

One economic benefit of the army's dominance in a large empire was that legions were only needed at the frontier. Rome's interior provinces in the West faced no threats and enjoyed peace, which greatly enhances the climate for trade and investment. The expansion of Roman territory during the Republican era brought with it transformations that at once confirmed the Roman identity and enlarged it. Roman values were understood to be universal, much in the manner that Americans believe their notion of fundamental human rights apply to all people, citizen and noncitizen alike. Consequently, it was easy for the Romans to assimilate advantageous aspects of other cultures while also assimilating conquered peoples into their own, often as slaves but over time as equals.

As Rome grew, its cultural identity took the place of an ethnic identity. Giving up pretensions of racial superiority is difficult for any conquering people, but the great success of Rome's empire is surely due to its ability to extend Roman citizenship to foreign peoples. Julius Caesar himself pioneered the Romanization of foreigners, that is, granting citizenship to non-Italians. By granting citizenship to the people in the province of Hispania (modern Spain and Portugal), Caesar established an institutional principle that strengthened the society for centuries. Doing so also resolved one of the key factors in the Social War of the first century B.C., but it also fueled the murderous hostility of ethnic elitists in the Senate. Despite his murder, the reform held fast under Augustus and became the norm of a conquering empire during the Principate. Within a century, the sons of Hispania were anointed as emperors, notably Trajan, Hadrian, and Marcus Aurelius.

The technological achievements of Rome are sometimes overlooked. To be sure, there was no Age of Enlightenment akin to the seventeenth century. Concrete may seem to be Rome's only major invention, but that is if we limit our definition of inventions to *hardware*. The *software* of Roman society—its professional army, federalist governance, property rights—actually matter more for economic growth. And one should not ignore the impact of concrete! It enabled commercial growth in two major ways. First, concrete made possible increasingly dense urban areas with taller buildings, better sanitation, and water from the aqueducts. Second, intercity trade was enhanced with stronger roads, while underwater concrete enabled better ports for sea trade.

Investments in public goods during the first century were constant, and probably worth much more as a commercial multiplier than the emperors realized. "I found Rome brick, and left it marble," Augustus boasted. His heirs did their best to match his infrastructural achievements. Tiberius (ruled A.D. 14–37) conquered new lands and secured them by building major military bases along the new frontier. The infamous Caligula initiated two new aqueducts in Rome during his brief four-year rule. Following him, Claudius (ruled A.D. 41–54) was an active builder of roads, aqueducts, and canals linking the provinces all across the empire. Until the treasury was diverted to other purposes in later centuries, this infrastructure was the primary expense of the state.

The one political institution that may explain the empire's longevity is, ironically, hostility toward hereditary rule. In 509 B.C., when it was a rather small city-state, there was a popular rebellion against the last king of Rome. A constitutional democracy was formed, with limited executive power given to two consuls who served a single year each. Also, as it eschewed monarchy, the Roman state left member cities administratively independent, an institutional arrangement that was maintained during the Principate. Economists Peter Garnsey and Richard Saller explain: "The secret of government without bureaucracy was the Roman system of cities which were self-governing and could provide for the needs of empire. The period of the *Principate* witnessed a striking multiplication and expansion of autonomous urban units, especially in those parts of the empire where cities had been few." [6] Romans enjoyed what we call a federalist governance structure. Even the early imperial administration had a tiny head count, according to writer Cullen Murphy.[7]

Federalism only made sense given the slowness of transportation and communications. Information traveled at about one mile an hour during the empire. We know this speed from a variety of methods, such as the average number of days it took for various parts of the empire to change the dating marks on official documents from an old emperor to a new one. The names of the older (deceased) appeared on official documents in the Roman province of Egypt for an average of fifty-six days after the new emperor had been named in the capital.[8] This constraint alone neutered later efforts to exert central control over the economy.

No Roman institution was more important, or celebrated, than its legal system, particularly its recognition of property rights. The rule of law, rather than the rule of men, no doubt encouraged Solovian investment (for example, purchasing capital equipment). The Romans also had vibrant markets for urban trade, markets unique in Europe. Heavy trading led to the development of a peculiar institution known as the collegium, which gave legal status to a private group, the direct ancestor in law of the modern corporation, trade union, and even nonprofit organization. Trade was further enhanced by the development of a kind of insurance for dangerous long-distance sea voyages.

All of these features gave the empire unrivaled economic advantages, but Rome never fully understood the power of free markets. The elites scorned merchants. There was no "bourgeois dignity," as the economist Deirdre McCloskey would say. "[T]he Romans looked down on entrepreneurship, which Americans hold in the highest esteem, and despised manual labor," [9] says Cullen Murphy. In fact, Roman senators were barred from engaging in shipping and other kinds of trade because it was considered undignified. This passage from Cicero is revealing:

Also vulgar and unsuitable for gentlemen are the occupations of all hired workmen whom we pay for their labor, not for their artistic skills; for with these men, their pay is itself a recompense for slavery. Also to be considered vulgar are retail merchants, who buy from wholesale merchants and immediately turn around and resell; for they would not make a profit unless they lied a lot. And nothing is more shameless than lying. All craftsmen, too, are engaged in vulgar occupations, for a workshop or factory can have nothing gentle about it. And the most shameful occupations are those which cater to our sensual pleasures, "fish sellers, butchers, cooks, poultry raisers, and fishermen," as Terence says. Add to these, if you like, perfume makers, dancers, and all of vaudeville.[10]

The heavy use of slaves also meant that Roman culture scorned manual labor. One out of three people in Rome may have been a slave. Some have argued that slavery made the Roman economy reliant on conquest to harvest a fresh generation of slaves, but that argument may go too far. Most societies had slaves until relatively recently in world history. Economists today would argue that slave labor is far less efficient than a labor market, and that the institution is a sign of economic weakness rather than strength. Overall, Roman attitudes toward different occupations represented a rigid occupational hierarchy, a kind of caste system culturally and sometimes legally, that was an unintentional but definitive barrier to progress.

This survey of the Roman economy accounts for its many advantages, nearly all of them *institutional software*. When a civilization experiences a century of technological growth, as for example modern America has, falling backward in absolute terms is unlikely. But when your growth is based on commercial scale (meaning a larger and more deeply integrated trading population), and then that scale is shattered, economic collapse is highly likely. As the economist Joel Mokyr says of the Roman economy: "its growth derived from those aspects for which the Greeks and Romans are famous: organization, trade, order, the use of money, and law. This kind of growth can take an economy a long way, and it did. When the political foundation on which it is built becomes shaky, however, the prosperity based on Smithian growth alone is rapidly lost."[11]

EVIDENCE OF THE FALL

There remains a popular theory that the emergence of Christianity during the later empire was a principal cause of Rome's fall. This explanation was prominent in Edward Gibbon's famous *History of the Decline and Fall of the Roman Empire,* published in 1776. Today, that theory has been largely debunked. "Most scholars have considered economic forces as critical," wrote Nobel laureate Douglass North in *Structure.*

One fashionable modern theory that grabs attention is this: Rome never fell. Forget searching for causes, these historians say. Rather, migratory pressures led to a gentle evolution of the culture. What's so great about empire, anyway? Historian Bryan Ward-Perkins made a definitive case for the traditional, politically incorrect viewpoint in his 2005 book, *The Fall of Rome:*

> It is currently deeply unfashionable to state that anything like a "crisis" or a "decline" occurred at the end of the Roman Empire, let alone that "civilization" collapsed and a "dark age" ensued. The new orthodoxy is that the Roman world, in both East and West, was slowly, and essentially painlessly, "transformed" into a medieval form. However, there is an insuperable problem with this new view: it does not fit the mass of archaeological evidence now available, which shows a startling decline in the western standards of living during the fifth to seventh centuries. This was a change that affected everyone, from peasants to kings, even the bodies of the saints resting in their churches. It was no mere transformation—it was decline on a scale that can reasonably be described as "the end of a civilization."

Ward-Perkins effectively traces the loss of complexity to a collapse of the scale of Rome's once vast, once frictionless, internal trade market. Without scale, specialization dried up. Whole towns died, and whole regions reverted to lower levels of development than they had been at *before* the Romans arrived. The maps of regions once dotted with Roman towns, now rural or even wilderness, are breathtaking.

Was the loss of scale the cause of Rome's fall? Here it is difficult to disentangle economic decline from military defeat and political decline. The demise of scale economies is perhaps better understood as a consequence, not a cause. Long before the fifth-century economic collapse described by Ward-Perkins, there were three centuries of *self-inflicted economic wounds*.

"There are almost as many causes cited for Rome's collapse as there are historians," writes Walter Isaacson.[12] One scholar in Germany tabulated more than two hundred articulated causes of the fall. Gibbon himself in 1776 had the common sense to suggest that the various theories were all working in concert. Most of these causes were fashioned before hard data were available.

Figure 12. World lead production, 750 B.C.–present.

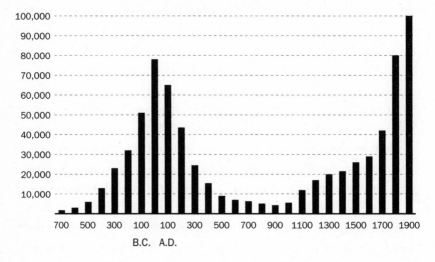

Source: Hong, et al., *Science* 265, No. 5180 (1994)

In 1994, four scholars reported in the journal *Science* the results of atmospheric lead pollution that had accumulated over the millennia as preserved in the Greenland ice sheet.[13] Lead pollution is a product of silver smelting, and the resulting data produced by the scholars is charted above, showing that lead in the atmosphere peaked during the early empire. Similar pollution levels did not occur until the 1750s. Another new piece of data is the discovery of shipwrecks in the Mediterranean, carbon dated to identify their age. Nearly two hundred wrecks can be dated to the first century A.D., and a similar number to the first century

B.C. The second centuries A.D. and B.C. have slightly smaller numbers. And although better ships might explain some decline, the number of wrecks discovered from the third century is just over 80, then 50 from the fourth century, and so on. At the least, this evidence shows how seriously, if gradually, trade in the western Mediterranean collapsed.

A third bit of evidence that catches the economist's eye is the archaeology of coinage, both its debasement over time and the areas where it ceased to be utilized. Ward-Perkins recounts detailed archaeological evidence of the decline of economic complexity throughout the *western* Roman Empire—the loss of advanced pottery, coinage, even basic mortar. The decline is limited to the western half, and even there was geographically sporadic on the third and fourth centuries. Decline becomes apparent in the fifth century, most abruptly in Britain, which "reverted to a level of economic simplicity similar to that of the Bronze Age, with no coinage, and only hand-shaped pots and wooden buildings." [14]

So the basic causes of Rome's weakened economy are not so mysterious anymore. We know when decline happened, and its general pattern. In a 1994 essay, the economist Bruce Bartlett laid out the economic explanation—food subsidies, rising taxation, inflation, and ultimately state socialism. "In the end, there was no money left to pay the army, build forts or ships, or protect the frontier. The barbarian invasions, which were the final blow to the Roman state in the fifth century, were simply the culmination of three centuries of deterioration in the fiscal capacity of the state to defend itself." [15]

IMPERIAL IMBALANCE

When something dies, there are many causes. Some are obvious, some are subtle. Some come at the moment of death, while most long precede the final moment. When it comes to Rome, the military victories of the Germanic tribes casts a shadow over all other explanations, but this one has light logical support. As Acemoglu and Robinson argue: "the success of the Goths, Huns, and Vandals against Rome was a symptom, not the cause, of Rome's decline." Indeed, Rome faced serious foreign military threats during its entire existence, but only in the century after its *internal economic stagnation* did the foreign threats prevail.

There are many kinds of economic imbalance. In our assessment, the

Roman economic imbalance was an ongoing inability to match its fiscal outlays with available revenues. Like most rich nations today, Rome made fiscal commitments that it could not square with taxation, with monetary debasement, or with dictatorial central planning. It tried all three in that order, before its collapse. Rome's fiscal problems and political erosion had origins in the second century B.C., when the satirist Juvenal ridiculed the selling of votes by an infantile public in exchange for *panem et circenses*—bread and circuses.

There were a hundred small errors made by Roman rulers during the centuries of empire, but three can be singled out as especially damaging. If any one of these three had been decided differently, a much richer history might have replaced a thousand dark years of economic regression.

The first error, begun in A.D. 122, was the building of Hadrian's Wall across the midsection of Britain. The wall is symbolic of Emperor Hadrian's reign, pulling back from the frontiers, from conquest, and turning inward. The second error was the debasement of the silver coinage by emperor Septimius Severus at the turn of the second century. We now know that thinning a hard currency can cause galloping inflation despite shoring up short-term budget deficits. The third great error was Emperor Diocletian's effort to command and control the economy as a "cure" for its weakness at the turn of the third century. The people side of the economy lost all flexibility. Like the other errors, this provided short-term advantages but with massive long-term costs.

The people of Rome may not have understood why the empire was weakening. Economic growth and decline moved in such slow tides that it wasn't even a topic of discussion. Hindsight is helpful, however. We see the people being entertained and bribed with "bread and circuses" while their constitutional institutions were chipped away.

THE BEGINNING OF THE END: TRAJAN'S ACCESSION

The beginning of the end of Rome is easy to pinpoint. It was August 9, A.D. 117. Emperor Marcus Ulpius Nerva Trajanus Augustus, known as Trajan, died that day, after a brief period of illness that began during his campaign to extend the empire in Mesopotamia against the Parthians.

Trajan was a beloved ruler, renowned for his tolerance of Christians, his just treatment of property owners, and above all his successful efforts to expand and strengthen the empire. Trajan is also one of the few Romans whose reputation has not diminished or varied across the ages. Every new emperor after him was welcomed by the Senate with the hopeful phrase "felicior Augusto, melior Traiano," which means, "Luckier than Augustus, better than Trajan." Later Romans, such as Pliny the Younger, lauded him. In the tenth century, Thomas Aquinas also lauded him, and Christian theologians described Trajan as a moral pagan. In Dante's *Inferno,* Trajan sits happily in heaven.

Despite his popularity, we see in his era as well some of the first threads of Rome's economic imbalance. Trajan initiated the first welfare program directed to relieve childhood poverty around Rome. Though not a widespread program nor universal in the region, it was more symbol than substance. Nevertheless, it established a principle of state obligation to compensate for unequal market outcomes. A three-month spectacle of gladiatorial games was also a costly, if not original, indulgence.

Immediately after Trajan's death, his adoptive son and the new emperor, Hadrian, immediately gave up the campaign in Mesopotamia and set about withdrawing Roman forces within a secure border. Hadrian is famous, of course, for the great Roman wall constructed on his orders across the island of Great Britain, which separated Roman Britain from the unconquerable and savage Celts of Scotland. That's the Hollywood version, anyway. The wall marked the terminus of the Roman state, but it was designed more to control and tax trade, not to seal off the Roman world. Psychologically, though, that is exactly what the wall did.

The transition of power from Trajan to Hadrian occurred in the midst of Rome's peak prosperity, known as the Antonine era, from A.D. 96 to 192. The geographic reach of Rome was greatest on the day Trajan died, in A.D. 117. After that, it would be drawn back over a smaller and smaller territory for the next three and a half centuries. On balance, Hadrian was a great emperor who subscribed to Livy's maxim that the foundation of a society's strength is the well-being of the people. Hadrian continued Trajan's policy of investing heavily in public goods, and his decision to *understretch* the empire was largely to redirect the treasury inward. For all the good Hadrian did, the completely inward orientation he established was intentional and set a negative precedent.

There is no point denying the archaeological evidence. This era was the economic turning point. The most obvious explanation is that the growth in economic scale and labor specialization came to a halt when the geographic expansion came to halt. Moreover, Hadrian surrendered Trajan's conquest of Mesopotamia and then lands on the eastern side of the Danube. What might have been if Rome had invested in assimilating those regions, particularly the Tigris and Euphrates with all their potential to conduct sea trade from the Persian Gulf to the Far East?

Another theory is that the Antonine Plague of A.D. 165–180 was the turning point. Contemporaries say that one in four infected persons died, though survivors were immune. Scholars now believe this was the first appearance of smallpox in Europe. The empire-wide epidemic wiped out an estimated five million people, but the theory that it was an economic turning point doesn't accord with the effect of other epidemics, which have a perverse counterbalancing effect of boosting wealth and income per capita. Wages should grow when labor is scarce.

Cullen Murphy favors the "overstretch" hypothesis, even though the timing is off the mark (Rome's economy turned nearly a century after the geographic stretch of Trajan). He cites the Romans' awareness of the fiscal trade-off between guns and butter. Cassius Dio called it a choice between "swords and bread," attributed to Agrippa, the right-hand man of Augustus. But so what? That Romans knew the short-term trade-off in finances but not the long-term Smithian economics is a sign of ignorance, not wisdom. More to the point, Murphy's otherwise insightful analysis of Rome's analogue to America makes a hash of the military pressures on civil society.[16] On the one hand, Murphy argues the loss of a conscripted army in the United States has created a cultural divide, but he then argues that Rome's military culture grew too strong, which then, on the other hand, led to oppressive conscription under Diocletian. So which is it? We agree with Augustus that an all-volunteer, professional military is better for the society's culture and its security. The late empire's readoption of conscription was just another form of state-sanctioned slave labor.

Within the state's borders, the economy continued to thrive, specialize, and grow, but the fortress psychology was soon dominant in civil affairs after Hadrian's ascension, an implicit assumption that the state should do more than protect the citizenry and build infrastructure. It should entertain. It should fight poverty. There was an enlargement of what benevolence by the ruler meant in practice. As economists, we have a strict and technical definition for what counts as a public good, but dictators (the cruel and the benevolent) have their own definitions, which suit their political ambitions.

Security is the singular essential public good, necessary by definition for a state to exist. Transportation, common currency, and basic utilities (fresh water and sanitation) are almost as essential. They are the basic conditions to enable private economic prosperity. Later-stage "public goods" challenge the limits of what a state can provide more efficiently than the private sector. Entertainment and food are productively, if not universally, supplied privately.

Hadrian's pullback was deeply unpopular in the Senate and among the people. Mike Duncan's 179-volume podcast *History of Rome* explains how carefully Hadrian disguised his intentions. He diverted popular attention with "games, games, and more games." He was slow to return from the frontier to the capital, arriving in July of A.D. 118. Before arriving, he ordered the murder of a handful of senators who opposed his foreign policy. He also coerced the Senate into justifying the murders with trumped-up charges against the victims. This precedent boded ill for Rome's political order.

A final move by Hadrian to curry popular favor raises economic alarms, in hindsight at least. He canceled "all outstanding debts taken out on any state loan taken out in the last fifteen years," explains Duncan. "And to prove his point, he had the Praetorians march the loan records out into Trajan's Forum and burn them all in a great pyre." [17] He also announced that financial burdens on municipalities would be funded directly by the central treasury, effectively bribing cities to sell their independence at a stroke. Although the moves made Hadrian popular, even the dullest citizen of Rome figured out that thrift after that day was for fools. Heavy debts became common for those citizens with the inside connections to get them. It would be centuries before economists formulated the theory of moral hazard, but it was clearly there in practice. Some historians may applaud the pacifism of Hadrian, but it was paid for by corrupting fiscal discipline, local independence, and senatorial autonomy.

Hadrian also became involved when foreign armies threatened at the borders, but he responded in a novel way. He paid for peace rather than war by bribing the Parthians to stand down. Word spread.

THE MIDDLE OF THE END: THE SEVERAN DEBASEMENT

Large as the empire was, the government was limited and the economy profoundly unregulated. "The period of Augustus and of his immediate successors was a time of almost complete freedom for trade and of splendid opportunities for private initiative," according to the famous Yale historian Mikhail Rostovtzeff (writing in the early half of the twentieth century, he pioneered the application of hard economic figures to ancient history).[18] Taxation by Rome was light, limited to 5 percent on inheritances and light tariffs on interprovincial trade.

Augustus, as you might expect, upgraded the Roman tax system from an abusive practice known as tax farming to a national monetized system. Tax farmers paid the treasury a lump-sum fee (often by auction) for rights to collect in-kind taxes from a specific neighborhood in whatever way possible. After the Augustan reforms, taxes continued to evolve over the next few centuries as Rome became hungrier for revenues to pay for its growing obligations. When no degree of tax collection was sufficient, emperors had limited options. Deficit spending was not an option because treasury bonds had yet to be invented. The ancients had a *cash* economy, or more precisely a *coin* economy. The revenue options in such an economy were to use the hidden tax of inflation known as debasement, or to steal. Selling state lands was the honorable method, but there was only so much state property, so confiscation of the assets of the wealthiest citizens occurred with greater frequency. Bartlett calls this practice the "war against wealth."

Another practice was to collect tribute from the people upon the ascension of a new emperor or a great victory. Emperors learned to declare even the smallest skirmishes as triumphs worthy of tribute, which Caracalla (reigned A.D. 198–217) did so frequently that the historian Rostovtzeff described it as "pure robbery." More ominous for future instability, the legions were given bonuses during these tribute times, and received ever-larger bonuses with each new emperor. Fresh emperors were eager to buy loyalty, naturally, but the legions learned that assassination yielded a bonus. Consider the incentives!

The reign of Caracalla is perhaps the single period on which the empire turned downward. He was part of the Severan dynasty, founded by his father, Septimius Severus. Both were thuggish in their approach to imperial rule. "Be harmonious [with your brother], enrich the soldiers, and scorn all other men," advised Severus to his sons on his deathbed. He espoused and embodied the philosophy of a zero-sum, paranoid, and constant struggle for political power.

Severus founded the dynasty in the year A.D. 193, also known as the "year of five emperors." The year began after a dozen years of increasingly erratic rule by Emperor Commodus, who was murdered on the last day of the year 192. His successor, Pertinax, was assassinated in March by the Praetorians after attempting to curtail their power and pay. Afterward, the Praetorian Guard auctioned off the throne. Senator Didius Julianus won by offering 25,000 sesterces per soldier (four brass sesterces equaling one silver denarius). His first act, apparently, was to order a debasement of the denarius from 87 to 81.5 percent silver purity. No matter. He was dead on June 1 at the hands of the ruthless military commander, Septimius Severus. Recognized as emperor by the Senate and the Legions of the Danube and Rhine, Severus had to fight two other generals with pretensions to the throne. To pay his troops, Severus debased the denarius to 78.5 percent. By the end of the year, both of his rivals were dead. Severus ordered the coinage debased once again to 64.5 percent purity in 194. It dropped to 54 percent by the end of 196. Assessing Severus, Edward Gibbon wrote: "Posterity, who experienced the fatal effects of his maxims and example, justly considered him as the principal author of the decline of the Roman Empire." [19]

In 211, Severus died, leaving control of the empire in the hands of vicious sons, Caracalla and Geta. The two brothers hated one another, and before long Caracalla had Geta murdered. The deed was done in front of their mother at a meeting she had organized for the two to reconcile peacefully. It was an accurate omen for his reign, but a half decade passed before Caracalla himself was murdered by one of his Praetorians. The Praetorian prefect Macrinus, another man bound to live just briefly in the role of Caesar, replaced him. The Severan family re-captured power after killing Macrinus and held it until the A.D. 235 as-sassination of the last Severan emperor, Alexander Severus, at the hands of his own troops sparked a half century of civil war and economic depression. Between A.D. 235 and 284, there were twenty-five differ-ent men recognized as emperor in what is known today as the Crisis of the Third Century, including periods where the empire was divided into two or three warring substates. The Roman Empire came close to imploding, but its preservation came at an institutional cost. Democracy had eroded to nothing, a sad parallel to the value of Roman silver. By 284, the denarius was a diluted token of 2–5 percent purity, while infla-tion burned out of control. Trade devolved to barter and taxation was in-kind. Without money, long-term trade is impossible. With the disap-pearance of its scale economy, prosperity contracted.

Walk around the ruins of Rome and you can understand the sad-ness that Gibbon described. Some structures are large, but not grand as you might expect. They are called ruins for a reason. To visitors from the New World, old cities such as Rome, Cairo, Kyoto, and Mumbai are fascinating because in our home countries we essentially never see buildings atop ruins a thousand years old. Most of Europe, for instance, is land littered with history. To this day in Europe, ancient coins are found by the dozens as a matter of course when construction crews unearth a fresh plot of land and begin to pour concrete foundations for a new home or building. Any hobby shop around the world houses hun-dreds of cheap, ancient coins born in the mines of the Roman Empire. You can purchase a silver coin from the reign of many Roman emperors rather cheaply. They don't hold much silver.

Earlier silver coins were truly silver—established by Augustus to a purity of 95 percent or higher. As Alan Pense explains, "To provide an idea of the value of this coin to Romans, a Roman army private in the time of Augustus earned between 200 and 300 denarii a year, paid every 4 months. An officer could earn 10,000 per year; a high officer, as much as 25,000." [20]

The first emperor understood more than his predecessors or succes-sors that the value of a minted denarius, sized slightly larger than a U.S. dime, was not its storage capacity for wealth. He saw its value in use by the people as the medium of exchange. A currency one can trust is a more solid foundation for an economy than the concrete that Romans invented. Nevertheless, like most foundations, it decays and depreciates if not maintained.

Debasing a currency is a process of lowering the quality of coinage by diluting the valuable metal. One might think a silver coin is pure silver, just as an American penny is supposedly pure copper, except for the unavoidable impurities. The modern American penny has only a trace amount of copper, being primarily made of zinc. No matter, American coinage has long been "fiat" money. Its value is based on trust in the wider society to honor the currency as valid, not as a manifestation of the underlying metallic value. Modernity is comfortable with this notion. We value mere scraps of paper, currency as well as checks with scribbled signatures. We trust the value of invisible digits that flow from plastic cards. Not so in ancient times, when coinage was metal, and metal was value.

Minting coins of gold, silver, and copper was not a pure process, but part of the ascension of an empire was the establishment of trust that its coinage was as pure as possible. Once the prestige of the state was established, however, the temptation was strong to mint coins with less than pure metals. Imagine 100 gold coins of 99.9 percent gold recast as 110 coins that look identical, but are only 90 percent gold blended with 10 percent copper. The state expands its money supply by roughly 10 percent, which is essentially free money for it to spend. What's the harm in that? Such debasement is what Trajan did.

The denarius was 93.5 percent pure during most of Trajan's reign, but was debased to 89 percent pure in A.D. 107, which was a net loss of 0.16 grams of silver per coin. He had more money to spend than any emperor before, and he used it primarily to fund military campaigns in the East. Some believe his debasement wasn't meant as a hidden tax, but rather that it was intended to keep the silver-gold ratio in line. Nevertheless, the debasement was minor enough that the Roman civilization was not affected. Citizens hardly noticed, and why should they? It had been more than a century since the Principate was founded. Nobody alive had ever known of life with impure coins.

Succeeding emperors resorted to debasement whenever faced with fiscal pressure. The expenses of the state grew, due largely to army demands. During the reign of Marcus Aurelius (A.D. 121–180), the denarius was minted below 75 percent pure and by the end of the Severan dynasty it was 40 percent. Eventually, symbolizing the fall of its civilization, debasement drove the silver content of the denarius down to 2 percent. These later coins were copper with a thin silver coating, eventually minted so cheaply that the coating often rubbed off soon after issuance.

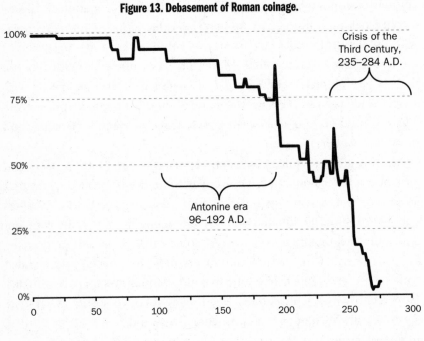

Figure 13. Debasement of Roman coinage.

Source: Kenneth W. Harl

The trick of debasing the currency soon lost its effectiveness once the public figured out what was happening. Merchants responded by raising the prices of their goods. Even if an emperor minted some small amount of thinner coins, their existence drove purer money out of the market. People hoarded the stronger coins, and spent the weak ones. The financier Thomas Gresham (1519–79) described this phenomenon to Queen Elizabeth I of England—"Bad money drives out good"—and urged her to restore the quality of the pound, a point now known as Gresham's law.

Debasement has a secondary effect as well. It inserts inflationary expectations in the public. Ten percent inflation may fool the masses one year, catch them unaware in the second year, but then be expected in the third year. Merchants won't wait for bad money to undercut their profits; they'll raise their prices in anticipation. And so will their peers upstream and downstream, letting inflation loose on the land like a plague. How should a government control that? It was a puzzle, never solved until economic theory and real-world experiments cracked inflation in the 1980s.

THE END OF THE END: DIOCLETIAN'S COMMAND ECONOMY

It would be wrong to believe that all of the Roman rulers during the Crisis of Third Century were tyrants. Aurelian stands out as noble and wise, but even his efforts to reunite the country and organize its defense against invading Persian, Vandals, Visigoths, and more came at a cost. Sovereignty no longer meant a secure border. It meant secure cities, which Aurelian walled. Even Rome. We know now that this was a forerunner to medieval feudalism's castles and towns. To his credit, Aurelian introduced a new silver coin with greater purity, but he survived just five years as emperor, falling victim to internal schemes of his own advisers.

The crisis didn't end until a soldier of modest origins named Diocletian came to power. He rose through the ranks of the army and wisely appointed a co-emperor after winning power. Seen by many historians as one of Rome's greatest emperors because he brought order to the state in A.D. 285, after a half century of military anarchy, his order lasted for two decades. To an economist who reads about Diocletian, the glowing tributes of some historians are a mystery. Diocletian established order in the Roman Empire in the way that Stalin established order in the Soviet Union. "Rome had its socialist interlude under Diocletian," remarked historians Will and Ariel Durant, which is the proper way to understand his peculiar type of order.

The new emperor doubled the strength of the army to counter barbarian invasions for good. Diocletian also added the residents of Italy to the tax roll—they had been immune before—but expanded the dole to include pork and oil in addition to grain.[21] To recruit and manage the supply of the army, which may have been 650,000 soldiers, the civil service had to be expanded as well, perhaps another 30,000.

In A.D. 301, facing hyperinflation and riots by the poor, Diocletian issued the famous *edictum de pretiis*—a list of price controls for all provinces. Ambitiously well-intentioned, the edict naïvely declared that wine in the vineyard regions would cost no more than wine in the desert, that bread in the cities no more than bread in rural towns. Merchants who priced differently were to be executed. Meant to quell inflation, his edict did what all price controls do. It drained goods from the markets, pushing even more trade into barter. Next, Diocletian's government, "which already owned most mines, quarries, and salt deposits—brought nearly all major industries and guilds under detailed control."[22] Because the free market wasn't working, the new bureaucracy intended to control it from on high, to manage it as central planners. The tax burden under this absolutism became so great that landowners and their tenant farmers simply abandoned the land. As the Durants noted, the problem with such high tax rates is their effect on "incentives to work or earn." Millennia before economist Arthur Laffer sketched out the downside of high rates on tax revenue in theory, Roman writers appreciated the destruction in practice.

It is maddening with our twenty-first-century knowledge to read the historical and contemporary accounts of the third and fourth centuries in Rome. There was no sense of paying a wage for labor or that taxation creates a wedge between supply and demand thereby reducing efficiency. These economic concepts were not imagined. Labor was in short supply in rural areas, and in oversupply in the cities. It made no sense, then. Diocletian established new public works programs in order to sop up underutilized labor, though such projects didn't resolve the urban glut, either. One might say that Rome was reaping the whirlwind of slavery. Slavery had dwindled over the years and many freedmen had been converted not-so-magnanimously into taxpaying citizens.

Diocletian had a more vigorous and simplistic approach to managing the Roman economy than any emperor had had before. He could not understand why people and markets did not operate as he wished, and so he reacted as an omnipotent child would in forcing his will. Early in his rule, Diocletian decreed that trade guilds should be nationalized. The shippers guild had been independent for centuries, running the Mediterranean trade that brought so much of the vital grain from Egypt to Italy. Diocletian nationalized it and further decreed that anyone who wanted to bring goods by sea into Italy had to join the guild. Government bureaucrats took a full accounting of the ships, men, warehouses, and so forth, all the better to control the business. To prevent an erosion of the skilled workers in the guild, Diocletian further decreed that no worker could leave the industry. Membership was compulsory, permanent, and, worse yet, extended to the sons of guild members. He liked the result, and he subsequently nationalized other guilds and trades.[23]

Perhaps in desperation to control other malfunctioning markets, the emperor made his biggest dictatorial blunder, the classic error of the central planner. He banned the free movement of rural Romans, and further ordered all male citizens to maintain the profession of their fathers. After many years of expanding the planning bureaucracy and taking over big pieces of the economy, he simply killed labor flexibility outright, enslaving the people of Rome.

And then, a few years after his price edict failed, he decided it was time to pass on the burden of imperial rule. By far, the best thing Diocletian did in his time as emperor was to retire, in A.D. 306, the first peaceful transfer of power ever known to most Roman contemporaries.

THE COLLECTIVE ACTION PROBLEM

Did Rome perish from overstretch? Hardly. There was an economic decline, no doubt, but its roots were clearly in fragile governing institutions. At first, the office of the emperor was not stable *between* emperors, and later not stable even *during* one's rule. Unless he was a tyrant. There was a constant risk of megalomania, corruption, and incompetence. This is not a fruitful environment for economic prosperity, let alone growth. That Rome lasted so long should be a credit to its innovations—universality, law, concrete, scale—but these innovations could not last.

The shift in the nature of the Roman legions took place over centuries but fits the public choice model of the economist Mancur Olson, who published *The Rise and Decline of Nations* in 1982. His principal idea was an extension of research he had done on the problem of "collective action," namely that special interest groups form naturally in a society to protect their status at the expense of the greater good. Labor unions and monopolistic corporations agitate and lobby for policies that secure "rents," often by limiting competition. Olson recognized that this tendency is a natural problem in democracy, where a policy with high gains that go to narrow interests has more support when the costs are shallow and broad. Over time, democratic institutions tend to become thickets of rent-seeking. The peculiar application of this behavior, where the government fosters rent-seeking, is what we see in ancient Rome.

The consensus assessment of historians is that the army's monopoly of power eroded the separation of civilian and military authority, such that the military was in complete control over imperial succession. The legions adopted rent-seeking tactics, maximizing their own pay and power at the expense of everything else—stability, prosperity, liberty of the citizens, and even national security. The army's appetites drove an escalation of taxes that ultimately destroyed the tax base, the currency, and even the money economy. As the Legions, particularly the Praetorian Guard, secured one small advantage in the design of the state, they fought hard to preserve it. Loss aversion makes rent-seeking institutions difficult to root out.

The Romans considered themselves the masters of the *oikumene*— the known world.[24] To be sure, the world they knew was extraordinary and large, but there was much about it they did not see. As Garnsey and Saller write, "It is difficult to accept that emperors and officials, their attention fixed on the short-term advantages of debasement, appreciated the long-term consequences. *They possessed only a limited empirical understanding of economic concepts and the working of the economy*" (emphasis added).[25] Economic ignorance by its rulers of changes in their rules set up Roman civilization for epic failure. It wasn't their fault, in one sense. Economics was an unknown science, and would remain so for another thousand years.

The ignorance of inflation's costs, of scale economies, of the dangers of rent-seeking, and of nationalizing industries was tragic. Even when emperors tried to make this right, emperors' ignorance of moral hazard often set bad precedents. Each new emperor tended to forgive all private debts of citizens that were due the state. Aurelian went so far as to haul out the public records of all such debts and have them set afire. Think about the incentive effects. Lesson one: rack up debt and never pay while the emperor lives. Lesson two: kill the emperor often.

SUMMARY OF DECLINE	
Great Power:	Imperial Rome
Turning point:	A.D. 117–317
Economic imbalance:	Fiscal, monetary, and regulatory
Political roots:	Growth of welfare state, centralized governance, military dictatorship
Behavioral dysfunction:	Bounded rationality in the extreme about inflation and free labor markets; collective action problem with the Roman army

5

TREASURE OF CHINA

The mind of the superior man dwells on righteousness; the mind of a little man dwells on profit.

— Confucius, *Analects*

 common academic saying is that the plural of *anecdote* is not *data*. No matter how powerful a narrative might be, it cannot compare to a comprehensive, peer-reviewed study using advanced statistics to analyze valid data that inform a testable hypothesis. That's the joke, anyway. The quote probably originated in its non-negative form in the lectures of the late Nobel laureate George Stigler, a famous economist who taught at the University of Chicago and often quipped "the plural of anecdote *is* data." The point is the same. People still hunger for narratives, probably because statistical thinking isn't natural, but heuristic thinking, based on anecdotes, is.

The familiar anecdote about Admiral Zheng He's naval missions during A.D. 1405–33 is that his massive "treasure ships" ventured as far as Africa, bringing back giraffes and other wild beasts to delight the imperial court. The anecdote practically opens the book for Paul Kennedy's *Rise and Fall,* though the admiral is referred to there by the Wade-Giles transliteration as Cheng Ho. This story has spread into mainstream culture as well. The Hugo Award–winning science fiction novel *Deepness in the Sky*, by Vernor Vinge, features an interstellar trading empire of humans known as the Qeng Ho.

Why are we so enthralled? Well, repetition, for one. The story of Zheng He appears in almost any popular account of global economics, and that is likely because its parallel with the explorations of Bartolomeu Dias and Christopher Columbus is so tantalizing. There is also the moral of the story of Zheng He, which to modern readers is simple: isolationism is self-defeating. In Paul Kennedy's words:

> From what historians and archaeologists can tell us of the size, power, and seaworthiness of Cheng Ho's navy—some of the great treasure ships appear to have been around 400 feet long and displaced over 1,500 tonnes—they might well have been able to sail around Africa and "discover" Portugal. . . . Despite all the opportunities which beckoned overseas, China had decided to turn its back on the world.[1]

While it is tempting to be contrarians, we tend to agree with the consensus. Just because something is an anecdote doesn't make it false. People tend to rely on heuristics as they often reinforce important truths, and this instance is one when the details clarify rather than obscure. In the case of China, Zheng He symbolizes rather perfectly that Great Power's economic imbalance *and* its political stagnation all in one. The admiral, however, isn't the principal actor in the story of China's momentous fall. Before we focus on that moment, let's consider the two millennia of rich cultural history leading up that fateful July in 1433, when the treasure ships returned to the mouth of the Yangtze River for the last time.

MASTER KONG

A Chinese man born in 551 B.C. by the name of Kong Qiu has a longer and wider traceable lineage than any other person in history. He has an estimated three million descendants, with the longest male-to-male family tree extending eighty-three generations. Legends say his family was of noble blood, but it has also been documented that the young Kong lived in relative poverty. Born in Shandong Province before greater China was unified, the boy was three when his father died. He worked petty jobs in his youth, but received an education, became a teacher revered for his wisdom, and eventually served as an adviser to local rulers. After his death, disciples collected his writings, which have shaped Chinese culture deeply ever since. In the West, "Kong Fuzi" (literally Master Kong) is known by the Latinized name Confucius.

Confucianism is not exactly a religion. But what it lacks in supernatural complexity, it more than makes up for in moral guidance and cultural impact. Confucius spoke of "Heaven" without distinguishing its origin in the natural or supernatural, and he was the first to articulate what we know as the golden rule, though in the negative: "Do not do to others what you do not want done to yourself." Whatever we call it, the influence of Confucian thought was enormous. In the words of Joseph Needham, the famous British historian, China was for two thousand years ruled by one party, the "Confucian party." [2]

Like any ancient wisdom translated across centuries and languages, Confucianism has elements that can be interpreted to suit the times, though some strong themes have been consistent through the ages. Confucius emphasized *benevolence,* which is especially relevant given that the roots of his teachings stem from his political observations. In particular, Confucius recommends the family as the model for the state, with all the former's positive and negative paternalistic implications.

Like Plato in ancient Greece, Confucius emphasized virtue and righteousness. According to the *Stanford Encyclopedia of Philosophy,* virtue in Confucianism is "a kind of moral power that allows one to win a following without recourse to physical force." [3] The emphasis on righteousness stands, like much of Christian teaching, in sharp contrast with supposedly greedy behavior of traders, merchants, and bankers. Agriculture was noble, but commerce was not—a moral theme that seems prevalent in all cultures.

One essential teaching of Confucianism is that leadership expressed through *moral example* is superior to rule through *law.* This principle is contrary to today's conventional wisdom about the importance of rule of law as a foundation for economic growth, but it served the dynasties well and shaped the development of Chinese institutions. The principle does not contradict the need for an administrative bureaucracy; rather it implies that bureaucrats use morality and subjective judgment to guide their decisions.

As Francis Fukuyama notes in *The Origins of Political Order,* Chinese politics developed in ways that were both superior and inferior to the democratic traditions of India and the West. Meritocracy was one potent guiding principle emphasized by Confucius, one that was often a counterweight to the human tendency toward nepotism and corruption. The system of examinations for talented youth to enter the imperial bureaucracy began during the Han dynasty (206 B.C.–A.D. 220), but never opened fully to the public until 1,100 years later, during the time of Zheng He. Exams varied over the ages. The economist William Baumol notes that the basic structure of the exams focused on impractical topics such as calligraphy and rote memorization. "In other words, the prevailing 'rules of the game' for Imperial Chinese economic activity seem to have been heavily biased against the acquisition of wealth and position through competitive and productive behavior." It was a meritocracy, but not one where merit in being productive counted for anything. Baumol further notes how elite and rare the exams were during the Song Dynasty, with "only a few hundred persons in all of China succeeded in passing" every third year.[4]

Due to its benevolent, top-down Mandarin hierarchy, China "never generated a rule of law or mechanisms of political accountability," Fukuyama writes. There were no corporate bodies outside of the state, nor independent cities. This point is vital. The institution of the corporation—limiting liability of the individual—was a keystone institution in Western growth. With corporate protection, entrepreneurs were freed to take more economic risks, to pool their resources while protecting their intangible rights to corporate property. That idea is impossible in a system where all property in the kingdom is the king's. A corporation expands the scope of profit-sharing beyond the family, which is perhaps why the familial *strength* of Chinese culture is overly appreciated. Moreover, the corporation enables innovation and competition, and it also normalizes failure without personal bankruptcy, another key to entrepreneurship. Without these elements of commerce enshrined in law, we cannot be surprised that China's great inventions were not capitalized privately, specifically that production technology did not shift "from the artisan's shop to the factory," in the words of economist Baumol.[5]

When asked to explain the principles of good governance by the ruler of the state of Qi, Master Kong replied: "Good government consists in the ruler being a ruler, the minister being a minister, the father being a father, and the son being a son."[6] This reply can be heard as a call for competency, as Confucius disdained rulers not fulfilling their primary obligation of loving the people, but it also comes across as a chilling affirmation of a static hierarchy. *Everyone should know their place.* This reckoning is the antithesis of institutional experimentation, innovation, and evolution.

As for imperial Chinese governance, it was always managed hierarchically, using the *prefectural* system whereby localities had appointed governors and mayors that were "agents of the center." Rival bodies jostled for the ear of the emperor. Consider the fate of the Han Dynasty. Four main rival groups for imperial influence were the great familial clans, military officers, scholar-bureaucrats known as mandarins, and the palace eunuchs. Although the Han era saw great economic progress—its coinage minted in the second century B.C. was the standard of monetary exchange for more than seven hundred years—the instability caused by palace intrigue led to a massacre of the eunuchs in 189 B.C. after the death of Emperor Ling. What happened next affirms the brittleness of central control: instability in the capital led directly to regional warlordism.

THE ONLY CONSTANT IS CHANGE

China is a particularly challenging case study. Could there be a more obvious example in history of a country that fell to *military* conquest by foreign barbarians, not once, but multiple times? Unlike Rome, with its long, slow demise, the history of China seems to reinforce military failure as the key factor in imperial decline, or at least a coequal factor alongside economics.

Roughly a dozen imperial dynasties have ruled China since the beginning of the Common Era. The communists under Mao Zedong defeated the Republic of China in 1949 through warfare, just as the Republic ended the imperial era in 1912. The Qing (aka Manchu) Dynasty took over from the Ming in 1644. The Ming reconquered China from its

Mongol usurpers (the Yuan) in 1368. And of course, the Mongols, led by Kublai Khan, conquered China from the separate Jin and Song dynasties in the late thirteenth century. The list goes on.

Regardless of these military incursions, we believe economics is the best explanation. China's dynasties should not be confused with China itself. The Great Power of China—its culture and institutions—survived and even thrived despite the shifting identities of sovereign dynasties at the top. Is the succession of China's rulers so different from Rome's many emperors? Confucianism and the Forbidden City swallowed up successive rulers, transforming *them,* not vice versa. Indeed, this firmness of Chinese culture explains the perseverance of its great power despite different dynastic heads. The firmness also explains China's later inflexibility and slowness to innovate economically. The Chinese *empire* itself, like the Roman Empire, only fell once. The difference is that Rome fell to its death, whereas China fell into permanent stasis.

The premise of military failure is flawed because it is superficial. Take a closer look at any of the dynastic successions, and each tells a story of military weakness fostered by economic imbalance. The Mongol power of the khans, notably Genghis Khan, reinforces the idea that military power rests on an economic foundation. Genghis "all but invented globalization," as the *Economist* claims.[7] He freed his lands from internal tariffs, with the express goal of establishing a trade corridor from Korea to Syria. Moreover, the Mongols ensured public safety for traders and commoners alike. According to Jack Weatherford, a leading biographer: "It was said that during this time a virgin could cross the length of the Mongol Empire with a pot of gold on her head and never be molested."[8]

Chinese dynasties often fell as a result of self-inflicted economic woes, however, most often due to the high costs of a centralized bureaucracy. One great advantage of China's more open internal geography was that a large state could be unified much more easily than Europe, South Asia, the Middle East, or the Americas, as those areas had thick natural barriers, such as the Alps in the heart of Europe. The ease of unification was also China's weakness. It made progress subject to the whims of a single ruler, with little comparative feedback. "European-style wars between internal political units became rare in China after 960 A.D.," explains Joel Mokyr. "The absence of political competition did not mean that technological progress could not take place, but it did mean that one decision maker could deal it a mortal blow."[9]

INNOVATION AND GROWTH

If Rome had somehow fostered an industrial revolution in A.D. 400, the Dark Ages would have been avoided, saving the world the horrible interruption of progress. But such thinking is fanciful. Roman society was an astonishing civilization relative to its time, but many other factors made unlikely a leap of technology that could overcome the Malthusian trap. The crack-up of Rome into fortified towns was both a tragedy and a blessing—a tragedy because of the millennium of regressive poverty and a blessing because of the unavoidable competition that followed. England versus France. Florence versus Vienna. China dominated the continent of Asia, more or less, and so lacked the competitive interstate climate of Europe.

Unlike the Romans, however, the Chinese had real potential to make the technological leap from agrarian to industrial. Many believe China could have and should have led the industrial revolution, not England. Angus Maddison estimates that Chinese GDP per capita was $450 per year from A.D. 400 to 1000—roughly a third higher than in Western Europe at the time. Because of its economic advantages, incomes rose steadily until A.D. 1300, to an estimated average of $600. After that, Chinese incomes stopped growing for the next five hundred years, nor did they shrink. China's high incomes relative to the rest of the world were not due to its expansive and peaceful commercial scale alone, though that was one pillar. It also had unique technology.

A court eunuch named Cai Lun invented paper in A.D. 105, and there is some evidence it had been invented long before (and then perhaps reinvented). The idea of the wheelbarrow occurred to someone in China as early as A.D. 232, a thousand years before its invention in the West. Woodblock printing was invented during the Tang Dynasty (A.D. 618–907), which made books available to the masses for the first time anywhere, as well as playing cards and paper currency. Genuine porcelain and a complex chemical industry were also invented and diffused during Tang rule. During A.D. 1041–1048, a commoner named Bi Leng invented movable type.

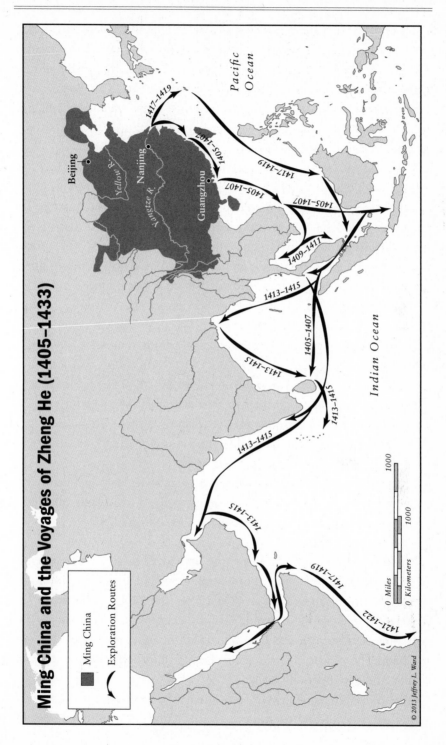

Ming China and the Voyages of Zheng He (1405–1433)

Ming China

Exploration Routes

Beijing

Yellow R.

Nanjing

Yangtze R.

Guangzhou

Pacific Ocean

Indian Ocean

1417–1419

1405–1407

1417–1419

1405–1407

1405–1407

1409–1411

1413–1415

1405–1407

1413–1415

1413–1415

1413–1415

1413–1415

1417–1419

1421–1422

0 Miles   1000

0 Kilometers   1000

© 2013 Jeffrey L. Ward

There is a persistent stereotype that Chinese were inventors but not innovators, meaning that their discoveries were not usefully commercialized. Worse, the stereotype holds that the Chinese thought of inventions as mere toys to delight the imperial court. The invention of gunpowder (fireworks, that is) is an example often cited, as it was not fully developed for projectile weaponry (muskets and cannons) until it reached the West. But this heuristic is false.

The modern horse collar was in wide use in China as back as 250 B.C. Not choking one's beast of burden would seem common sense, especially in an economy dominated by agriculture, but the horse collar was never used in Rome or anywhere else in Europe until a thousand years after its Chinese invention. Other useful innovations widespread in China include toothbrushes, umbrellas, and matches. In his comprehensive history of technology, Mokyr lists no fewer than ten major innovations made in China before anywhere else. In his words:

> Major improvements in the cultivation of rice revolutionized Chinese agriculture.
>
> The casting of iron was known in China by 200 B.C.; it arrived in Europe at the earliest in the late fourteenth century. Although the exact dates of the beginning of cast-iron production in China are unknown, there is no doubt that in the Middle Ages iron production in China far exceeded Europe's even on a per capita basis.
>
> In textiles, the spinning wheel appeared at about the same time in China and the West—the thirteenth century (possibly somewhat earlier in China)—but advanced much faster and further in China.[10]

Maddison's data show a surprising end to Chinese growth around the time of the Ming empire. Population grew, but GDP per capita did not. While incomes were flat in China after the 1400s, productivity in Western Europe grew slowly and steadily, century after century. By the early nineteenth century, average European incomes were double those in China. The industrial revolution that started then widened the gap further, and exponentially faster.

Why did China not grow? "The greatest enigma in the history of technology," according to Mokyr, "is the failure of China to sustain its technological supremacy. In the centuries before 1400, the Chinese developed an amazing technological momentum, and moved, as far as these matters can be measured, at a rate as fast as or faster than Europe." [11] This debate is lively. An older, orthodox view holds that China was simply backward compared to the West, a view passed down through nineteenth-century colonial prejudices. The excellent work of archeologists and historians of technology summarized above challenged that orthodoxy. China may have seemed backward two hundred years ago relative to the industrializing West, but that obscured China's power half a millennium before. Another challenge to the orthodox view has less merit: the argument that China remained economically on par or even ahead of the West until the industrial revolution in England. Historian Kenneth Pomeranz articulated that viewpoint in his book *The Great Divergence,* which divergence he argues occurred after 1800, not before. While the question about the divergence between the East and West is often hot, it is misplaced. Echoing Mokyr: "The question most in need of an answer is not why China differed from Europe, but why China in 1800 differed from China in 1300." Something happened, something decisive during the early Ming era, that changed China's destiny. Using the new data assembled by Angus Maddison and our measure of economic power, the turning point is self-evident (see Figure 14).

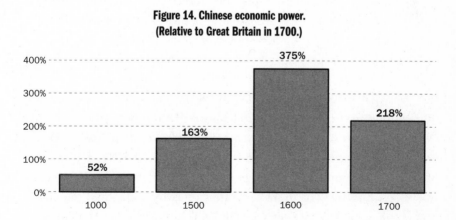

**Figure 14. Chinese economic power.
(Relative to Great Britain in 1700.)**

Source: Glenn Hubbard and Tim Kane, Data from Angus Maddison

THE REAL STORY OF THE TREASURE SHIPS

Of all China's innovations, the most economically important may have been its shipbuilding. Seamanship had been central to the way of life in Southeast Asia since prehistoric times, particularly the Malay Archipelago, with the 17,000 islands of Indonesia and the 7,000 islands of the Philippines. By the time of Zheng He's seven epic voyages from 1405 to 1433, imperial Chinese ships had ventured far and wide across the Pacific and Indian oceans. The Tang and Song empires traded with Persians and Turks. In eighth-century Guangzhou, a major port city in southern China, there was a Bureau of Merchant Shipping, which monitored the sea trade. And taxed it. The city was home to hundreds of thousands of Arabs, Indians, and Persians, peoples who thrived for centuries there.

The imperial navy was first established in 1132 by the Song emperor. Within a century, this seaborne "great wall" not only provided a defense against foreign armies, but it had also cleared the coast of piracy, allowing trade to flourish. Scholar Louise Levathes describes its development this way:

> The emperor offered cash rewards to spur innovation in ship design, and a variety of new boats, as well as naval gunpowder weapons, were created. Ten different oceangoing junks evolved and ten types of warships, as well as ferryboats, water tankers, floating restaurants, horse transport ships, manure boats, and a dozen other specialty craft. Along with creativity came open-mindedness. Abandoning their superior stance toward other cultures, Chinese scholars studied Arab and Hindu contributions in navigation and geography. . . .[12]

When Genghis Khan overturned the Song empire, naval warfare was more important than popularly remembered, but it was only made possible by defections of Song merchants and naval commanders. Marco Polo, the European explorer who befriended Kublai Khan (grandson of Genghis), reported seeing large junks with four masts. These giant sea vessels had sixty or more separate cabins for individual merchants to use on long trading voyages. Imagine a floating mall with sixty stores independently owned rather than a single superstore. As for technological prowess, the Chinese made the junks with "watertight bulkhead compartments, which would not be introduced into European shipbuilding for another six hundred years." [13]

The khans ruled China and many other regions for only a century (actually, three years shy of a century). Kublai Khan proclaimed the Yuan Dynasty in 1271 and established the new capital in Beijing. But the Yuan dynasty was chaotic. A succession of emperors was one sign of instability, but few if any of Kublai Khan's successors had much economic sense. Taxes were high, infrastructure decayed, and ethnic repression was constant. The Yuan Dynasty crumbled. The Ming successors were less victors over the Mongols than over competing rebel groups. The decisive victory was a naval battle in 1363 on Lake Pyang, China's largest freshwater lake. The rebel leader of the Ming, Zhu Yuanzhang, led a force of two hundred thousand sailors to victory over the rival Han forces that were three times larger. He used fireships against the slower-moving siege vessels of the Han. In 1368, after securing control of the rebel forces under his command, Zhu took control of the capital from the fleeing Yuan ruler and proclaimed the mandate of Heaven to form a new Ming Dynasty with himself anointed as the Hongwu emperor. An excellent but paranoid wartime leader, he enacted domestic policies that helped rebuild the Chinese economy, but he established a precedent of even more centralized control than normal.

During the cleanup battles against Mongol forces in the southwestern Yunnan Province, the emperor's top general captured a particularly intelligent and surly Muslim boy named Ma He. The boy's father may have been assisting or fighting for the Mongols, and had been killed, so Ma He was enslaved. A few years later, in 1385, he was castrated and sent to serve the emperor's fourth son, Zhu Di. For the next decade, rather than living as a court eunuch, Ma He became friends with Zhu Di and traveled with him on military campaigns in the south. Zhu Di went on to fight for the throne against a murderous nephew after his father died. He proclaimed himself the Yongle emperor in 1402, third in the Ming Dynasty, and promoted his faithful servant Ma He with the honorific name Zheng He. One year later, Zhu Di ordered the construction of a vast fleet of trade and war ships. Tellingly, the new emperor reversed his father's restrictions on foreign trade.

What made Zheng He's seven voyages to the West noteworthy was not their originality, but their size. A fleet of 317 junks, with an average crew size of ninety sailors, formed his first voyage from Nanjing in 1405. Its six-, seven-, and eight-masted merchant ships carried tons of silk, porcelain, lacquerware, and more. To put their size in perspective, the largest junks were wider than the ships of Columbus were long.

Many historians characterize these voyages as a show of force by an emperor, indeed an empire, with a superiority complex. But this characterization defies common sense as well as archeological facts. These were trading missions. To be sure, the language of the Chinese was (and is) euphemistic. They spoke of giving tribute from the treasure ships to foreign rulers. But they expected "tribute" in return. The best evidence is, in journalist and writer Louise Levathes's words, "Zhu Di's immediate repudiation of his father's strict tribute and trade policies upon becoming emperor." She writes:

> He allowed private trade and lifted the restrictions on pepper and gold. To the horror of his Confucian advisers, who subscribed to the ideal that China's prosperity rested in agriculture alone, Zhu Di threw China's doors open to foreigner merchants, saying, "Now all within the four seas are as one family." The emperor decreed, "Let there be mutual trade at the frontier barriers in order to supply the country's needs and to encourage distant people to come." [14]

Zheng He cemented trade relations with Calicut and western India, which was Zheng He's destination. But he also opened trade with Japan (which had twice resisted massive invasions by the Yuan Dynasty). He cleared the seas of pirates. As a result, China became the economic hegemon of Asia while Zhu Di ruled.

Is this imperial overstretch? Some historians contend that the voyages of Zheng He were so expensive that they created a fiscal burden. Fukuyama cites taxation, which tripled under Zhu Di, though we would counter that this was largely for public works—canals and the construction of the Forbidden City—not just the navy. Matt Ridley is particularly harsh in his assessment, though his criticisms hit harder at the Hongwu's policies ("an object lesson in how to stifle an economy: forbid all trade and travel without government permission; force merchants to register an inventory of their goods once a month . . ." [15]), which his son, Zhu Di, reversed, only to have them flipped back by successors.

Our assessment is that trade is, in the economists' parlance, the handmaiden of growth. Making the seas safe for trade entails costly public investment, while the gains from trade go much more to the private sector. Contemporary critics of Zhu Di, however, focused on the imperial politics rather than public finances. The Confucian mandarins distrusted him, and vice versa. He forced the mandarins to open the administrative examinations to the public rather than just their own elite families. His most trusted allies were eunuchs like Zheng He. The mandarins schemed against him patiently, laying the groundwork for their ascendancy with his successor. Consider the fragility of the political institution in play after Zhu Di's death:

> Upon becoming emperor, [Zhu] Gaozhi . . . surrounded himself with a group of traditional Confucians, including Qian Yi, his tutor who stressed the importance of benevolent rule, and Yang Rong, another tutor, who believed in curbing the power of the eunuchs and withdrawing from [Southeast Asia]. . . . On September 7, 1424, the day he formally ascended the throne, the emperor issued his first edict, which clearly reflected the philosophy of his tutors and advisers: "All voyages of the treasure ships are to be stopped." [16]

Gaozhi's son ascended to the throne less than a year later and reversed that last decision. While also surrounded by the same Confucian advisers, Zhu Zhanji struck a balance between the eunuch faction, which oversaw trade and the military, and the scholar-bureaucrat faction, which administered the state. Zhanji favored trade and openness, but not wars of conquest. Zheng He's voyages continued for another decade under Zhanji, until 1433, when he died and was buried at sea. Unfortunately, the emperor died three years later, and his successor fell sway to the mandarins. The final termination of exploration and trade was not a "fit of pique" by an emperor, or a fiscal necessity. It was the consequence of an internal power struggle in an excessively centralized government.

What happened next is fascinating, and a case study in how imbalance leads to decline. A near civil war between the eunuchs and mandarins burned for decades. The tribute trade collapsed. The unrivaled Ming fleet rotted away in port. Meanwhile, people in coastal towns continued to profit from foreign trade for decades, but their prosperity was seen as offensive and threatening by the Ming court. The mandarins did what any myopic, economically ignorant bureaucracy would do: they undercut their potential rivals. So much for benevolence. Levathes describes the situation:

> By 1500, it was a capital offense to build boats of more than two masts, and in 1525 an imperial edict authorized coastal authorities to destroy all oceangoing ships and to arrest the merchants who sailed them. By 1551 . . . it was a crime to go to sea in a multimasted ship, even for purposes of trade. In less than a hundred years, the greatest navy in the world had ever known had ordered itself into extinction. Why? . . . Seafaring and overseas trade were the traditional domain of the eunuchs, and in striking down those enterprises, the Confucians were eliminating a primary source of their rivals' power and income.[17]

THE GREAT DIVERGENCE

The myth of Chinese as inventors but not innovators is a hangover from the era when Europeans first ventured to China. The appearance of Jesuits with their mechanical clocks shocked a court that considered its emperor the supreme authority on time and the heavens. The Manchu Dynasty likely felt threatened by superior foreign technology. Confucianism held that foreign barbarians were inferior, but these Europeans brought cannons, kerosene, manufactures, and ideas—astronomy, mathematics, engineering. Manchus reconciled this dilemma by often pretending publicly that there was nothing new or useful in the toys of the Europeans. Internally, however, a battle raged. Some members of the imperial court advocated reforms, but losing these battles often meant personal loss as well.

"The would-be modernizers were thwarted, moreover, not only by brittle insecurities but also by the intrigue of a palace milieu where

innovations were judged by their consequences for the pecking order,"
explains the historian David Landes. "No proposal that did not incite
resistance; no novelty that did not frighten vested interests. At all levels, moreover, fear of reprimand (or worse) outweighed the prospect of
reward." [18] In the judgment of political economy, this scenario is proto-
typical institutional stagnation. The mandarin order with all of its well-
defined interest groups locked the Manchu institutions into inflexibility.
Call it loss aversion on a national scale, or a dynastic collective action
problem, but it led to weakness and then exploitation at the hands of
imperial Europeans who carved up the Middle Kingdom.

To many eighteenth-century visitors, the depth of poverty in China
was without peer. It had once been a great power, and the size of its
population and cities was both impressive and the ultimate Malthusian
trap. But the Qing (Manchu) Dynasty (A.D. 1644–1911) had let the innovative natural spirit of the Chinese people fade along with the depre-
ciation of public goods. As Mokyr writes, "It did not provide the usual
elements of the infrastructure necessary for economic development,
such as standardized weights, commercial law, roads, and police." [19]

OVERSTRETCH OR INWARDNESS OR . . .

In Paul Kennedy's assessment, the Ming fleet's decay was a symbol of
Chinese inwardness, end of story. In fact, Admiral Zheng He is not the
story. Manchu conservatism is not the story. Overstretch is not the story.
Rather, the underlying politics explain why decline happened. Emperor
Zhu Di's policies explain China's economic rise, and his erratic progeny
explain China's fall.

Inwardness as a Chinese characteristic explains everything and nothing. There was a seesaw of expansion and contraction, aggression and
cooperation, curiosity and disdain. But the same story can be told about
any Great Power. Again, let's imagine the history of America written five
hundred years from now: "Eisenhower led a conquest of Europe and
Asia, consolidated during his rule, then his protégé retreated from Asia,
etc." The thing that truly doomed Ming China was *institutional fragility*. The Chinese call this the "bad emperor" problem, but even that
term doesn't do justice to the underlying danger of centralization. Bad
emperors happen (as do bad U.S. presidents). But like Roman history,

China's history is marked by eras where the checks on imperial power were absent. The political institution of Chinese emperorship, designed to serve the greater good, morphed into a zero-sum struggle for influence among interest groups. This outcome echoes the Praetorian Guard, which warped imperial rule over Rome.

Fukuyama concludes that institutions cannot be the explanation because "China during the Ming Dynasty had most of the institutions now regarded as critical for modern economic development."[20] But this argument is not correct. Yes, the institutions were in place, but they were much more fragile in ancient China than in modern China. We believe the Ming empire would have continued to expand its power if its political institutions had been stable, perhaps with less centralization.

One of these interest groups, the mandarin scholars who worked to turn the Ming emperors inward won the short-term game. And they surely believed their policy of autarky was wise. What we see in hindsight is their cultish devotion to heuristics—farmers are noble; merchants are not. We also see that sea trade was creating prosperity for the people in 1436, but mandarins' benevolence was blind to commerce as a source of wealth.

The rise and fall of Ming China happened quickly. The Yongle emperor reigned for just two decades, and his grandson for one more. These emperors were followed by instability, which was destructive to Smithian commerce, indifferent to Schumpeterian learning, and chilling to Solovian investment.

Confucius was correct that leaders should be benevolent and righteous, which is fine guidance for the open-minded ruler. But it is empty advice for the design of one's politics. The political question is how to design a society that will yield benevolent and righteous leaders. Entrance exams are not enough. This question is no rebuke of a great philosopher, because Confucius himself can be understood to call for a social compact between the ruler and the ruled.

China's economy today has shrugged off many of the habits and institutions of its imperial past, many of which were discarded by Mao Zedong and the much wiser Deng Xiaoping. The modern one-party state cherishes stability, perhaps to a fault, but with great effect. There is administrative balance in Beijing, absent in the fifteenth century, which diminishes the vulnerability to abrupt and doctrinaire policy swings. And yet the Chinese economy remains centrally organized rather than federally, a feature that makes institutional progress less likely. The nation is primed to grow further in the twenty-first century, but there are questions about how high that growth can go without a more open political system. Only time will answer those questions, not history.

SUMMARY OF DECLINE

Great Power:	Imperial China
Turning point:	Fifteenth century
Economic imbalance:	Severe contraction in foreign trade
Political roots:	Centralized governance, autocratic policy-making, and factionalized bureaucracy
Behavioral dysfunction:	Loss aversion by zero-sum-thinking bureaucrats; identity heuristics hostile to merchants, profit, and foreign ideas; ignorance about importance of trade for growth

6

THE SUN FADES ON SPAIN

I have placed under the sovereignty of the King and Queen our Lords, an Other World, whereby Spain, which was reckoned poor, is become the richest of countries.

— Christopher Columbus, Letter to Doña Juana del Torres, October 1500

Spain (1469–1898) was the worst empire in history. We don't mean that the Spanish empire exploited its colonial lands most severely, or exhibited the most horrifying treatment of native peoples in the lands it conquered, or spilled the most blood. Other powers can make claim to those dishonors, including contemporary European peers Portugal, France, the Netherlands, and Britain. The ancients themselves offered no shortage of inhumane terror. Egyptians? Aztecs? Huns? There are no winners for that kind of worst.

Spain was the worst empire in terms of fumbling its position of dominance. Never did a great power embody such potential to prosper or to lead the world. Spain achieved great power, but it never understood how to translate that into productivity or prosperity. "It is difficult to see how so undeveloped a nation could have 'declined' before ever becoming rich," wrote historian Henry Kamen.[1] What a shame that this ultimate cautionary tale obscures moments of brilliance, courage, and nobility.

After its discovery of the New World in 1492, the silver-fueled riches of the Spanish empire gave the newly unified crown of Spain unexpected economic power. Yet a century later, the Spanish crown had declared bankruptcy twice, which it would do many more times in the seventeenth century. A relentless philosophy of mercantilism had filled its treasury with a mountain of silver while leaving the productivity of its people—and long-term living standards—empty. Lacking modernized science, technology, and innovation, Spain fell backward both relatively and absolutely. None of this history is controversial. There is widespread consensus on the facts of imperial Spain's rise and fall:

1. Spain's ascent as a power was based on economics, primarily the discovery of New World riches. A series of fortunate marriages consolidated many disparate lands in Europe, which gave the crown the potential for power, but American silver funded its armies and navies in the sixteenth and seventeenth centuries.
2. Spain neglected capitalist development. Hostile to many of its own merchants by design, Spain expelled thousands of Jewish citizens and other non-Catholics.
3. Fiscal imbalance doomed Spain to default on its debts, more than once. By the close of the seventeenth century, the empire had lost most of its major conflicts, lost control of Portugal, lost the Netherlands, and lost any financial credibility. Spain went quickly from world hegemon to middling nation-state.

The reason we include Spain as one of the case studies in this book is that it might appear to represent the strongest counter to our theory of imbalance. A critic would point to Spain's reckless and constant warring with France and other powers as the cause of its decline. It was on the wrong side of the Eighty Years' War (1568–1648), when its Low Countries fought for independence, *and* the Thirty Years' War (1618–48), the continent-wide bloodbath between Protestants and Catholics. The critic would say that discovery of silver in Mexico and Peru early in the 1500s may have made Spain rich, but war made it poor. There is also the religious intolerance of the Spanish Inquisition, and the babbling disunity of its many different Hapsburg lands. Imbalanced? Yes. Economically imbalanced? No. And that's just the economic half of our theory. The critic would hold special scorn for our theory of political dysfunction. To mimic Kamen, there was no development in Spain's monarchial absolutism, thus nothing to stagnate. Indeed, imperial Spain seems to be a perfect prototype of the war-loving and exploitative European empire.

A CENTURY OF (GEOGRAPHIC) GROWTH

The nation-state of Spain formed when Isabella, queen of the region that includes the northern Atlantic coast known as Castile, wed Ferdinand, king of the region of Aragon along the southern Mediterranean coast as well as parts of Italy. Their union in 1469 eventually settled the intrigue that had haunted the country for more than a century. Ferdinand and Isabella controlled the nascent Spanish empire when Christopher Columbus came to the court to beg for their investment in his vision of a voyage of discovery beyond the edge of the western Atlantic map.

During the next century, Spain grew dramatically, at least by way of geographic expansion. The princess Joan became queen regnant of Castile when Isabella died in 1504 and of Aragon when Ferdinand died in 1516. Her marriage to the young Hapsburg Philip I fused his kingdoms in the Low Countries and Burgundy with hers in Spain. Philip's death in 1506 left Joan the supreme ruler for the next half a century alongside her son, Charles V, who became the ruler of the entire Holy Roman Empire. His son, Philip II, ruled during the greatest extent of Spanish power, from 1556 to 1598. During this golden era in the sixteenth century, Spain was called "the empire on which the sun never sets." We wrongly remember this line today as something said of the British, but they were the second Great Power to wear this crown. Spain was sovereign over territories on every known continent, territories that included the whole Iberian Peninsula, major parts of the Netherlands and Italy, Hungary, half of North and South America, the Philippines (named after the king), and Portuguese trading ports dotted all along the coasts of West Africa, East Africa, and India, as well as Malacca and Macau.

The viewpoint expressed by Paul Kennedy, and perhaps common among historians, is that Spain *almost* achieved European hegemony. If the Spanish Armada had defeated the English in 1588, the balance of power on the continent may have been decisive. If the Portuguese had not revolted at worst possible time (1640), perhaps Spain could have won its openly declared war against France. Instead, weakness

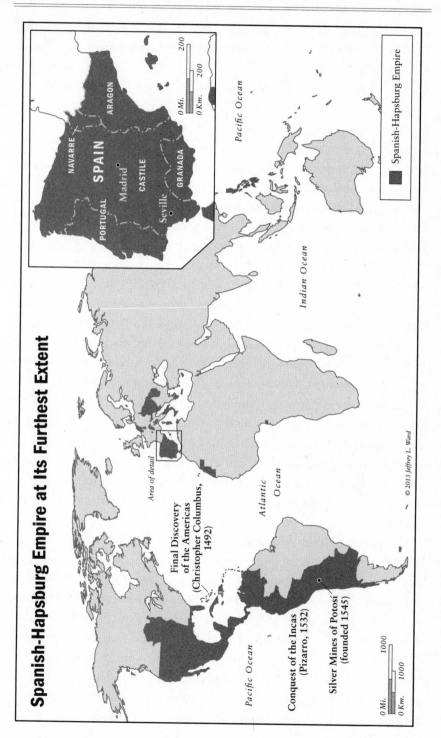

Spanish-Hapsburg Empire at Its Furthest Extent

Spanish-Hapsburg Empire

SPAIN
NAVARRE
ARAGON
CASTILE
GRANADA
PORTUGAL
Madrid
Seville

0 Mi. 200
0 Km. 200

Pacific Ocean

Indian Ocean

Area of detail

Final Discovery
of the Americas
(Christopher Columbus,
1492)

Atlantic
Ocean

Conquest of the Incas
(Pizarro, 1532)

Silver Mines of Potosí
(founded 1545)

Pacific Ocean

0 Mi. 1000
0 Km. 1000

© 2013 Jeffrey L. Ward

forced the Spanish crown to grant full independence to the Netherlands in 1648 to focus its full energy against the antagonistic French.
If only, goes the thinking, a more competent admiral or general or
musketeer . . . who knows what might have been.

A century and a half of war did cost the empire dearly, in blood and
treasure. Paul Kennedy claims Spanish weakness was exposed by the
"spiraling costs of war." True, the raw numbers of soldiers in the field
rose due to the military revolution of the era. New kinds of weaponry
and tactics diminished the long-standing primacy of cavalry in favor of
democratized warfare with large infantry formations. When Charles V
repulsed the French invasion of his Italian territories in the 1520s, he
fielded no more than 30,000 soldiers. In the 1530s, he fielded 60,000.
By the 1550s, he commanded a sprawling army of more than 150,000.
Spain doubled its military manpower to 300,000 over the next eight
decades, yet by the 1640s that number had collapsed to just 100,000.[2]
The civilian population, particularly in Castile, had been ground down.
The wars were a leading cause, but pressure on the private economy
and religious discrimination were also major factors. An influential
paper published in 1938 by the economic historian Earl J. Hamilton
described how the Spanish population decreased by 25 percent in the
seventeenth century, but little of that was due to war. Economic migration hollowed out the Iberian Peninsula. "Almost all manufacturing cities suffered a catastrophic decline in population between the census of
1594 and 1694; Valladolid, Toledo, and Segovia, for example, lost more
than half of their inhabitants,"[3] the economic historian Earl Hamilton
noted.

By the time Philip IV and Louis XIV of France agreed to the Treaty
of the Pyrenees in 1659, the dream of Spanish greatness was long gone.
The king had to address the splintering rebellions within the kingdom
still under his control. Spain was, surmises Kennedy, "paying the price,
as it were, for its original strategical overextension."[4] This conclusion
itself seems a stretch, and not in line with many other observations
Kennedy made about Spain. If only Charles V had humbly accepted
the balance of power in 1519, all would have ended happily? No, the
nation-states of Europe were in a deep-set competition. Military competition was just a part. We would submit that war was "an extension

of politics by other means," as the great Prussian strategist Carl von Clausewitz declared. The blood flowed horribly on all sides, no doubt, but behind all that was an economic competition even more important to the final outcome. Why did the constant wars not exhaust the Dutch or English? France declared bankruptcy in 1557 alongside Spain. Ninety percent of the English budget was dedicated to military expenditures. Yet those nations grew stronger.

ALMOST A SUPERPOWER

So, why do we think Spain declined if it was more than just military overstretch? *Ignorance.* For starters, there was no body of economic theory in 1492 (three centuries before Adam Smith and two before William Petty). Literacy was rare, superstition mighty, and the Church encouraged people to focus on moral goodness instead of material goods. That could be done by ousting infidels from Europe (the Reconquista of the previous centuries) and spreading the faith to savages over the oceans.

Despite the lack of understanding of economic growth by the rulers of that era, there was ample growth. In the sixteenth century, most of the states of Europe exploded with an unprecedented increase in prosperity. Growth rates were small compared to today's standards, but they were real. The synergies of new technologies, new crops and farming techniques, and expanded trade in the competitive continent of Europe mixed with a much larger world following America's (re)discovery by Columbus. Between 1500 and 1600, the average per capita income across twenty-nine countries in Western Europe rose from $771 to $890 per year, according to Angus Maddison's figures. This increase was 15 percent. Spanish incomes grew faster from a lower base, from $661 to $853, a 29 percent increase. Only two countries grew faster. The United Kingdom grew by 36 percent over the century, the Netherlands by an astounding 82 percent.

Growth during the seventeenth century differed greatly. The following figure shows how GDP per capita stagnated between 1600 and 1700 in Spain and France, in sharp contrast with Britain and the Netherlands. It is a graphic representation of some economies breaking free of the Malthusian trap, leaving others behind:

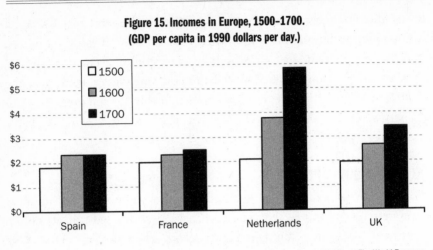

Figure 15. Incomes in Europe, 1500–1700.
(GDP per capita in 1990 dollars per day.)

Source: Angus Maddison, The World Economy

Using our measure of economic power (that mixture of GDP, GDP per capita, and GDP growth), the next figure shows an ever bigger contrast. Spanish power declined after 1600, compared to a doubling of British power and nearly trebling of Dutch power. In relative terms, Spain was barely competitive in 1600, though note that these figures do not account for the whole empire, only Iberian Spain.

TABLE 4. EUROPE'S ECONOMIC POWERS, 1600–1700

Power = GDP × Productivity × Growth$^{1/2}$

	1600	1700
Spain	40	29
France	78	85
Netherlands	29	71
United Kingdom	51	102

With its new territories in the Americas, Spain imagined creating a kingdom that would rival all of the power in Europe combined. Perhaps if it had managed its colonies differently—without exploitation, slavery, and crazed commodity extraction—New Spain would have been realized in place of Mexico, Brazil, Argentina, and even the United States. Instead, the emperors engaged in religious wars. They saw armies as the measure of power, not commerce. Worse yet, those Spaniards who did see another path failed to convince the crown.

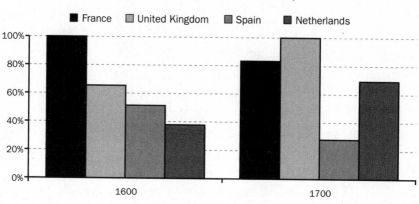

Figure 16. Economic power in Europe, 1600–1700.
(Percentage relative to the world leader.)

Source: Glenn Hubbard and Tim Kane, Data from Angus Maddison

SILVER FOUNDATIONS

Fourteen ninety-two was not only the year that Christopher Columbus discovered the Americas. The year was also economically significant for the empire for two unrelated reasons. After eight centuries of fighting to reclaim the Iberian Peninsula from the Muslims, the Catholic armies of Castile defeated the holdout emir of Granada. He surrendered to the forces of Ferdinand and Isabella on January 2, 1492. This year was also the one in which the crown decided to expel Spain's Jewish population, an extension of the Spanish Inquisition under way for more than a decade. The king and queen handed down the infamous Alhambra Decree on the last day in March, driving 150,000 or more Jews out of Spain within four months. Those who stayed were forced to convert to Christianity (*conversos*) and allowed keep their possessions, but they remained at high risk of being persecuted.

Nevertheless, 1492 will forever be remembered as the year that Columbus discovered the New World. Historical revisionism has downplayed the significance of the discovery, or tainted it with the horrors that followed. Even the word *discovery* raises hackles. How can you be said to have discovered a place that was teeming with native human beings? Perhaps the correct way to think about and describe the discovery is by inverting the Genoan's place in the order of explorers. Columbus will always be the most significant man to discover America, not because he was *first* but because he was the *last* man to do so.

Columbus died in 1506 believing he had found Asia, but his many voyages to the islands of the Caribbean and south-central America set a bad precedent. It wasn't just the institution of slavery that Columbus introduced, against the express wishes of Queen Isabella; it was his misguided search for treasure. The Spaniards introduced flora and fauna from the Old World that would transform New World society: horses, cattle, sheep, pigs, sugarcane, wheat, and coffee. And of course they brought back wondrous things: corn, potatoes, tomatoes, tobacco, chocolate, and vanilla—all unknown in Europe until then. Nevertheless, the main objects of the explorers' desire were Asian spices and gold, so they set about a brutal hunt. They found silver.

Francisco Pizarro was the most notorious of the conquistadors, due to his success in defeating the Incas in Peru with a force of just twenty-seven horses and 180 men. After many voyages to the New World, he set sail in 1530 on a mission of conquest and vanquished the Incan emperor Atahuallpa two years later. The Incas secured tens of thousands of pounds of gold and silver to pay for the release of Atahuallpa. Instead, in one of the least honorable acts in history, Pizarro executed him in the summer 1533, after he had determined the available supply of precious metal had been exhausted. A decade later, in 1545, the conquistadors discovered high in the Peruvian mountains the world's greatest mother lode of silver. At the same time, Charles V was entering the last decade of his reign, and the Hapsburg Empire was already an emerging superpower.

Spanish conquistadors founded the city of Potosí at the base of the mountain, and it soon became one of the most important in the empire, with a population as high as 200,000 (bigger than most European cities). The mines of Potosí sent some 45,000 tons of pure silver back to Spain over the next two centuries. The conquistadors found other rich

veins of precious metals, but only the Mexican mines at Zacatecas rivaled Potosí.

The centralization of the silver "trade" explains how the Spanish
crown took advantage of its fortune. "The convoys of ships—up to a
hundred at a time—which transported 170 tons of silver a year across
the Atlantic, docked at Seville," writes Niall Ferguson in his recent
history, *The Ascent of Money*. "A fifth of all that was produced was
reserved to the crown, accounting for 44 per cent of total royal expenditure."

The imperial stereotype established by Spain was this one: live by the
silver, die by the silver. The empire prospered so long as the silver mines
were productive, but it "could not survive the withdrawal associated with
drastically reduced imports of precious metals in the 1620s and 1630s." [5]
The historian Dennis O. Flynn argues that the surge of silver "propelled
Castile to greatness," but indirect fiscal distortions more than the direct
monetary supply caused its decline. That "fifth" of silver the crown
skimmed from American specie may have risen in quantity throughout
the sixteenth century, but it decreased in value simultaneously.

Charles V was ignorant, as were his advisers, of the inflationary effect
that his silver would have on prices. Flynn applies standard economic
logic and makes the point that "silver's market value plummeted inexo-
rably to its production cost." This lesson is one in supply and demand:
push out the supply curve on a commodity and lower prices result. That
is, silver prices will be lower relative to prices of everything else. American silver instigated what is called the *price revolution* in Europe. According to historical composite price data, prices of almost everything
doubled between 1500 and 1550, then rose another 50 percent by 1585.
A silver coin bought far less food or clothing in 1585 than in 1500, a
shift felt throughout Europe after three centuries of price stability. This
inflation eroded living standards, hitting the poor especially hard.

One can imagine the puzzle facing the Spanish court. How is it that
tons of high-quality silver caused inflation? Hadn't Rome suffered
inflation because it debased its silver *denarius*? Or does inflation happen whether you thin or thicken a coin's minted quality? The answer,
we know now, is that the inflations were different, and here's why. In

both cases—Roman and Spanish—the *real* economy was unchanged. And in both cases, the nominal prices of goods rose dramatically. Now consider, using a loaf of bread as an example, how the inflations were different. In the Roman case, the price of bread that rose was the coinage price, *not* the silver price. Reduce your coins' content of silver by half and you will see the price of bread (and everything else) double. The amount of actual silver exchanged for the bread holds steady. The sixteenth-century price inflation in Spain was altogether different, because the glut of silver meant that its value eroded, year after year. In that case, the amount of silver in the economy doubled but the amount of bread held relatively steady. Too much money chased too few goods, which the market resolves by a natural increase in prices.

In the list given by Carmen Reinhart and Kenneth Rogoff in *This Time Is Different* of twenty-three pre-industrial national defaults through inflation, Spain was not the worst case but it was the earliest. In the year 1521—the year Hernán Cortés conquered the Aztecs in Mexico—Spain's prices inflated by more than 40 percent.[6] However, American silver's biggest gift to Spain was debt, raised from the major banking families around Europe in exchange for future promises of even more silver. As soon as the silver was unloaded at the ports, Spain still needed more, and needed it faster, to pay for its military expansion. Charles used that flow of silver to obtain large new loans from investors across Europe: wealthy Flemish, German, and Portuguese families, Spanish merchants, and Italian bankers. Debt on a national scale had never been available to Spain before, and such debt had particular appeal to the emperor because it required no approval by Spain's legislature. This turn of events served as an institutional cautionary tale—an executive with unrestrained ability to raise the national debt practically guarantees fiscal chaos. Reinhart and Rogoff note that the Spanish crown typically owed payment on its debts equal to half of its total revenues. Imagine if interest payments on the debt of the United States equaled $1 trillion per year, five times as high as they were in 2010.

Spain's first debt crisis hit in the 1550s. A letter from Prince Philip II to his father mentions that the budget deficit of three million ducats could not be met with New World funds—"money from the Indies, [which] by reason of the letters of exchange assigned against it, remains unavailable for several years." With debt payments in excess of revenues, Charles abdicated the throne in 1556. The empire defaulted the next year. It declared bankruptcy again three years later in 1560, then again in 1575 and 1596 under Philip II, then three more times under his successors, in 1607, 1627, and 1647.

How was the state able to declare bankruptcy so frequently? One would think that after its first declaration in 1557, lenders would be cautious about lending a second time, a third time, or a fourth time. One reason is that the default in 1557 was not a repudiation of the principal, only a stoppage of payment until the debt could be restructured through negotiation. Recall also that many of the debtholders were subjects of the empire, without much political leverage. The mechanism invented by Spain for writing down its debt was the creation of *juros*, long-term bonds that paid out a fixed interest rate against a specific revenue stream, such as a city's sales tax. The *juros* were a safe investment, never defaulted on by Philip II, but they squeezed what we might call the crown's general budget even tighter.

Spain might have been better off if it had never discovered Pitosí and Zacatecas. Indeed, many economists would say those resources were a curse. Classical economics held that the key factors of production are land, labor, and capital. Land includes all of a country's resources: timber, ore, gems, rivers, safe harbors, oil, and so on. But economists in the past century conducting empirical research have noticed that countries with abundant resources tend to be poorer. The United States is an exception, but consider the case of Japan. It has few natural resources but set the standard for growth "miracles." Singapore is an even starker example, a swampy island that was effectively kicked out of Malaysia but went on to prosper under the leadership of Lee Kuan Yew. Switzerland is not wealthy because of oil or diamonds or timber, nor is Luxembourg. At the other extreme, some resource-rich countries in Africa with massive diamond mines and oil fields are trapped in poverty. Likewise, oil-rich countries such as Russia, Venezuela, and Iran have developed slower than expected.

In 1977, the *Economist* noticed that the discovery of a large natural-gas field in the Netherlands led to national economic boom that masked a decline in other sectors, notably manufacturing. The magazine called it the "Dutch disease." The influx of foreign currency to the resource sector made other sectors less competitive for labor internally, and also made exports from other sectors less competitive. This resource curse was compounded further in imperial Spain because the booming profits from American silver did not go into developing a financial sector. They went to the crown and into the military.[7] A military career had more prestige and also more income than any other job.

One might expect a booming shipping industry in the empire that discovered the New World and monopolized its oceanic silver trade. Its disappearance from Spanish ports symbolizes how the nation became structurally imbalanced. According to Hamilton, in 1585 "the Spanish merchant marine rivaled, if it did not outrank, the Dutch, doubled the German, and trebled the English and French." Yet over the next century, the tonnage of its ships fell by roughly 75 percent. The vast majority of sea trade into Spanish ports was carried on foreign vessels. As for ship-building, Hamilton says that it "virtually ceased."[8]

The situation on land was hardly better. Hamilton reports there were contemporary critics of the economic policies in place. He mentions the "crushing burden of taxes" repeatedly. Debasement of the currency was common as the seventeenth century progressed, "largely due to a chronically unbalanced budget." Hamilton lists seven Spanish economists of the seventeenth century who "denounced most of the evils leading Spain to ruin—such as primogeniture, mortmain, vagabondage, deforestation, redundance of ecclesiastics, contempt for manual labor and arts, indiscriminate alms, monetary chaos, and oppressive taxation."[9]

PROPERTY RIGHTS AND WRONGS

Conquest and control of sovereign land was seen by the Spaniards as a principal activity of the state. It would be natural to imagine that Spain enjoyed scale benefits of trade as a result, but this gain was not the case. Tremendous gains from the importation of gold, and especially silver, should have fueled growth in the microeconomy. Simply put, if the people of Mexico today became suddenly richer, they would probably invest the newfound wealth. Invest it where? The stock market or perhaps directly as venture capital—in other words, into the market.

But our imagination assumes a whole universe of finance and commerce that did not exist in those times.

It's odd from our modern perspective to see how the Spanish crown applied its instinct for controlling and taxing commerce on internal trade as well as foreign trade. Burgundy and Castile and Hungary had just as many trade barriers after uniting under Charles V as before. "The Spanish were probably the most constrictive of the three [compared to Britain and France], establishing a mercantilist system of trade that allowed colonies to trade only with Spain herself," writes economist Robin Grier. "Seville was the only port allowed to engage in transatlantic trade. The Seville merchants, the most powerful guild in Spain, controlled all incoming and outgoing trade with the Indies. In Mexico, Veracruz was the only legal port for international trade. The powerful Mexican guild, called the *consulado,* controlled all goods that entered or exited through Veracruz."[10]

Requiring all trade with the Americas to dock only in the port of Seville established a new, rich guild that Charles V could tax and control, as well as a mechanism to exert control over his colonies. The city of Seville prospered, growing to a million inhabitants as sailing ships from around the continent flocked there to trade for New World wonders. But this monopoly broke down when foreign ports competed for his approval, particularly Italian ports. Those Italian city-states offered loans to the crown.

This way of thinking—that the government's role is to grant permission for business activity—still lingers today. Occupational licenses, for example, are a common form of rent-seeking that affects a third or more of American workers today by some estimates. What a government charter, license, permit, or approved guild represents in any economy (ancient or modern) is a kind of property right. Modern conventional wisdom holds that property rights are good and necessary for economic development, but only because that has become vernacular for rights that protect one against centralized power, public or private. Douglass North has observed that there are negative property rights as well as positive.

In his seminal work, *Structure and Change in Economic History,*

North makes the point that the industrial revolution "followed rather than preceded" structural change in property rights in the seventeenth century. He contrasts the kind of property rights that emerged in two nation-states within the unified Hapsburg-Spanish Empire. Under Charles V, the Low Countries of northern Europe progressed while Spain regressed, because the two empires had different conceptions of property, notably rights to one's income. In Spain, income was considered ripe and right for the crown to take as needed, which explains why tax revenues rose twenty-two-fold in Spain between 1470 and 1540, for example. North explains that in the successful countries that achieve high levels of individual prosperity, property rights "provided incentives to use factors of production more efficiently and directed resources into inventive and innovating activity." [11] Hence the outcomes in Figures 17 and 18 we showed earlier in the chapter.

Spain's notion of economic rights can be traced back to the *mesta*, one of the most powerful and earliest guilds. The *mesta* were granted a monopoly right for country-wide land use in herding sheep. They were given this in exchange for a steady source of revenue for the crown. As a consequence, "the development of efficient property rights in land was thwarted for centuries." Other guilds followed suit. Guilds by definition are in the business of restricting competition and innovation, that is, growth in GDP per capita.

In the Netherlands, personal property and the rights of merchants were predominant over guilds. In the fifteenth century the Duke of Burgundy had avoided guild or trade restrictions. There was low, broad taxation of commerce, which encouraged rather than discouraged the efficient use of labor. And as we know now, labor freedom is the mother of labor productivity. These policies were kept in place once Burgundy (and the attached Low Countries) were inherited by Charles V, for the simple reason that the free markets of Antwerp provided more tax revenue than any region in Spain.

When he became hungry for revenue after the Dutch rebellion that started in 1648, Philip II turned to confiscation of land and treasure of his own people and the granting of new monopoly guilds in the cities of Castile, restricting free commerce further. Revenue for the crown was also raised by the sale of noble titles, the value of which was enhanced because nobles were exempt from future taxation.[12] Spain enhanced property rights, but these property rights were anti-growth. They were licenses sold in exchange for fees—licenses on a way of doing business that acted as disincentives for innovation. The economic incentives established in the mid-fifteenth century made unproductive careers more attractive: soldier, clergy, colonizer, or guild member.

POLITICAL CROWDING OUT

The English political philosopher Thomas Hobbes used the term *Leviathan* to describe the power of the state, unmatched by any other power on earth. The term comes from the Old Testament, where it is understood as a horrible creature that represents the power of Satan.

For economists, a large government risks distorting the broader economy in a handful of significant ways. Taxation is the most obvious and direct intervention of a state, taking funds away from private citizens who would otherwise use it to spend or save. Lower consumption and less saving both have deleterious effects on aggregate activity. Insofar as the state's consumption or investment of those funds replaces the lost private activity, there is no net loss. That's one theory. However, a secondary effect of expansive fiscal activity is understood within economics as *crowding out,* a technical term for the discouragement of private investment because of higher interest rates. Let's step back and appreciate that the inverse relationship between interest rates and investment is a narrow case of crowding out, while the broader theory applies to any state action that distorts economic incentives of any kind. We can be sure that the banking sector in imperial Spain remained underdeveloped as a direct consequence of the crown's voracious appetite for debt.

However, Spain was guilty of distorting incentives in many other ways. It distorted the market for talent most clearly. "[T]he Inquisition drove innovators in business, science, and technology (both military and navigational) out of the Habsburg lands, spurring development in Protestant Holland and Britain," observed the sociologist Richard Lachmann.[13] Estimates are that two hundred thousand Jews were "crowded out" of Spain. And its policies also crowded the labor market away from entrepreneurship and toward military and government employment.

Recall the skeptic of our theory whose final argument is that Spain was politically absolutist, so there was nothing to devolve. Our theory of Great Power imbalance holds that political decay locks a society into a status quo economy, resistant to productivity growth through disruptive new technologies. One critic asserts that Spain in the imperial era was economically and politically behind from the start. The British, for example, pioneered individual liberty for its people as early as 1215, when King John agreed to the Magna Carta. England had a relatively smoothly operating centralized kingdom centuries before the formation of Spain as a nation-state. The Netherlands was far more advanced economically but also had developed a tolerant religious culture quite the opposite of Spain.

These are valid points, but they overlook Spanish institutional innovation. Overlooked in particular is the Cortes Generales, the legislature of Spain. The system of Cortes originated in the kingdom of León in 1188, the first parliamentary body in Western Europe. It was an assembly of the landed aristocracy, and it had the power of the purse. As urbanization occurred, the Castilian king expanded representation in the Cortes to include the richest merchants, for the simple reason that he needed more money than the rural nobles could provide. In exchange for their revenue to the state, cities and regions were granted *fueros*, or contracts that we might think of as legal autonomy to maintain their own economic regulations. A *fuero* established nothing less than a medieval charter city.

As we saw in other Great Power case studies, in Rome and ancient China, the centralization of revenue collection during the first stage of growth is coupled with a loss of local autonomy. In the case of Spain, the powers of the bourgeoisie and the Cortes in Castile were undercut by Ferdinand and Isabella. Those powers did not want to fund the voyage of Columbus, for example, and Queen Isabella chafed under their restrictions. The crown moved to buy off resisting interests with special favors—tax exemptions and guild monopolies. This task may have been easier as there were different Cortes for distinct classes—one for aristocrats, one for urban merchants, and so on. It wasn't long until the Catholic monarchs had won the power of the purse. Soon after their conversion to compliant rent-seekers, the Cortes "ceased to function as a serious check on state power," according to political scientist Francis Fukuyama.[14]

The kind of taxation implemented by the crown was, as we know, oppressive, but how it came to be is a tale of imbalance. The Cortes preferred a system where they were responsible for tax collection, known as *encabezamiento*, which was granted by Isabella but repealed by her grandson, Charles V. The Cortes did not accept this action obediently. It instigated a costly revolt that the newly crowned Holy Roman Emperor smashed. So much for autonomy. The outcome was a centralized tax system that was insensitive to the commercial impact of its levies, only sensitive to maximizing revenues. Eventually, 80 percent of the empire's revenues were drawn from the people of Castile, which meant it was drawn from the poorest Spaniards, who had no royal exemptions. Its cities soon depopulated.

What's most alarming as we survey the lost opportunities of imperial Spain is that it not only set back development in its colonies by establishing antigrowth institutions in the countries of Latin America that haunt them still today. The alarming realization is that the restrictions on free markets and free labor that were part of Spanish culture in the fifteenth century also remain part of the dominant economic culture of twenty-first-century Spain. Consider the current economic crisis in the Eurozone. The Netherlands and Germany are member states, along with Spain and Italy. And the unemployment rates in those four countries correlate far more closely with their scores on the World Bank *Doing Business* report (Spain ranks 44th in the world, Germany 19th) than with their debt levels. In Germany, as we write, unemployment is five percent. In Spain, with riots in the streets, the national unemployment rate is five times higher. The good news is that many Europeans, indeed many Spaniards, recognize what has happened, and they are demanding an end to the "easy money" solutions that Charles V and Philip II championed centuries ago.

SUMMARY OF DECLINE

Great Power: Imperial Spain

Turning point: 1550

Economic imbalance: Fiscal deficits and state bankruptcy; wrong kind of
                            property rights

Political roots: Centralized monarchy

Behavioral dysfunction: Locked in guild loss aversion; bounded rationality
                            about the nature of productive opportunity

7

RULE OF SLAVES

The Ottoman Paradox

The Egyptians had a great secret, which they did not forget for thirty centuries. They feared and hated change, and they avoided it wherever possible.

— Charles Van Doren, *The History of Knowledge*[1]

Ancient Egypt was the first great human empire, but it lasted for three thousand years by committing to stasis, not progress. If we were to write a chapter about ancient Egypt to affirm our thesis, it would be no more than a few pages, which we could summarize more efficiently with a few abbreviated sentence fragments: Agricultural monarchy based on rich lands and the seasonally flooding Nile River. No strategic peers. Complete and purposeful institutional stagnation. Hold for three thousand years until superior power emerges. Hail Caesar.

Parts of India were united many times under different empires, and often those were powerful, but the subcontinent never created a modern state before contemporary India. Many of its empires merit closer scrutiny, to be sure. The Gupta Empire ruled during India's golden age from A.D. 300 to 550. The Mughal Empire dominated the subcontinent from the 1500s to the 1700s, and its Muslim rulers descended from Genghis

Khan. But it is Ottoman Turkey, more than any other Middle Eastern civilization, that stands in history as a truly great power.

For many in Europe, Ottoman was synonymous with Muslim. The Ottoman Empire, with its astounding capital in Istanbul, was one of the longest-lasting empires in history. It survived for six centuries, from 1299 until 1923. Like Rome, the rise of the Ottomans is a story of an aggressive, conquering tribe that took its name from the leader of that tribe, in this case Osman. The difference is that the rise of Osman's tribe feasted on the remains of Rome's eastern half, known to us as the Byzantine Empire. When the Western Roman Empire collapsed in the fifth century, the Eastern half survived for another thousand years with its capital in the great city of Constantinople. By the time Osman was born in A.D. 1258, the Mongols were advancing from the East, conquering Baghdad, while the old Byzantine Empire was in shambles. One of the Turkish tribes, led by the fierce twenty-three-year old warrior Osman, conquered neighboring lands in the name of the Muslim faith. The importance of Islamic fervor in advancing the expansion of the Ottomans cannot be overstated.

Turkish cavalry were unrivaled in their time, but advances in naval technology allowed the empire to conquer much of Greece and ultimately Constantinople in 1453, finishing off Roman civilization at last. The Ottomans conquered the eastern Mediterranean, including Egypt, in the early 1500s. By the time of Suleiman the Great, who ruled the Ottomans from 1520 to 1566, the empire had amassed a territory rivaling ancient Rome. It included all of modern Turkey, Greece, Hungary, Syria, North Africa, the entire Black Sea, Red Sea, and Mesopotamia down to the Persian Gulf. One might argue that the economy was based on spoils of war, or "extractive" institutions, in the words of Daron Acemoglu and James Robinson. This observation is fair, but a culture of conquest does not explain how Istanbul (Constantinople) and its new empire became so sophisticated.

During the time of the empire's dominance in the sixteenth century, the Turks were in most ways the most civilized people in the world. "Its cities were large, well-lit, and drained, and some of them possessed universities and libraries and stunningly beautiful mosques," wrote Paul Kennedy. "In mathematics, cartography, medicine, and many other

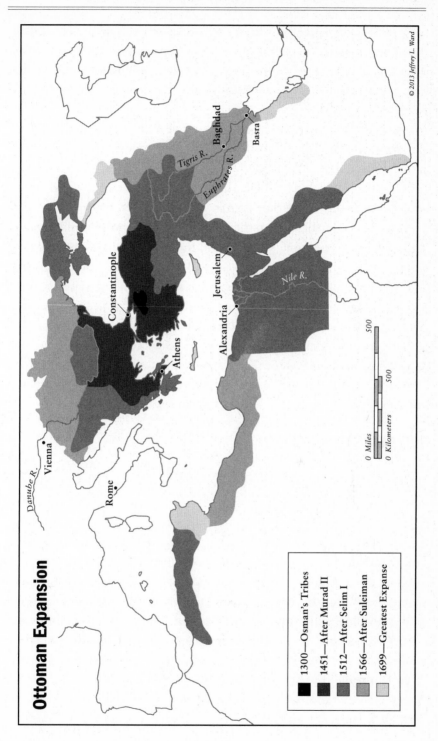

Ottoman Expansion

Vienna

Rome

Danube R.

Constantinople

Athens

Baghdad

Basra

Tigris R.

Euphrates R.

Alexandria

Jerusalem

Nile R.

0 Miles 500

0 Kilometers 500

1300—Osman's Tribes
1451—After Murad II
1512—After Selim I
1566—After Suleiman
1699—Greatest Expanse

© 2013 Jeffrey L. Ward

aspects of science and industry in mills, gun-casting, lighthouses, horse-breeding the Muslims enjoyed a lead."[2] Modern numerals are known even today as "Arabic" numerals even though they originated in India. They were brought to the West through the vast cultural and trade network of the Ottomans.

As such a long-lasting empire, it faced and overcame many existential crises, but by the 1800s it was described as the "sick man of Europe." Indeed, the defeat of Ottoman Turkey in World War I capped a centuries-long economic decline. How did the power of the Turks peak so early (arguably under Suleiman in 1566) and then linger for so long?

There was a renaissance in the West, the Protestant Reformation, and an industrial revolution. Yet watching those tectonic cultural and economic shifts, during all those centuries, the sultans did nothing. As just one example, usury became acceptable under progressively reformed Christian financial institutions but banned under reformed Islamic ones. We do not think it is sufficient, though accurate, to point to the lack of private property, or that there were first- and second-class citizens (the former paying no taxes), or the widespread practice of tax farming. The definitive issue is this one: why were Western European empires *innovative* during 1600–1800, while the Ottomans were not?

TOLERANCE AND DIVERSITY

Turkey is the forgotten empire. The Western European stereotype about Turks is that their empire was a mess, and the underlying culture brittle and weak. These negative attitudes formed during the Ottoman Empire's later years. They are fundamentally wrong. In particular, Westerners mocked the quilt of cultures, languages, and ethnicities that made the Ottoman Empire *obviously* ungovernable. The term *Balkanized*— originally referring to the breakup of the Balkan Peninsula into smaller states after Ottoman rule—now describes an intractable mix of peoples that is hopeless politically, destined for strife and unhappiness. But what a curious heuristic this critique represents—nothing less than hostility to diversity.

In truth, the diversity of the early Ottoman Empire was its genius. When foreign peoples were conquered by the unmatched Turkish cavalry, they were not culturally repressed, but in fact were allowed to maintain their faiths and local traditions. Success "owed much to their willingness and ability to adapt, to utilize talent and accept allegiance from many sources, and to make multiple appeals for support," according to economic historian Sevket Pamuk.[3] The early sultans were models of tolerance. That tolerance included explicit messages of openness to Jewish and Christian immigrants being oppressed in Western Europe during the 1400s. Legal scholar Amy Chua credits Ottoman tolerance during the 1500s in her book *Day of Empire,* noting that Jews and Christians faced no restrictions on where they could live or what occupations they could choose, that their property was protected under the rule of law, and that they could even sue Muslims in Muslim courts.[4]

The occupational guilds, a major force in the urban economy, were open to all religions. Likewise, non-Turks were active entrepreneurs, "playing prominent roles in banking, shipbuilding, wool and tobacco production and the luxury trades."[5] Even though the government was open only to Muslims, Chua reminds us that the Ottomans considered Muslim converts as equal to born Muslims. This right is no small thing, and contrasts with the unequal treatment given to Christian converts throughout Europe.

The distinguishing degree of tolerance changed only after Suleiman's death in 1566 and the subsequent rise of Shia Islam in Persia under the Safavids. Chua remarks that Suleiman was succeeded by thirteen sultans, whose talents ranged from "incompetence to idiocy." The Shia-Sunni split, which still rages today, diminished intrafaith tolerance in seventeenth-century Turkey. Orthodoxy and conservatism became more important, and the heuristic of cultural superiority that became dominant in the sultanate "closed it off to new ideas coming from the outside," according to political scientist Francis Fukuyama.[6] Culturally, then, just as Europe began to offer Enlightenment science, Istanbul closed its eyes and ears.

Another aspect of Ottoman flexibility remained in place, however: governance. Earlier we described China's institutions as strong but fragile. Arguably, Turkish politics were the reverse—weak, but flexible. Although both empires suffered from the "bad emperor" problem, China did so under dozens of dynasties. The Ottomans had just one. The distinction can be found in their politics. The Ottoman governing hierarchy is best understood as a *federal dictatorship*. Yes, the sultan was supreme. Early sultans of the empire made a point of killing off the landed aristocracy. Like the Chinese administrative system, the Ottomans adopted a prefectural system, appointing provincial governors (*beys*) from Istanbul and rotating them every three years. This system prevented the reemergence of a landed aristocracy. Further, the provinces (*sanjaks*) were not treated uniformly. The closest regions in Anatolia, the Balkans, and Greece were the most Turkish, while others had more flexibility in local institutions. Consider how Niccolò Machiavelli describes the unique form of Ottoman politics under the sultan compared to the king of France:

> The entire monarchy of the Turk is governed by one lord, the others are his servants; and, dividing his kingdom into sanjaks, he sends there different administrators, and shifts and changes them as he chooses. But the King of France is placed in the midst of an ancient body of lords, acknowledged by their own subjects, and beloved by them; they have their own prerogatives, nor can the king take these away except at his peril.[7]

For all the contrasts between French and Turkish culture, the treatment of land rights may be the one that mattered for their Great Power trajectories. There is almost no point in distinguishing whether the institutions organizing land under the Ottomans were military, economic, or political in nature. They were intertwined. Yet in another sense, land ownership was cleaved in two.

One of the institutions that the Turks adopted and implemented in newly conquered lands was the *timar* system. Timars were plots of land, not of fixed size, rather of roughly equal value. Under this system, the sultan owned the land but gave residential rights to the people while giving administrative rights to his cavalrymen, known as *sipahi*s. With 90 percent of the population being agrarian, the norm for a preindustrial economy, the importance of the timar cannot be overstated. An individual sipahi and his family lived on his timar along with the people. He collected tax revenues in-kind to subsidize himself as well as equipping and training a small contingent of soldiers. Dispersed throughout the empire, the Sipahis convened annually for seasonal warfare. Meanwhile, locals on the timar had hereditary usufructuary rights, meaning rights to use the land and keep its produce, or fruits.

The sipahis were a unique kind of military aristocracy. Some have called them a one-generation aristocracy. Their status and rights to the timar were not heritable. Timars, and larger plots of land, were awarded based on military valor and service to the sultan. It was a remarkably stable order that prevented a concentration of power from developing that could threaten Istanbul or other urban power centers. Moreover, the sipahi-timar structure served as a constant incentive and reward for merit. In an era in which aristocracies dominated most countries, Turkey thrived with its sipahi meritocracy. The cavalry-heavy army of the Ottomans was without peer during the fifteenth century. Of course, only ethnic Turks were permitted to be sipahis. Tolerance goes only so far.

THE JANISSARIES

The Janissary Corps was a second political-military institution that counterbalanced the provincial influence on the throne. This meritocratic institution was also adopted whole from a conquered land early during the empire's expansion in the fourteenth century, when it was most open to good ideas from the outside. In this case, the sultanate recognized that having an elite personal guard like the Egyptian Mamluks would be invaluable in countering tribal, ethnic, and other interests that might otherwise scheme to usurp the sultan.

Christian boys aged ten to twenty, primarily from the Balkans, were selected once every five years to become military slaves in a process known as *devshirme*. The strongest boys went to Istanbul, cut off from their kin and homeland. Forcibly converted to Islam, they were trained as warriors and if worthy became members of the *askeri* class (the first-class citizens, translated as "military" class). The askeri were a functional equivalent of China's Confucian mandarins and court eunuchs. It may seem odd that only non-Muslims could join the askeri, but it makes sense for the singular reason of ingraining them with complete devotion to the sultan (and internally to their own brotherhood). It was also impermissible to enslave Muslims directly. Most served in the elite infantry corps, known as the Janissaries, which numbered twenty thousand men in the 1500s. Janissaries were the first army to wear a uniform. They received a cash salary and were honored within the empire. But they could not marry and all of their wealth was passed along to the corps. The best among them rose to serve in the sultanate, often to the top administrative position of prime minister or *grand vizier*. Eight of the nine grand viziers serving Suleiman, for instance, were non-Turk askeri.

The combination of Janissaries in the full-time infantry and the sipahis in the part-time cavalry served the Ottoman sultanate for centuries. This dynamic, also balanced by religious elites, urban guilds, and others, may have lasted longer if not for the economic pressures that emerged in the seventeenth century. Or it may have decayed inevitably. Pamuk argues that economic interests (landowners, merchants, and financiers) had little influence.[8] Although none of the interest groups had much capacity to develop self-serving interests as individuals—Janissary children could not serve as Janissaries—they did develop class interests. As happened in imperial China, the servants matured over time into masters, fighting a zero-sum game of power politics rather than serving the greater good. This imbalance is *regulatory,* the well-known problem of rent-seeking, which we discussed previously in the context of Rome's legions.

The Janissaries became rent-seekers over the centuries. Once an army of slaves to the sultans, they eventually became the de facto rulers, and worked hard as a class to protect their privileges. One sultan relented as early as the late sixteenth century on marriage, and within a century Janissary children were permitted to join the corps. Although the internal balance of power was well designed to serve the sultan, a major weakness of Ottoman politics was the ambiguity of succession rules. With their proximity to the center and their prestige, the Janissaries became kingmakers. It wasn't long before they were staging palace coups, establishing puppet sultans, and in some cases ruling directly.

The institution of devshirme was abolished in 1638, which was undoubtedly humane but also presaged a shift in institutional incentives. In the eighteenth century, Janissaries numbered more than one hundred thousand. Some had become merchants and tradesman, blurring their role and loyalties. No longer effective at fighting war because of outmoded technology in the eighteenth century, the Janissaries crushed all efforts to reform their own military organization or the development of alternative military bodies.

Recognizing the empire's relative weakness after Napoleon's invasion of Egypt in 1798, a reform movement pushed against the Janissaries. The well-respected sultan Selim III was dethroned by a Janissary revolt in 1807. He was taken captive and murdered. His reformist successor, Sultan Mahmud II, learned by that example to be patient. Two decades later, when his non-Janissary forces were strong enough, he had his revenge. Mahmud fostered a revolt among the Janissaries as a pretext, then set fire to their barracks under a cannon assault and massacred them by the thousands.

In retrospect, the Janissary Corps is the institution most responsible for the political stagnation of Istanbul. Their conservatism held up all kinds of reforms that might have let the empire modernize, and not just in military reforms. If the rest of the world were standing still, the Ottoman institutions could have helped preserve the operational stability of the sultanate grip on power for thousands of years. But that internal stability came at a price of economic dynamism. As Pamuk explains, the Janissaries were really a symptom of a larger economic bias toward the status quo. Pamuk describes what we interpret as a case study of hostility to Schumpeterian creative destruction: "[T]he government took pains to preserve as much of the traditional structure of employment and production as possible. It tended to regard any rapid accumulation of capital by merchants, guild members, or any other interests as a potential disruption of the existing order." [9]

Perhaps this conservatism was natural. Fukuyama dissects it at length and makes the insightful observation that the institution of military slavery is by nature not conducive to the development of capitalism. Coercive labor is in the antithesis of free markets, and the rise of free markets internationally correlated with the demise of slavery. This internal contradiction could not be resolved by the Ottomans, precisely because slaves managed the state.

TAX FARMING

Although we attribute the political stagnation of Turkey to the sclerotic askeri bureaucracy, the economic imbalance and unrelenting fiscal troubles that faced Istanbul were all too typical of decaying Great Powers. No doubt the cost of paying the salaries of the corrupt and bloated Janissaries was a burden, but the empire's fiscal troubles may have started on the tax side. As the economy evolved, the sultanate suffered from understandable ignorance about how to balance its budgets. Driven by necessity, it allowed itself to create national debts of a unique nature, debts that it ultimately could not pay.

A myth persists that Islam itself is a barrier to the development of financial markets because of its prohibition of usury. A similar condemnation of usury exists in the Old and New Testaments. Likewise, usury was denounced by Plato, Aristotle, Buddha, Thomas Aquinas, and so on. We only attribute the rule to Islam because it continues in many countries to this day, yet financial markets have developed throughout the modern Middle East as well. More to the point, scholars have unearthed credit records from many urban areas in the sixteenth century, revealing a network of lending among all classes of Ottoman society, not just elites or merchants.

Some attribute Istanbul's economic decline to Spain's discovery of the New World and Portugal's exploration of the Indies by sea, which ended the Ottoman Empire's natural overland trade monopoly at the intersection of Eurasian geography. The flood of Spanish silver also inflated prices everywhere in the Old World. This channel makes sense as a proximate cause of decline. Portuguese explorers rounded Africa in 1498. Spanish explorers discovered the Americas in 1492. And there is evidence of a quadrupling of grain prices in the Ottoman Empire during the course of the sixteenth century, as well as debasement of the silver currency. The height of Suleiman's reign—peak Turkish power—coincided with the undercutting of his empire's trading economy.

But trade alone is not a sufficient cause for growth or decline. There were increasing costs of to equip the military, especially after the gunpowder revolution. Gunpowder was used early by the Ottomans during their rise to power, but their primary land force was the cavalry. As the

finer and finer gunpowder weapons of the 1500s and 1600s made cavalry irrelevant, it became increasingly costly to pay for a professional
infantry (recall that imperial Spain struggled with the cost of its infantry
as well). The sipahi-timar system was diminished along with the cavalry's centrality to warfare. Yet the bulk of the state's tax revenues were
being collected locally, in-kind through the timar system. Although the
loss of tariffs from Eurasian trade might have been small relative to the
whole economy, it was not small relative to the monetized economy.
To collect revenues during the sixteenth century, Istanbul had to transition to a system of tax farming to collect agricultural revenues directly
rather than in-kind.

Tax farming is a peculiar institution to many modern readers, so here
is a quick summary. The sultanate would sell rights to collect taxes in a
region, usually to the top bidder. Normally contracts were for a single
year. But in the seventeenth century, the Ottomans sold tax-farming
contracts of five years and asked for large portions of the contract to be
paid up front. The tax farmers were free to keep whatever excess revenues they could squeeze from the land. As a side note, the Romans also
used tax farming. Its abuses there are partly to blame for disenchant-
ment of the Roman provinces with imperial rule.

The transition away from the timar system was anything but smooth.
Many cavalrymen formed bandit groups that harassed the countryside,
an internal problem that plagued the empire. Meanwhile, tax farmers
became increasingly utilized and powerful in the provinces. In 1695,
the sultan introduced a new institution called *malikane* in the pursuit
of state revenues. Malikane was the lifetime contract for tax farming,
intended to raise significant funds for the sultan in the short term, but
also to align incentives of the tax farmer toward prosperity of the local
people to foster long-term growth. Malikane was also extended to other
state-based revenue sources such as monopolies of trade and industry.
Perversely, however, malikane crowded out private investment. Turkish money was much more likely to be sunk into buying these financial
products than into investing in industry or agricultural improvements.
Meanwhile, the role of peasants remained limited to usufructuary rights
only, while the title-holder role evolved from sipahi to tax farmer to
malikane owner.

The malikane was owned for the lifetime of the individual who purchased it, by law. When the Russians declared war on Turkey in 1768, the sultan permitted a diversified malikane with multiple owners called the *esham,* sold for six or seven times the annual revenue stream. Unfortunately for Istanbul, esham were natural commodities to trade. A man who initially purchased it would naturally want to sell it as he grew older, a transfer that made enforcement of the lifetime limit on its revenue stream difficult. Although this evolution of a financial market is fascinating in retrospect, it served the interests of Istanbul poorly. The system was ultimately scrapped in the 1840s as part of the Tanzimat reforms—which we can think of as a perestroika of the era. But by that late date, the empire had fallen far behind the development of the West.[10]

TOO LITTLE, TOO LATE?

To be sure, the Ottomans made tremendous reforms during the nineteenth century to catch up to the technological frontier being set by the growing empires of Western Europe and North America. Samuel Morse received his first telegraph patent in 1847 from the Ottoman Empire, issued by the sultan himself. But the empire's first railways were not built until 1856, a half century after the technology was pioneered in Britain.

Was Turkey playing catch-up too late in the game? It is tempting to say yes. The truth is that it is never too late for any country to make pro-growth reforms. Five hundred years after Ming China's introversion, Mao's communism arguably made the nation of China poorer. But it wasn't too late for Deng Xiaoping to initiate market reforms that sparked world-beating growth rates. Likewise, during the final decades of the Ottoman decline, 1870–1910, other countries around the world were sparking economic reformations from a much lower starting point. Japan's Meiji Reformation of 1868 is a good example.

What hurt Turkey was that the institutional stagnation had made it vulnerable as well as weak. Japan was an island, and therefore insulated in its weakness. In contrast, Turkey was exposed to enemies on all sides. The Crimean War in the early 1850s, with Russia on one side and Turkey along with Western European allies on the other, revealed how sick the Ottoman state was. The Russians attacked again in the war of

1877–78, this time fighting Turkey alone. The Ottomans lost much in that war, and even more territory was ceded to rising nationalist movements in the Balkans and the rest of Eastern Europe. As it had so many times in the past, the Ottomans resorted to creative debts to pay for self-defense, this time borrowing from foreign lenders. Economic historians trace the first foreign borrowing by the Ottoman government to 1854; borrowing accelerated in two decades to such high levels that debt service accounted for half of the budget. Turkey soon declared bankruptcy and even stopped debt payments altogether.[11]

The sultan suspended the nascent parliament in 1878, but a revolution in 1908 restored it. It didn't matter. The empire was splintering. Its inferior economy and military relative to the rising European powers made the dissolution of the empire all but inevitable. The episode worth pondering is not the century of collapse, from 1820 onward, but the century prior when Istanbul lost its balance.

SUMMARY OF DECLINE	
Great Power:	Ottoman (Turkish) Empire
Turning point:	1550–1600
Economic imbalance:	Fiscal; technological
Political roots:	Centralized governance, theocracy, rent-seeking bureaucratic class
Behavioral dysfunction:	Loss aversion by zero-sum bureaucrats; identity heuristics hostile to foreign ideas; bounded rationality about importance of technology for growth

8

JAPANESE OPENING

One popular concept is that the Japanese have never been anything more than a race of borrowers and imitators. The truth is quite the contrary. Although geographic isolation has made them conscious of learning from abroad, it has allowed them to develop one of the most distinctive cultures to be found in any area of comparable size.

—Edwin O. Reischauer, *Japan: The Story of a Nation*[1]

The click of a white stone as it is played by the *meijin* (master player) on a wooden board is a distinctive sound of Japan's ancient culture. Often compared to Western chess, the board game of Gō is distinct in many ways and also centuries older. Chess originated in India as early as the sixth century, though its modern layout was only settled in Europe during the late fifteenth century. Chess is a game of movement by a preset number of unique pieces with a simple goal to kill the enemy's king. By contrast, the Gō board is empty at the beginning of a game, a grid of nineteen by nineteen lines, making 181 intersections. Players slowly fill the board by alternating moves with black and white stones that never move again. The patterns of the stones grow and interconnect to achieve one of two objectives worth equivalent points—swallowing up as many enemy stones as possible or securing free space. The opening moves are like fresh paint on an untouched canvas; the midgame is where the literally incomputable dynamics are ripe for innovative play. The endgame is where the ultimate point balance is beyond doubt.

Figure 17. Gō.

Japan's rise and fall is a story that can be understood in three parts, somewhat akin to a game of Gō. Part one is the surprisingly rapid modernization from 1860 to 1905, in which the feudal society shocked the world by being the first non-European people to adopt "liberal" institutions and the first to war against a European power and win (against Russia in 1905). These opening moves, known as *fuseki* in Gō, revealed a pattern of state-managed, export-driven capitalism that other Asian nations, often rivals, copied with great success in the late twentieth century. Part two is the century of convergence, which includes Japan's brutal and successful colonization of the Pacific region and its similarly brutal defeat in World War II. The mid-century conflict was, however, essentially irrelevant to Japan's long-term convergence arc—from 29 percent of the U.S. income level in 1900 to 65 percent in 1970. The century is notable because it confirmed the successful institutions of state-managed capitalism and involved numerous creative plays known as *tesuji* along the way. Part three is the equilibrium since 1990—known pejoratively as the "Lost Decades." We believe this period should be interpreted as the limits of the Japanese economic supermodel. The end-game here has Japan settled into a set pattern. It seems set to follow the technological lead of the United States. In Gō, this stasis happens when a player loses *senté* (the active lead) and is forced into *goté* (passive re-action).

During the first two parts of the story, Japan was a prodigy among nations, but it became prodigal during the third part, squandering its economic promise. The Japanese need to accept the outcome of the game they have played. It was well played. It changed the economic game for all nations. But the institutional model that Japan pioneered has reached its limits. The challenger has remained at roughly 80 per-cent of the strength of the productivity frontier. If Japan hopes to escape what is becoming a fiscal and demographic trap, it must empty the board and start again. Japan must invent a new fuseki.

FUSEKI: JOHN MANJIRO AND THE MEIJIN

Young Americans have no memory of Japan as a bitter enemy during the four years of fighting in the Pacific that followed the attack on Pearl Harbor in 1941. They instead think of Japan as one of their nation's closest allies. And when they think of feudal Japan's transformation into a modern society, they probably have two Hollywood productions in mind. Most recent is the movie in which a cynical American officer from the Civil War becomes a mercenary in 1860s Japan. He rediscovers his sense of honor after being captured by the samurai warriors in their struggle against the greedy, capitalist bureaucracy that has corrupted the emperor. In the 1970s, the image of Japan was set in the television miniseries *Shōgun,* based on a novel by James Clavell of the same name. A Dutch trading ship crashes on the Japanese coastline around 1600 while trying to circumnavigate the globe. Its intrepid pilot, played by Richard Chamberlain, becomes a trusted adviser to a warlord vying for rule against the established shogun. Both movies celebrate the beauty of Japanese culture, but the 1970s version has a more honest presentation of the special interest incentives at stake.

Japan had a unique sociopolitical form of feudalism during the Tokugawa shogunate (1600–1867) that historians describe as more sophisticated than European variants of the same era.[2] The brilliant general Hideyoshi (1537–98) emerged victorious after decades of internal wars among Japan's fractured warlords, although his peasant roots prevented him from personally assuming the title of shogun. Tokugawa Ieyasu achieved full national unity after Hideyoshi's death (legend has it the two friends played Gō together) during a battle in October 1600. Peace settled over the country following that victory as a result of Tokugawa's generosity toward his enemies. He established stability and peace by allowing autonomy among the local warlords, or *daimyo*, which appeared to be a sign of weakness. But it worked. In addition, Tokugawa's direct control of one-quarter of the land included the Kanto plain, Edo (Tokyo), Kyoto, and "all the major Japanese cities, ports, and mines."[3] He also established a competent central bureaucracy and instituted agricultural reforms that enriched the people. Thus the reformed nation had what amounted to a federal structure internally, not to mention free internal trade, which gave it a mixture of competition and cooperation among the daimyo domains.

Urbanization, a surging population, and high literacy rates were just some of the many signs that Japan had emerged from the Malthusian trap as the nineteenth century began. Income per person in Japan rose between 1820 and 1870 from $669 dollars per year to $737, compared to stagnation at lower levels elsewhere in Asia and a real 10 percent decline in China. To be sure, we can point to many shogunate policies that probably hindered progress—Acemoglu and Robinson list strict occupational controls, centralized monopolies, high taxes on farmers, and autarky—but the point is that the policies were *relatively* growth-enhancing for that era.

But not all Japanese citizens were happy with the country's progress and peace during the two and a half centuries of the Tokugawa shogunate, even before the European empires arrived. The status of the samurai class, roughly 7 percent of the population, was based in the rural, agricultural economy, which was diminished and threatened by the emerging commercial culture. Although merchants were technically the lowest class, samurai became increasingly in debt to urban financiers. Though we think of samurai as a symbol of Japan's high culture, economically the status meant something more reactionary. Status protected by violence shrouded by ritual is a common theme that we have seen in Roman, Ottoman, and just above every premodern empire. In all places, it stands for traditional elites versus progress. It was no different in Japan.

TABLE 5. COMPARING JAPAN'S GDP PER CAPITA AT KEY MOMENTS (1990 INTERNATIONAL DOLLARS)[4]

	1820	1870	1900	1913	1938	1950	1960	1970
U.K.	1,706	3,190	4,492	4,921	6,266	6,939	8,645	10,767
U.S.	1,257	2,445	4,091	5,301	6,126	9,561	11,328	15,030
Japan	669	737	1,180	1,387	2,449	1,921	3,986	9,714
Korea	600	604		862	1,459	770	1,105	1,954
China	600	530	545	552	562	439	673	783
India	533	533	599	673	668	619	753	868

Only outside pressure—or rather the cautionary tales of the treatment of China, India, and Indonesia by the European powers—convinced many daimyo that Japan must change or be conquered. The arrival of advanced ships bearing superior cannons was not enough to convince the samurai to give up their high position in the social hierarchy (where, naturally, merchants had to bow low before them). Japan at this time was fiercely isolationist. The law decreed "death for all intruders." Repeated efforts by British, Russian, and American navies to negotiate trade and port access were rebuffed. Oddly enough, the shipwrecked sailor who reshaped Japan's orientation toward the West was not, however, a British pilot, American whaler, or Russian merchant. It was a Japanese fisherman.

His name was Manjiro, and he was born in 1827, far south of Tokyo in Kochi prefecture, as the second son of poor fishing family. When he was fourteen, Manjiro's small fishing vessel was destroyed in a storm, and the sailor swam for days until landing on a deserted island. After surviving there for a half a year, he and his shipmates were found by an American ship as it passed by. The other survivors were dropped off in Hawaii to live out their days, while young Manjiro was adopted by the captain and taken to live with the latter's family in the United States. After a decade in America, where he had received an education, John Manjiro, as he was now known, wanted to return home, but to do so

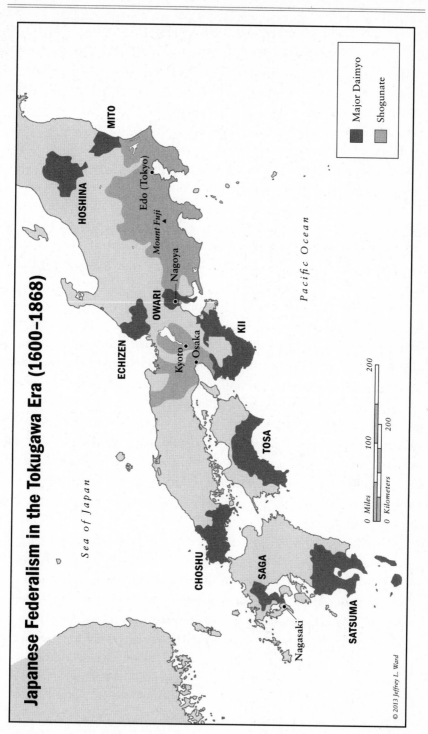

Japanese Federalism in the Tokugawa Era (1600–1868)

Sea of Japan

MITO

HOSHINA

Edo (Tokyo)

Mount Fuji

Nagoya

OWARI

ECHIZEN

KII

Kyoto

Osaka

Pacific Ocean

TOSA

CHOSHU

SAGA

SATSUMA

Nagasaki

Major Daimyo

Shogunate

0 Miles   100   200

0 Kilometers   200

© 2013 Jeffrey L. Ward

was to risk death. No foreigners, even Japanese migrants, were allowed to set foot in Japan. But Manjiro overcame the suspicions of the shogunate after interrogations upon his return in 1851 and went back to his home village. For many years, he was the only person in Japan who could speak English, making him instrumental as an interpreter when the American "black ships" led by Commodore Perry arrived in Tokyo in 1853. Manjiro explained the industrialization of the United States and its political culture in favorable terms, which perhaps led to progressive reforms rather than a doomed confrontation with the Americans.

Even though the emperor nominally ruled the nation, he held a religious and ceremonial role during this era. The ruling shogun used the title *taikun* in foreign dealings, which was a nuanced title that emphasized economic control. This word became the root for one of the few English words of Japanese origin, *tycoon*. Perry's black ships forced Emperor Edo to submit in 1853 to American naval visitation and trading rights, which were soon expanded to the Russians, the British, and others. The next decade saw the shogunate agree under duress to more and more foreign demands. The xenophobic public reaction, fanned by restless and conservative samurai, put the shogunate in an impossible bind. A calculating group of revolutionaries used the public anxiety to topple the shogunate with the pretext of restoring the emperor to power. The emperor was a boy of fourteen at the time, known as the *meiji*, hence the rebellion is known to history as the Meiji Restoration. It was the opposite of a reactionary shift to traditional policies; nor was it a rebellion against the intrusive Westerners. As U.S. Ambassador Edwin O. Reischauer explains:

> In theory the movement may have "restored" the imperial rule of antiquity, but nothing of the kind actually took place. While paying utmost deference to emperor, the group of young samurai and court nobles who were in actual control ruled in a collegial manner, as had become customary in Japan, and they took their models of innovation not from ancient Japan, but from the contemporary West. . . . The real changes they made were the abandonment of the feudal structure of Tokugawa society and government and the piecemeal adoption of Western institutions of modern centralized rule.[5]

In a sense, the displaced shogunate had been beholden to conservative, class-conscious special interests, inhibiting its capacity for economic reforms. Japan of 1853 was stuck in a trap described by Mancur Olson: unable to break out of its political and economic sclerosis without a revolutionary event. By playing on classist resentments, the Meiji "rebels" made necessary reforms possible. In 1869, the new rulers abolished feudalism. Political power was centralized and enforced with a prefectural system. Daimyo were given ceremonial roles for a few years, then ousted bloodlessly with fat state pensions. Individuals were given broad property rights, and classes were formally abolished, as were occupational and migratory restrictions.

Following the example of John Manjiro, Japanese officials fanned across the globe to visit, befriend, and learn the best practices of the Great Powers. The rechristened capital of Tokyo sparked a nationwide effort to industrialize the economy and educate the masses. "By 1890 Japan was the first Asian country to adopt a written constitution, and it created a constitutional monarchy with an elected parliament, the Diet, and an independent judiciary," according to Acemoglu and Robinson.[6] Furthermore, it designed a navy based on the British model and an army based on the German model. And so three decades after the Meiji Reformation, Japanese GDP per capita had grown by 70 percent, and by 1913 it had doubled outright (Table 5). By 1938, it had nearly doubled again. Victory during the Russo-Japanese War of 1905 put the world on notice that its stereotypes of Asian inferiority were flawed. The continued growth of Tokyo's industrial and naval might were the foundations of an entirely new empirical supermodel of how a poor nation can grow mighty, and mighty fast.

TESUJI: KEY FEATURES OF THE ASIAN MIRACLE

In 1993, the World Bank published a book that explained in great detail a phenomenon that had captured the world's attention. *The East Asian Miracle* examined a virtual contagion of double-digit growth rates in nearly a dozen countries. Like a virus, these miraculous growth rates spread across the Pacific region during the 1960s and 1970s, and they could be traced back to a series of common institutions and policies that had started in Tokyo. Although, even a half century after their brutal occupation had ended, the South Koreans thought of the Japanese as bitter rivals, they respected the supermodel that the Japanese economy had become. And so they copied it, by and large. In Singapore, in Hong Kong, in Malaysia, in Thailand, in Taiwan, even in nominally communist China, the features of Japan's state-managed economy were copied.

At its prewar height in 1940, Japan's per capita income level had risen to 40 percent of the U.S. level. Despite the utter devastation of the war, including two nuclear attacks, the economy rebounded. By 1960, Japan had recovered to the same relative 40 percent level (and absolutely, a much higher level of income). Not to oversimplify, but this recovery belies the notion that the Japanese "miracle" of the 1960s was simply a matter of repairing damage from the world war. Japanese firms and workers had grown radically stronger. In a single decade, from 1960 to 1970, Japanese productivity levels closed the remaining gap with U.S. levels by half.

Industrialization was the watchword of economic development for many decades, and the Japanese model proved superior to the alternative model across the East China Sea. In 1957, Mao Zedong promised that Chinese industry would produce more than Britain within fifteen years, which justified his Great Leap Forward, a tragically misguided national effort. A zealous focus on producing steel forced peasants to leave their farms and even to melt down everyday items such as pots and pans. More than half a million Chinese were executed for resisting in the first year, and somewhere between 15 and 40 million people starved to death before the Great Leap Forward movement ended four years later.

The Japanese model was different, emphasizing free markets for final goods that were supplied by government-guided private corporations. Catching up to the West had been a national mantra since the Meiji Restoration, a focus that continued to give a missionary zeal to the economy unmatched by any other society. "There were close solidaristic links between Japan's highly educated bureaucratic elite, politicians of the Liberal Democratic Party, big business and the banking system," wrote Angus Maddison in commentary accompanying his compendium of world historical data.[7] Some also credited so-called Japan Inc.'s unique set of "communitarian" rules, in the words of Lester Thurow,

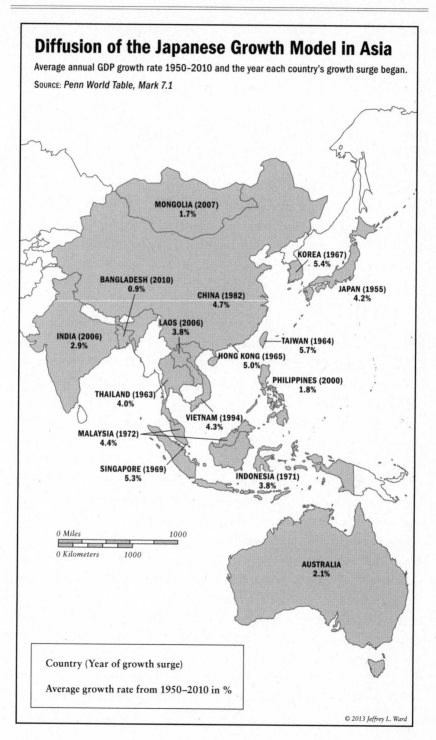

Diffusion of the Japanese Growth Model in Asia

Average annual GDP growth rate 1950–2010 and the year each country's growth surge began.

SOURCE: *Penn World Table, Mark 7.1*

MONGOLIA (2007)
1.7%

KOREA (1967)
5.4%

BANGLADESH (2010)
0.9%

CHINA (1982)
4.7%

JAPAN (1955)
4.2%

LAOS (2006)
3.8%

INDIA (2006)
2.9%

TAIWAN (1964)
5.7%

HONG KONG (1965)
5.0%

PHILIPPINES (2000)
1.8%

THAILAND (1963)
4.0%

VIETNAM (1994)
4.3%

MALAYSIA (1972)
4.4%

SINGAPORE (1969)
5.3%

INDONESIA (1971)
3.8%

0 Miles   1000

0 Kilometers   1000

AUSTRALIA
2.1%

Country (Year of growth surge)

Average growth rate from 1950–2010 in %

© 2013 Jeffrey L. Ward

contrasting the nation's "producer economics" with Anglo-Saxon "consumer economics." Although much of Thurow's admiration was overwrought, he accurately identified Tokyo's heavy interventionism as a key factor that differentiated its economic policies. By manipulating currency exchange rates to favor exports over imports, and by subsidizing and directing production in certain sectors, the Japanese government pursued economic growth through the supply side of the economy.

Culture was a factor as well. Personal saving rates of the Japanese people were 15 percent of annual after-tax income on average during the 1980s, and were vital in generating a pool of internal capital investments at the expense of consumer appetites. Japan also had an educated workforce imbued with norms that reinforced hard work, late nights, and infrequent vacations. The other key feature of industrialization ignored by experts in the West was an emphasis on agricultural reforms that liberated labor, in sharp contrast to the coercive approach under socialism. Taiwan, in particular, instituted rigorous land reforms in the postwar years that broke up monopolistic and overly concentrated holdings after World War II, just as Japan did on the advice of the American advisers.

For all that, official policy can only explain so much. We believe the efficiency in production of Japan's large industrial firms was a vital driver of its rapid convergence to American GDP per capita. "The first thing to notice about Japan's modern industrial structure is that it has always been dominated by very large organizations," writes political scientist Francis Fukuyama. And its large corporations were interconnected vertically and horizontally in the production chain, first as massive, family-run conglomerates (*zaibatsu*) and later as networks of firms with cross-held equity stakes (*keiretsu*). "Before World War II, the ten largest zaibatsu accounted for fifty-three percent of total paid-in capital in the financial sector, forty-nine percent in the heavy industrial sector, and thirty-five for the economy as a whole."[8] These firms dominated the nation's economy.

This bigness had an upside and a downside. As an upside, firms provided secure and stable meritocracies for the hardworking population, while also producing a kind of safety net for elderly and less productive workers. The guarantee of lifetime employment was a cultural norm across all Japanese companies and was thought to be one of the cultural secrets that might explain high Japanese productivity growth. Thurow and others urged the adoption of this institution to help Western capitalism survive, which turned out to be an overreaction. The downside of corporate gigantism is a paucity of entrepreneurship. Japan had plenty of small businesses, but they tended to be restaurants and retail establishments, not the kind of start-ups that develop and deploy technological innovations. High saving rates likewise imply a risk aversion that hinders entrepreneurship. The feature of *pioneering* innovation in America was generally lacking in the Japanese supermodel, even as its large firms excelled in *marginal* innovation through R&D. It must also be said that the rare organization of new Japanese corporations proved to be successful in many cases despite government favoritism for established firms. The iconoclastic entrepreneur Soichiro Honda (1906–91), for example, defied the guidance of government officials in 1962 to pursue his dream of producing automobiles, in competition with favored Toyota, Nissan, and Subaru. Today Honda produces some 14 million internal combustion engines annually, more than any other company in the world, and is the seventh-largest automobile manufacturer in the world (producing more cars on U.S. soil than Chrysler).

Dismissed often in the West as a nation of trinket-makers, Tokyo's export-fueled economy converged toward America until the early 1970s when the global recession caused the Japanese economy to shift into a lower gear. An OPEC oil embargo sparked by the Arab-Israeli War in 1973 hurt Japan more than any other industrialized power. Some 80 percent of its energy imports came from the Persian Gulf, and the price of oil quadrupled after OPEC learned how much power it held during the crisis. Nevertheless, convergence by Japan toward America continued in this lower gear, from 76 percent in 1976 to 90 percent in 1990, according to Penn World Table data, shown in Figure 18. Japanese productivity hit its relative peak one year later, at 94 percent. Then the bubble burst.

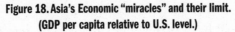

Figure 18. Asia's Economic "miracles" and their limit.
(GDP per capita relative to U.S. level.)

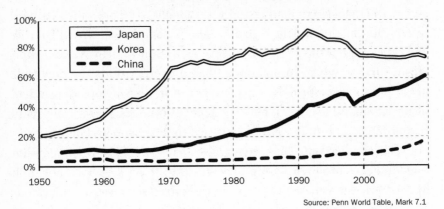

Source: Penn World Table, Mark 7.1

A huge pool of private savings—fueled by a combination of frugality and unprecedented incomes—had a perverse downside in the form of a nationwide asset bubble. It's odd to say that Japan grew too fast, but the suddenly wealthy Japanese citizens of the late 1980s had more money than they could spend. Real estate prices inflated dramatically, reaching twenty thousand dollars per square foot in Tokyo's Ginza district. Excess demand met perhaps one of the most limited supplies of land anywhere. One offhand estimate of the price of the imperial palace at the center of Tokyo, its manicured gardens surrounded by curved walls and moats, suggested it was worth more than the island of Manhattan, though neither was for sale. The Nikkei stock index experienced a similar bubble, which came crashing down in late 1989. Today the Nikkei composite is only one-quarter of its peak value. Property in Tokyo's financial districts collapsed, losing more than 99 percent of peak value, while Tokyo residential property lost 90 percent. Nationally, the value of residential land—a store of wealth for middle-class citizens—dropped by one-third.

Paul Krugman was one of the first to call out the limits of the so-called miracle economies of Asia. In a 1994 article for *Foreign Affairs*, Krugman wrote that "the realities of East Asian growth suggest that we may have to unlearn some popular lessons." [9] In particular, Krugman cast doubt on "industrial policies and selective protectionism" while applauding the simple common feature of "delayed gratification" of a public willing to trade consumerism for a high national saving rate. Soon after Krugman's prescient essay, it became obvious that the recession and burst real estate bubble in Japan were more than temporary setbacks in a business cycle. There was a "new normal," and critics began warning that Japanese policymaking was so bad that a whole decade was being lost. Overall growth rates fell behind the West during the "lost decade" of the 1990s, with a growth rate of 1 percent per year. After that stuttering recovery, another decade has since been declared lost as well. Productivity is no longer converging. But this common observation is not quite true: the actual performance of Japanese GDP growth has been almost exactly in line with Western Europe, on average. What has been lost is not economic growth, but the extraordinary growth of a mythical supermodel that never existed.

NEW FUSEKI: WILL JAPAN RISE AGAIN?

Japan's peculiar mix of managed capitalism was rightfully celebrated by Lester Thurow and others for achieving rapid economic growth, but most analysts in the 1980s did not understand or distinguish between catch-up capitalism and entrepreneurial capitalism. The Japan supermodel proved there is a successful way to develop from any level of poverty up to 80 percent of the frontier (defined in our era as the level of U.S. GDP per capita), but that catch-up model relies on coercive and centralized management of industry, export manipulation, and heavy infrastructure investments. Each of these approaches stops being effective for an economy near the frontier. The ceiling hit by Japan will soon be hit by Korea and will be hit by China in the next two decades, though in each case at different velocities. Think of it this way: building a national highway infrastructure is an essential step in expanding internal scale, but the marginal benefit of doubling the highways is much lower. A frontier economy needs *de*centralized competition in cutting-edge sectors (the antithesis of picking "winners" centrally), a strong consumer culture, and relatively lower government expenditures.

In 1997, when the country was halfway into what became a lost decade, a number of analysts pointed out that there were two Japans.[10] One was just as productive as any nation on earth, and it was made of world-renowned multinational corporations such as Sony and Toyota. The other was backward, more like a middling nation that had yet to experience the "miracle" of modernization. "Look closely at the Nikkei's latest sell-off," said *Business Week* in a 1997 cover story, "and you'll see a reordering of Japan's $5 trillion economy into divergent camps—cosseted, uncompetitive domestic industries vs. a core of highly competitive multinationals." [11] Tokyo, where the first Japan has always been on display, holds a quarter of the nation's population and is the center of finance, entertainment, and government sectors. It's like Hollywood, New York, and Washington, D.C., all in one. When Japan was growing at 10 percent a year, even at 4 percent, Tokyo was able to mask the less productive regions, but no longer. The multinationals globalized, as did their competitors in Europe and America, sourcing new factories and work closer to their customers abroad, a move that exacerbated the downturn at home.

Our assessment is that Japan's economy needs much more internal competition. The root problem economically is that there are interest groups aligned against sectoral evolution of the economy. Small farmers and small retailers have blocked reforms (in other words, big-box retailers) that would allow larger competitors to bring greater efficiency to the domestic economy. Worse yet, the government in Tokyo holds complete control over the regulatory environment. Competition among cities and prefectures to experiment with different regulatory and tax environments is a nonfactor. Lacking competition, the economy has settled into a steady pattern of followership in the global pecking order. This pattern implies stability not decline, but the country faces a second challenge stemming from its behavior since 1990.

Despite being a positive role model in rapid development, Japan is now in the midst of a crisis that is turning the country into a negative role model. The way Japan responded to the asset bubble and lost decade—misdiagnosing its recession—has created a bubble potentially more dangerous: a debt bubble, equal to 200 percent of GDP, and rising. That level is twice as high as most economies' in Europe.

The government responded to the 1990 recession with a massive, textbook Keynesian response. It increased expenditures, particularly on infrastructure, funded by selling debt. Expenditures have been higher than revenues by so much that the annual Japanese deficit has averaged roughly 10 percent a year for more than a decade. Is this a concern if interest rates on government debt are phenomenally low? The interest rate on ten-year Japanese government bonds is below 1 percent, the lowest in the world. True, 95 percent of Japanese national debt is held by Japanese citizens, but someday soon those savers will want their funds back.

Remember those high saving rates? Although the Japanese maintain a large stock of personal savings, the flow of new savings dwindled below 5 percent in 2000 to roughly 2 percent today. This decline is partly to compensate for lost wealth, but it is mostly because of the aging demographic of the population. The working-age population peaked at 87 million in 1995, and, with a birth rate of 1.2 children per woman (about half of the replacement rate), will shrink to 52 million by 2050. Harvard economist Martin Feldstein warns that the "combination of low household saving and substantial government dissaving would normally force a country to borrow from the rest of the world," but the low interest rate and high corporate saving allows Japan to remain a net creditor, for now.[12]

Feldstein's warning was taken seriously in a 2012 academic paper by Takeo Hoshi of the University of California, San Diego and Takatoshi Ito of the University of Tokyo. These scholars asked: "How long can Japanese bond prices defy gravity?" By extrapolating demographic and saving patterns forward, the authors predict the net household saving rate to hold steady at 2 percent for two more decades, then drop over ten years to a net negative saving rate of –3 percent of GDP. They anticipate Japan's debt-to-GDP ratio would rise to 400 percent by 2034 under the optimistic scenario in which interest rates and growth rates are equal. It seems unlikely foreign lenders will be willing, or able, to make that investment.

To be clear, Japan is cruising forward on a familiar road of Great Power decline because of unsustainable national debt. Stimulating the economy with fiscal deficits and currency manipulation would be somewhat understandable if the time it bought was used to engage in structural reform. But Japan's supermodel institutions remain the same, as successive prime ministers have promised reform and then failed for one reason or another to follow through. Monetary policy has foundered on conflicting goals: stimulating the domestic economy with low nominal interest rates while also trying to keep the yen's exchange rate low to stimulate exports. For years now, the nation has been suffering from price deflation, which some see as a symptom of a liquidity trap. Structural reform may have to occur once the artificial stimulus is withdrawn. In truth, the supposedly easy money available at low interest rates has not been available to smaller firms. Appeals for bank loans are common in Japan, what with listed rates being so low, but the artificial price of money is reserved for politically connected big firms, the antithesis of the kind of financial system necessary for entrepreneurial capitalism.

The Japanese dilemma confirms our thesis that economic imbalance is rooted in political stagnation. Japanese voters are fatalistic and have been for years. *New York Times* reporter Martin Fackler explains that people's "high-flying ambitions have been shelved, replaced by weariness and fear of the future, and an almost stifling air of resignation. Japan seems to have pulled into a shell, content to accept its slow fade from the global stage." [13] Rent-seeking by a troika of big companies, big banks, and a big bureaucracy have hindered the political system from making structural reforms. In essence, Japan seems to be stuck in the same dilemma today that it faced a century and half ago. The economy cannot reform until a crisis shakes up the existing political structure. Japan needs a twenty-first-century version of the Meiji Restoration.

Lacking a federal structure for its politics, Japan's prefectures cannot provide institutional experimentation that might foster the entrepreneurial leap the economy needs. Greater federalism would ironically be a "restoration" of how the shogunate organized its domains. Is it time for daimyo to be restored in place of the prefectural hierarchy? In retrospect, we have learned that the Asian model pioneered by Japan is fine for an economy aiming to catch up to the technological frontier, but not of much use in trying to surpass it. Using our Gō metaphor, Japan did something truly special in creating the fuseki for a developing economy. But now the board is full. Its institutional pieces and patterns are no longer moving. Japan needs to clear the board and construct a new fuseki for an advanced economy. The country's biggest mistake now would be to see China's double-digit growth rates as some kind of new model to copy. That mistake is a double reflection of its old self, and there can be no return to the glory days of 1905 or 1960. To restart real growth that will bridge the final 20 percent gap to the technological frontier requires an entirely different mix of institutions that emphasize entrepreneurship and innovation, with a heavy tolerance for individual failure, and capital markets open to small start-ups.

SUMMARY OF DECLINE

Great Power:	Japan
Turning point:	1994
Economic imbalance:	Fiscal, structural
Political roots:	Weak democracy relative to special interests and centralized bureaucracy
Behavioral dysfunction:	Heuristic of neo-mercantilism as growth; loss aversion by big banks and corporations

9

BRITISH DECIMATION

Britannia, that unfortunate female, is always before me, like a trussed fowl: skewered through and through with office-pens, and bound hand and foot with red tape.

— Charles Dickens, *David Copperfield*

ickensian London was a miserably impoverished place, as the author made clear in his sympathetic novels. In books such as *A Christmas Carol* and *Great Expectations,* he exposed the stark wealth inequality of the early stages of the industrial revolution. His ambition to "strike a sledge hammer blow" for the poor through his fiction in the mid-1800s paralleled the idealistic work of another Londoner, Karl Marx. Indeed, the only places worse than London in that era were just about every other city in the world. And the only era more impoverished was just about every one prior.

A good historian will be the first to warn you about applying today's standards to yesterday's civilizations. Our moral revulsion to slavery fails to appreciate how common it was in all of the world's cultures not so long ago. And when we question the actions of Great Powers, we often forget how constrained those societies were. Books were non-existent in Europe until the invention of Gutenberg's press in 1440, while illiteracy of half the population was the norm through most of the eighteenth century. The scope of human knowledge was narrow indeed. A similar hindsight bias, more dangerous to our project of judging and assessing leaders of the past, is the presumption of knowledge even among kings and queens. David Hackett Fischer, a professor of history at Brandeis University, described the *historian's fallacy* as the mistaken view that leaders in the past had access to the same information we have in the present day.

One cannot help but be impressed, for example, by the array of tables that Paul Kennedy prepared for *Rise and Fall of Great Powers,* which covers the rapid changes in the European balance of powers between 1885 and 1918. He reports the total population of the eight major powers at seven moments in time, from 1890, when Russia had 116.8 million people compared to America (62.6 million) and Britain (37.4 million), up to 1938, when Russia had *added* 65 million, America added 76 million, and Britain just over 10 million. This recitation may be powerful documentation of shifts in size, but it is something we know with an exactness contemporaries could not. Other tables Kennedy assembles include similar time-series on urban population, per capita industrialization, iron and steel production, energy consumption, manufacturing shares, military personnel, and warship tonnage. These observations are invaluable, but they were unknown at the time, and also unknown when most of the early retrospective history was being written during the twentieth century.

We nonetheless ponder the decisions of those long-dead rulers and their nations. And no modern Great Power is more interesting (or controversial) than Great Britain itself, particularly its sudden *relative* decline a half century after Dickens's greatest novels were published. The world hegemon in 1880, Britain lost its colonial empire in the decades after World War II. India became independent in 1947, Malaya and Ghana in the 1950s, and the African territories in the 1960s. Capping the century of decline, it handed off control of Hong Kong to China in 1997.

The historian Niall Ferguson argues that the cause of Britain's decline was not colonialism's defeat at the hands of "freedom fighters," a theory many others have embraced. He makes a good argument that colonialism versus freedom is a false dichotomy. The alternative to being a British colony for much of the world in the nineteenth century was not independence, but to be suffering under a much different imperial master in Belgium, France, Portugal, or Germany. Economic scholarship affirms that indeed membership in the club of ex-British colonies is correlated with much higher prosperity than any other colonial club. British institutions were different. No, says Ferguson, the real reasons for decline are rather noble: World War I and World War II. "It was the staggering cost of fighting these imperial rivals that ultimately ruined the British Empire," he writes.[1]

Most would agree that Europe's self-destruction from 1914 to 1945 was unparalleled in modern history. Paul Kennedy would agree with this thesis, adding that Britain had overstretched itself in the late 1800s and was unable to afford its global navy. At the least, the demise of European strength overall because of the world wars seems beyond debate.

Yet we still wonder. As we look at the data on British GDP, productivity, and growth rates, the whole narrative of British decline seems less convincing. To be fair, Kennedy stressed that Britain's decline was merely relative to the catch-up growth of its European neighbors. Average daily income in the United Kingdom in 1700 was the equivalent of $3.40, which rose rather dramatically to $4.70 in 1820, and then to $12.30 in 1900. Britain maintained this lead until the beginning of World War II, though the other European powers were catching up by 1938. As a point of reference, daily income in 1938 Britain was $17.20, compared to $16.80 in the United States.

But that's not the point. Our skepticism is much larger than the distinction between *relative* and *absolute* decline. The initial plan for this book included no chapter on Britain because, in our eyes, the narrative of Britain's imperial decline is lacking what every murder mystery needs—a dead body. Nonetheless, knowing that it is impossible to discuss Great Power decline while ignoring the British Empire, we will make our case. First, the economic data that are available freely on the Internet today but were not known by most historians until recently show that the United Kingdom never really declined in absolute terms. Further, its "power" decline was probably inevitable in a world where other countries have vastly larger populations and under most plausible scenarios where those larger nations converge toward frontier technological levels. Lastly, we believe that Britain did experience a self-inflicted economic and political imbalance along the conventional lines, with loss-averse interest groups and political stagnation, just nothing extraordinary.

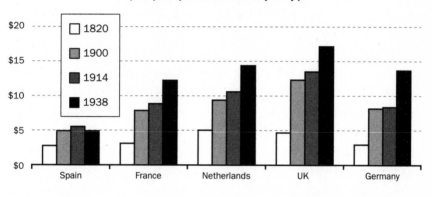

Figure 19. Incomes in Europe, 1700–1938.
(GDP per capita in 1990 dollars per day.)

Source: Angus Maddison, The World Economy

Great Britain was imbalanced in the end by its human capital policies, or rather its concept of citizenship. By treating the residents of its colonies in America, India, and elsewhere as subjects, rather than citizens, London seeded a crack-up. Britain may have had coaling stations all across the seven seas, but the bottom line in terms of human resources was that it *understretched*. The British Empire could still be a superpower today, we believe, if it had been more expansively British and less imperial.

HOW DID BRITAIN GROW?

In 1909, the British Empire encompassed one-quarter of the world's landmass, three times more territory than what was controlled by the French. It also ruled one-quarter of the world's population, though not as British citizens. This hegemonic reach was powered by an economy that was unrivaled in size and technological sophistication.

The Netherlands in 1700 had a higher per capita GDP than the

United Kingdom by about 40 percent, but a large global trading empire drove its high incomes. As Figure 19 shows, the U.K. industrialized faster and overtook Holland in the nineteenth century, maintaining its lead at critical points in the early twentieth century over other European nations as well. These figures should be kept in context: measures of per capita GDP do not consider all of the people in an empire's possessions, only the nation proper. England had something much different on top of its vast imperial trading scale, which was a technological breakthrough known as the industrial revolution. Often dated as "occurring" in the year 1820, economic historians trace the origins of industry to many changes a hundred years before that. The first steam engine came into use in the 1720s, probably at a mine in Cornwall, and was improved dramatically a half century later when James Watt added a separate cooling mechanism that cut coal usage by two-thirds for the same amount of power. The revolution in industry shows up for the average British citizen when the supply of textiles increased (and their prices declined) thanks to innovations such as Richard Arkwright's spinning frame in the 1760s. Arkwright's innovations brought the production of thread from raw cotton fiber out of the cottage and into the world's first factories. In contrast to Karl Marx's interpretation of the social effect of the nascent factory system, the new arrangment was not a sharp division of labor *from* capital. It was a tremendous expansion of opportunity for low-income labor to *use* capital equipment and consequently enjoy a higher level of productivity (and pay).

University of Illinois at Chicago economist Deirdre McCloskey argues that the shift that girded all the hardware innovations was more important still, and that was the cultural embrace of the merchant class as something heroic rather than ignoble.[2] This cultural story we find convincing, but we don't make the hard distinction between economic institutions and cultural factors that McCloskey seems to make. There is no denying that merchants were driving the early British expansion. In 1686, there were 702 London merchants "exporting to the Caribbean, and 1,283 importing," according to Acemoglu and Robinson.[3] A similar number were importing and exporting with North America. Rather than try to have the final word on which factors were more fundamental in Britain's rise, let's appreciate that there were mutually reinforcing liberalizations in governance, property rights, culture, commerce, religion, and science a full century before the year 1820. The Industrial Revolution was a many-pivoted fulcrum, the lever of Britain's rise.

One can appreciate the rise of Britain using our measure of economic power. Consider 1900 as a benchmark. British GDP per capita was $4,492 per year (in 1990 equivalent international dollars) compared to $2,826 in France. Overall GDP was $185 billion in Britain, versus $117 billion in France. And the annual growth rates averaged over the previous two decades were 2.2 percent and 1.5 percent, respectively. Combining these three factors through our formula, the United Kingdom in 1900 had an economic power score three times higher than that of France. To emphasize, these are power scores for the nations alone, not including colonial territories. These scores make sense in relative terms, which is what we calculated for five European powers in Table 6. What is astounding here is not just the dominant economic power of the United Kingdom in 1900, but the fact that its power increased twentyfold in only eight decades.

TABLE 6. ECONOMIC POWER (RELATIVE TO THE UNITED KINGDOM IN 1900)

	1600	1700	1820	1900	1914	1938
Germany	1%	0%	2%	57%	118%	162%
United Kingdom	0%	1%	5%	100%	125%	136%
Netherlands	0%	1%	0%	7%	12%	37%
France	1%	1%	2%	36%	39%	130%
Spain	0%	0%	1%	5%	8%	3%

Germany's power growth in the nineteenth century was also impressive, rising from 2 percent of the 1900 United Kingdom level in 1820 to 57 percent in 1900. Germany then doubled its power between 1900 and 1914. And although it lost 5 percent of its population during World War I (Britain lost 2 percent), Germany's economic power recovered quickly, surpassing England in the 1920s and 1930s. France also emerged from its agrarian slumber and industrialized with great speed in the early twentieth century, matching the relative economic power of Britain in 1938.

Was this then the British decline? There is some truth to that observation. British growth rates averaged 0.8 percent per year between the world wars, compared to 3.6 percent in France and 2.9 percent in Germany. Britain's *technological* lead was indeed surrendered in the first few decades of the twentieth century, but to the United States, not its European rivals. There was, however, no absolute decline. Britain emerged victorious in 1945 along with its much larger allies, the United States and the Soviet Union. More to the point, it continued to grow at a healthy pace from 1950 onward. Consider Figure 20, which shows real GDP per capita for the United Kingdom, United States, and Japan. Although the United Kingdom had one-twentieth of America's economic power in 1960 (as we measure it), that was almost all because of the difference in population. And the United Kingdom's power grew during the next fifty years because per capita GDP rose from $10,000 per person (1990 dollars) in 1950 to $35,000 per person, a 250 percent increase. To use our earlier metaphor, the body of Britain was not at all dead before *or* after the world wars. It just stopped being extraordinary. Why? That's the puzzle.

British intellectuals understood in the 1870s—even as they marvelled at their own economy—that other nations were catching up. And they were befuddled about how to stay in the lead. The vaunted free-trade consensus began to crumble, as just one example. The political scientist Aaron Friedberg's book *The Weary Titan* explains how Britain wrestled with declinism in four areas—economic, naval, army, and financial—with successes on many fronts but not all. "At the close of the nineteenth century, Britain's leaders shared a belief in the importance of 'national economic power,' but they lacked agreement on exactly what that concept meant or how it should be measured."[4] Imagine if the prime minister in 1900 could have turned to the diagnostic framework of economic growth that we have today—scale, innovation, and investment with an emphasis on human capital and institutions that fulfill its development. He might have been able to arrest the relative decline. But there was no grasp of GDP then, or of productivity. The metrics they did have were imperfect trade accounts and a mishmash of production figures for various commodities such as steel and coal. The lack of good economic metrics led to a false confidence and hindered development. Of course, the same logic holds if applied to the king in 1776, at a time when the seeds of British weakness were first embedded.

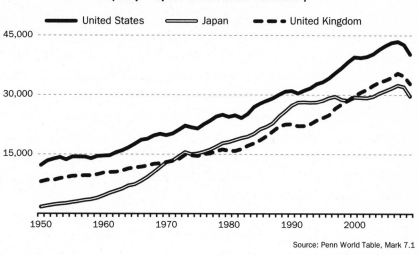

Figure 20. Comparing British, American, and Japanese postwar productivity. (GDP per capita in 1990 international dollars.)

━━━ United States   ⊂══⊃ Japan   ■ ■ ■ United Kingdom

45,000	
30,000	
15,000	

1950   1960   1970   1980   1990   2000

Source: Penn World Table, Mark 7.1

PROPHECY IN VAIN

British identity is a crucial factor in understanding the mentality and decisions of Britain's politicians throughout the late nineteenth and early twentieth centuries. "Possession of such a vast and obviously alien empire encouraged the British to see themselves as a distinct, special, and often superior people," writes historian Linda Colley in an essay on Britishness. "They could contrast their law, their standard of living, their treatment of women, their political stability, and, above all, their collective power against societies that they only imperfectly understood but usually perceived as far less developed."[5] These feelings of national pride extended to the economic models of free trade and the teachings of Adam Smith and John Stuart Mill. Much of the hegemony and success of Britain throughout the majority of the nineteenth century was attributed to doctrines of "laissez-faire" economics as a fundamental part of the British identity.

Unfortunately, the British conceit of themselves as a free people was only partially true. Their concept of freedom was narrow. The British Parliament recognized the hypocrisy of slavery in a free society long before other Great Powers and did something about it. Banning the Atlantic slave trade in 1807 is perhaps the most shining example of a Great Power acting as a *good* power regardless of its own short-run economic interests (the trade in slaves was indeed profitable, even if the practice of slavery was a barrier to economic growth). But in too many other ways, the United Kingdom was not so free as its leaders thought.

As a pioneer in the development of self-government and recognition of human rights, the United Kingdom did not convert to a fully fledged democracy in a day, or in a century. Indeed, when it first developed the institutions of representative democracy, Britain made an operational distinction between *citizens* who had the right to vote and more numerous *subjects* who did not.

The Stamp Act of 1765 and other similar revenue bills highlighted the lack of rights of British subjects who were not residents of the British Isles. The act seems harmless enough, a direct tax imposed by the British Parliament on its subjects in North America for the express purpose of helping pay for the expense of troops stationed there and to replenish the heavy costs of fighting against France during the Seven Years' War. However, such action had been considered and rejected by many former governments until the brief administration of George Grenville. Its impact was significant indeed. The act required that any piece of official paper used in the colonies be imported from London with an official stamp that symbolized its tax and certification. Even paper stock for newspaper was included, but there were much higher fees for official papers such as college degrees and attorney licenses. There was clear intent to curb the growth of the native professional classes, which smacks of occupational controls and central planning more than it does revenue raising. Americans were outraged because they had no representatives in Parliament, a minimum standard for taxation under British law. Protests erupted throughout the colonies, often violent, and so the use of stamped paper was never enforced.

William Pitt "the Elder," who twice served as the virtual and popular prime minister in England, was aghast when the Stamp Act passed. He and other members of Parliament warned that it was a bad idea. In January 1766, just over a month after it had been put into effect, Pitt spoke:

Greater Britain Dreams of Pitt the Elder?

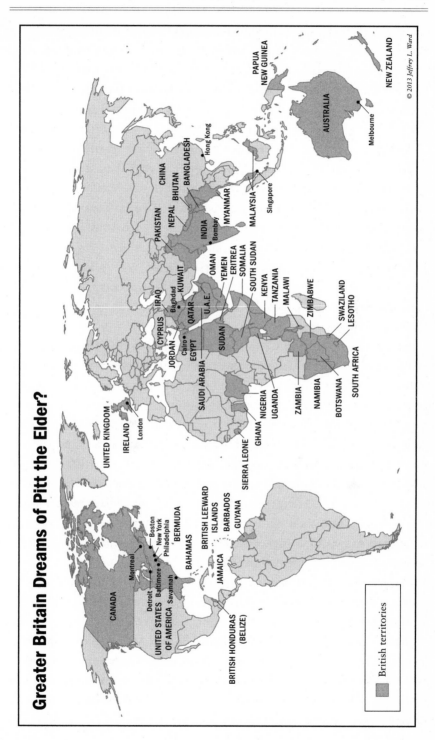

© 2013 Jeffrey L. Ward

British territories

They are the subjects of this kingdom; equally entitled with yourselves to all the natural rights of mankind and the peculiar privileges of Englishmen; equally bound by its laws, and equally participating in the constitution of this free country. The Americans are the sons, not the bastards of England! Taxation is no part of the governing or legislative power.[6]

The fury of the colonists caught Parliament by surprise, even though many sympathetic voices such as Pitt warned that the act violated the core principles of the British Constitution. They pointed to the Bill of Rights of 1688, which guaranteed there would be no taxation without consent of the governed. Even though representation in Parliament was limited to a small proportion of landowning residents on the British Isles, the principle of democratic representation was treasured. Parliament had the sovereignty to tax English lands, whereas local representative bodies in the colonies had sovereignty to tax their colonists. The Stamp Act violated that line.

As we all know, King George III and his government were offended at the violence in the colonies and overreacted. Pride was on the line. Parliament tried to lower the tax burden first, then repealed the act altogether, while asserting its sovereign absolutism with the Declaratory Act. What did it declare? That Parliament could tax the colonies "in all cases whatsoever." Within a year, Parliament passed a series of five additional revenue bills, the so-called Townshend Acts, which the elites in London assumed would be less objectionable because they were indirect tariffs on imports. One of the more contentious bills lowered the tariff on British tea in Britain, so as to make it more competitive with Dutch tea, compensated by a higher tariff on tea in the colonies. Could there be a more explicitly unequal treatment?

Next came the boycotts of British tea, which, if you'll forgive the pun, brewed resentment. British troops were sent in 1768 to impose martial law in Boston. In 1770, British soldiers killed five protesting colonists in what became known as the Boston Massacre. At that time, the colonies were still dominated by loyal subjects, but the harsh treatment by the crown pushed more colonists toward open rebellion. Even five years later, when armed rebels engaged in open combat with British troops for the first time, at Lexington Green, it was not understood as a battle between British and American forces. As Niall Ferguson reminds us, that battle was preceded by Paul Revere's famous ride when he shouted: "The regulars are out!" not as is popularly thought, "The British are coming!" Of course, they were British on both sides of the line. Ferguson's point is that the Declaration of Independence in 1776 should be understood for what it was, a civil war.

In retrospect, the American War of Independence of 1775–83 was the singular moment of economic and political imbalance for the British Empire. It would never recover. The war was never winnable for London, an observation that Pitt the Elder made in one of his last speeches in the House of Commons in 1777. "You may ravage—you can not conquer; it is impossible; you can not conquer the Americans."[7] Suppose British soldiers had killed George Washington and suppressed the revolution—would the spirit of liberty have stayed suppressed? Adam Smith, Pitt the Elder, and others argued that the Americans would have carried their resentments a generation, then revolted anew. And once the larger landmass of Greater Britain was lost, even before the industrial revolution started the global economic transformation to modernity, it was all but inevitable that the smaller British population would be eclipsed by economic convergence in larger nations.

The mystery is why London neglected to expand its citizenship to include colonial representatives in Parliament. This fantasy is not merely retrospective, but a genuine puzzle. Consider, first, that Parliament expanded soon before and soon after the American Revolution. In 1707, the English Parliament became the Parliament of Great Britain by uniting England and Scotland. A similar act of union gave the Irish representation in the newly christened Parliament of the United Kingdom in 1800. Consider, second, that there is a historical record in the papers of Pitt the Elder of proposals to expand Parliament to include the British colonies in the New World. One proposal of particular interest can be found in an undated stack of his papers from the years 1764–74. This "scheme for better uniting" proposed that there be four members of Parliament to represent Virginia, as well as four for Pennsylvania, four for Massachusetts, three for Jamaica, three for New York, two for Canada, one for each of various Caribbean islands, and so on.[8] We can only imagine that this proposal was circulated by Pitt and his allies but found so few supporters that it was never seriously considered.

Adam Smith's *The Wealth of Nations* also includes a similar recommendation discussed at length in Book IV, Chapter 7. Smith anticipates that British America, if independent, "will become, and which, indeed, seems very likely to become, one of the greatest and most formidable [empires] that ever was in the world." While asserting British sovereign authority, Smith appeals again and again to the dignity of free people "on that side of the water" and concludes that "Great Britain should allow such a number of representatives" from those lands in Parliament. He even made multiple references to the Roman Empire's expansive treatment of citizenship. One can tell from the text that Smith was sensitive to the actual concern of London's elites—becoming outnumbered by the Americans—and so proposed a revenue-based scheme for representation to forestall that. Absent representation, he predicted, all colonies would become more trouble than they were worth and rebel besides. His prediction, like Pitt's, was not persuasive enough to overcome the loss aversion of those legislators and the merchants holding the Atlantic trade's monopolies.

GREATER BRITAIN REDUX

Despite losing the thirteen colonies of the United States, the greatest extent of the imperial territory was still to be realized. England's territorial control reached its zenith in 1909. Parliament had a second bite at the apple of economic scale. Rather than consolidate its expansive lands in an integrated federation—granting citizenship to its colonial subjects in Australia, New Zealand, India, Africa, and Canada—it chose to maintain a more hegemonic relationship. Thus the imperial British continued to pursue a human capital policy wholly opposite that of the imperial Romans or the Ottomans.

The main opposition to the imperial-colonial structure was not voiced by expansionists, however, but by Britons such as liberal parlimentarian William Gladstone, who served as prime minister on four occassions during the span of 1868–94. Many English leaders considered the overseas possessions to be "costly, burdensome, and unnecessary," which no doubt they were, in the narrowest accounting. Only a few voices imagined a "Greater Britain," in the words of Charles Dilke, a liberal member of Parliament. In 1881, Cambridge professor John Seeley called for a larger union. Seeley lectured that Britain had an opportunity to successfully govern such a vast territory thanks to the new technologies of steam power and electricity, which were effectively shrinking the globe. Against these sentiments for more union was the immovable, self-satisfied status quo. Britain's industrial revolution was the envy of the world, and its naval power as well.

As we know now, and some dared say then, Britain was losing steam. The leader of the Liberal Unionist party in the 1890s, Joseph Chamberlain, was an especially strong advocate for the creation of an "imperial economic union" that would be a federation of English-speaking colonies. His was a tragic campaign, one that caught up English intellectuals in a debate between two sides that were both wrong. To make his case for change, Chamberlain had to champion the idea of Britain's relative economic decline, warning of astounding industrial growth of continental powers. Skeptics pointed to the one statistic they could use to refute Chamberlain's declinism, which was the absolute increase in foreign trade. As Friedberg documents in *The Weary Titan,* Chamberlain made the fateful decision to disagree and subsequently called for a policy of trade protectionism, or rather, favoritism withing the British sphere. Think of it as a walled garden that would favor trade inside the walls. Chamberlain was right to emphasize the benefits of a stronger, larger anglosphere, but he should have looked for internal barriers to lower, rather than for external barriers to raise. His opponents were right to defend Britain's bedrock principle of free trade, despite sharp criticisms that their laissez-faire policies were worn-out. None of the parties took the logical step of calling for deeper integration, beyond mere trade, within the British Empire.

Meanwhile, the economy on the British Isles was falling into patterns of special interest rent-seeking. Mancur Olson's classic theory is informed by the British case study explicitly. Ever since vanquishing Napoleon at the Battle of Waterloo in 1815, Great Britain enjoyed peaceful hegemony over not just its global territories, but Europe as well. With a navy often twice the size of its closest rival, it established a ninety-nine-year Pax Britannica until the outbreak of World War I. This long peace was the most fertile environment for the development of special interests, says Olson. "In short, with age British society has acquired so many strong organizations and collusions that it suffers from an institutional sclerosis that slows its adaptation to changing circumstances and technologies."[9]

By falling into the technological wake of the more innovative U.S. economy, the British shifted into a much less entrepreneurial economic structure than it had had during its heyday. To be fair, England has produced many great scientists and inventions, but there is no denying its relative stagnation in the late twentieth century. Its expansive national health system is a cautionary tale—expensive to the taxpayer, famously inefficient, and difficult to reform. True, Margaret Thatcher pushed back against the Leviathan when she served as prime minister in the 1980s, but the status of British GDP per capita hardly budged relative to United States, remaining at the 80 percent level. In some sectors, such as high finance, London has maintained its global leadership. The United Kingdom has done well in maintaining an independent currency while integrating with the European Union in other ways.

So what does its future hold? The United Kingdom seems most likely to muddle along, tied to unstable partners on the continent, also tied in its special relationship as the mother country to the United States as well as many other offspring. But its future will not be decided by any of these relationships; rather, it will be shaped by London's capacity to rediscover its identity as an institutional pioneer.

SUMMARY OF DECLINE

Great Power:	United Kingdom
Turning point:	1770–80
Economic imbalance:	Territorial
Political roots:	Loss aversion by class and geographic elites in England
Behavioral dysfunction:	British identity too narrow, distinguishing citizens from subjects

10

EUROPA

Unity and Diversity

I have ever deemed it fundamental for the United States never to take active part in the quarrels of Europe. Their political interests are entirely distinct from ours. Their mutual jealousies, their balance of power, their complicated alliances, their forms and principles of government, are all foreign to us. They are nations of eternal war.
— Thomas Jefferson, letter to President James Monroe, June 11, 1823

The achievements of Europe are considered by many to be the greatest achievements of humankind, from the art of the Italian and Flemish masters such as Leonardo and Rubens to the philosophy of Kant, Pascal, and Locke. To be sure, the Renaissance was an era of Great Powers on the continent of Europe, but should we consider the whole of Europe as a Great Power? As we near the end of our case studies for this book, the current financial crisis in Europe weighs on our thoughts. Is it too early to draw lessons from the crisis? Is it too late for the Eurozone to learn the lessons of the past?

Thomas Jefferson was not alone in his suspicions of the "eternal war" among European nations. Who from that time would not be surprised at the continent's current union, let alone unity? In fact, Europe as a single sovereign body is an old idea that has become realized once again in our time. The continent was first unified by the gravity of the Roman Empire in the second century, then by Charlemagne at the turn of the ninth century, then almost by Hitler's Germany in the middle of the twentieth century. Perhaps because the continent was fractured into competing polities, Europe's aggregate economic power made it the unrivaled leader of the world—pioneering in the sciences, domineering in the ways of war, and imperial in its diplomacy.

Only a few outside civilizations could stand up to the Europeans after 1500, usually by playing one European power against the others. The North Americans stood strongest, and the South Americans rebelled soon after. The Asians and Africans bristled, and waited.

Then, during the twentieth century, Europe was the scene of one tragedy after another. Genocides, total wars, and tyrannies more complete than could have been imagined by our forefathers. Gravity pulled inward again, and violently. Industrialization, some believed, made that gravity stronger. In the novel *1984,* George Orwell anticipated a dystopian future in which technology empowered the state's control over individuals and a geopolitical trend toward gigantism of region-states. It was published just a few years after World War II, when pessimism on the continent was at its height.

Fortunately, Orwell's prediction was off. Totalitarian states did emerge in North Korea, China, Russia, and Eastern Europe, but the larger impact of technology was to empower individuals and to expand economic growth. Instead of imperial gigantism in the second half of the twentieth century, colonies splintered into dozens of independent states, often rough and raw. For the ex-colonies, it has been a difficult half century of liberation, but the promise of freedom is slowly being matched by prosperity. For Europe, the notion of a violent unification seems to have been retired to the ash bin of history, but not the dreams of a peaceful union.

STATISM IN TWO STATES

When we first discussed the idea of this book to some colleagues, they objected on the grounds that it did not explain Nazism. Was Hitler's Germany not a Great Power? Didn't its defeat on military grounds prove the thesis incomplete at best?

Adolf Hitler had imperial ambitions. And German scientists were some of the best in the world. The Messerschmitt Me 262 was the world's first operational jet-powered fighter aircraft. The unpiloted V-2 rockets bombed London. The Nazi economy of the late 1930s was one of the most advanced in the world, but it must also be said that little of the progress was thanks to Nazi institutions. The heights of the Third Reich's technological achievements were based on excellent German universities, developed long before Hitler's dictatorship began in 1934, and that institution fell into decline with overt racism repelling Jewish scholars as well as non-Jews of conscience. Albert Einstein was on a visit to the United States when the Nazis seized power in 1933. He decided, wisely, not to return. There is an anecdote as datum.

The meta-institution of Nazism represents a governing philosophy that most economists now recognize as hostile to growth. The word *Nazi* is the short form of *National Socialism*. The *National* (Na) stood for central authority and the *Socialism* (Zi) stood for a heavy-handed role for the state. While fascist economics may have respected corporate property, it also established that the highest obligation for citizens was to the state, not to private profits, private workers, or the free will of the owners. With its emphasis on corporate control, Nazism had little appreciation for the entrepreneur.

It can never be known if Nazi Germany or fascist Italy could have thrived in peace, though it seems unlikely. Rather, the growth of those economies in the brief run-up to 1939 fit what is now a familiar model—the *statist* takeover. When a government transitions to a more interventionist role, transforming a free economy to a command economy, it thrives on a one-time extraction of wealth from formerly independent, private companies. But like any sudden wealth tax, aggrandizement by a dictator diminishes the incentives of the private sector to *create* wealth going forward.

The Nazi economy existed for barely twelve years. We can only speculate that its statist model would have slowed and imploded. However, a longer-lived statist economy did exist worth remembering—the Soviet Union. Established after the 1917 revolution, the Soviet Union industrialized, fought as an Allied power against the Nazis (and briefly the Japanese) in World War II, and then grew to become one of the two superpowers that defined the bipolar balance of power from 1945 to 1991.

The Soviet Union was a planned economy. It attempted to command the total and diversified supply of goods through a centralized committee in Moscow, known as Gosplan. Gosplan was established in the 1920s as an advisory organization, but its "advice" became mandates. It was the integral control mechanism for the communist party's Five-Year Plans, which began in 1928, and it merged with the national statistical agency in 1930. Bureaucrats from Moscow issued orders for every conceivable product, and their plans were designed to spur heavy industrial production at the expense of consumer goods. Prices in this system did not reflect market equilibrium. They were accounting tools skewed toward favored products. And accounting tools were not the worst of it. The founding fathers of the Soviet Union established concentration camps for slave labor, partly as punishment for political nonconformists, partly to extract value for their industrial utopia. Prison laborers numbered up to 70,000 in the 1920s. But this pales in comparison to the millions of peasants who starved to death in the forced famine of 1920 and 1921, the years when Lenin consolidated his power.

When the Soviet dictator Joseph Stalin took over in 1924 after Lenin's suspicious death, the slave camps grew. Economist Bryan Caplan explains: "By 1930, [inmates] numbered 1,000,000. By 1940, the Gulag Archipelago housed fully 10,000,000 pitiful souls. The death rate was extraordinary: 10–30 percent per year, for the prisoners performed demanding labor such as mining and timber-cutting with minimal food and clothing in freezing temperatures. The slaves were ruled by an elite of secret police, now known as the NKVD."[1]

Despite the horror, the Soviet Union grew dramatically, and it seemed to many to represent the future. Not only did Stalin's armies grind down the bulk of the Nazi war machine, but they also conquered the eastern half of Europe.

Now, imagine if you could travel backward in time. What if somehow you found yourself in the White House in January 1953, given a half hour to talk with the newly inaugurated president, Dwight D. Eisenhower. The burden of history that weighs on Eisenhower in that moment is probably greater than any president ever carried. It goes something like this:

There is a hot war in Korea between the communist north and the combined forces of the United Nations, less the Soviets, in the south. Although that war is stalemated, there remains the adversarial relationship with the Soviet Union, armed for four years now with nuclear weapons. For the next eight years, the Central Intelligence Agency warns that the Soviet arsenal is growing ever stronger, just like its industrial economy, which is growing at a faster pace than America or Europe can match. Soviet premier Nikita Khrushchev gloats that his country will "bury" the West. Americans are paranoid about their relative decline, exploited by Senator Joe McCarthy and the despicable hearings on "Un-American" activities. There are reports that the Soviets are even working on rockets that will launch weapons into space. In 1957, Sputnik will become the first man-made satellite to circle the globe, taunting not just technological equality with the West but outright superiority.

With your knowledge, what would you say to President Eisenhower? What advice would you offer as he confronted the Cold War between communism and capitalism? We would say this: "Yes, Mr. President, communist power embodied by the Soviets appears daunting, but that is a mirage. It will not end well for Russia, especially if Americans stay calm. Communism is an ill-fated experiment that enslaves its people for industrial expediency in the short term. But that system will break down on its own in just a few decades." Our answer, with the benefit of hindsight, is nothing more than a summary of our thesis—Soviet communism's institutions are inferior.

Everybody is a cold warrior now, but back in those days, many commentators believed communist institutions—one-party autocracy with central economic planning—were superior to old-fashioned constitutional democracy and free markets. "I have seen the future," proclaimed American journalist Lincoln Steffens after a visit to the Soviet Union, "and it works." Indeed, there was a widespread overestimate of the rate and durability of Soviet growth among economics textbook authors in the West.[2] Nobel Prize winner Paul Samuelson's leading textbook, *Economics*, motivated readers with a discussion of Soviet versus American potential. In the 1961 edition, the textbook included a chart projecting the Soviet GNP overtaking U.S. GNP over the four decades 1960–2000, with an initial starting ratio of 100:50 in the year 1960. Subsequent editions changed the starting date for the chart, but not the GNP ratio. It was still 100:50 in the 1970 edition, while in 1980, it had been revised to 100:55. For years, that image was the first economic chart many students saw. In the later editions, the lack of Soviet catch-up was blamed on "bad weather," which was changed to an "unfortunate past" in 1980. In the 1989 edition, the textbook included this line: "The Soviet economy is proof that, contrary to what many skeptics had earlier believed, a socialist command economy can function and even thrive."

We know better. Statism offers a timeless appeal, but empirical experience reveals its promise to be built on coercion. Coercion of labor goes by many names, but slavery in the private sector and slavery in the public sector are never efficient, let alone moral. Soviet institutions allowed Russia to industrialize quickly, at great sacrifice of both its people and the people of its conquered neighbors, from Ukraine to Latvia to Croatia. We see now that its "growth" was based on catching up to about the 50 percent level on the productivity frontier, a typical short-term boost in total GDP at the expense of institutional incentives. Thankfully, President Eisenhower understood even without the benefit of time-traveling advisers that a state-managed economy wouldn't work.

THEORETICAL MODELS AND EUROPEAN SUPERMODELS

If the Soviets represented an extreme approach to organizing a national economy, it was convenient for many Western Europeans to think that the Americans represented the other extreme. Some called it "cowboy capitalism," but most just laughed at the hubris and inequality of "laissez-faire" in the United States. Look at their urban slums, they scoffed. Intellectuals in France, Germany, and England liked to think that they occupied the moderate middle ground between the two extremes, which was called a "mixed economy." Its institutions would respect private ownership of productive assets but would also be regulated and taxed by the state.

This mixed economy, as a contrast to that of the United States, is an appealing fiction, but it is a fiction for two reasons. First, American capitalism was far less wild than its critics (or defenders) would admit. Like most modern economies, the United States had national programs for old-age pensions, for unemployment insurance, for medical care for the poor, as well as laws thick with protections for laborers, the environment, and social justice. All this was in place half a century ago. Second, economic theory can trap us into thinking too simplistically. That's why economists are always looking for real-world evidence to prove or disprove competing theories. As for the mixed economy, real-world institutions are much more complex than a one-dimensional choice between anarchy or statism.

As we discussed in the opening chapters, economics can run few experiments in the lab. It looks instead to history. To data. Because of the advances in national-level data, economics has shifted in our generation away from chalkboard models and toward real-world empiricism. It is easy to think that *theoretical* models matter less than they did in the heyday of formal theory (basically 1940 to 1980), but in the context of global affairs, we like to think of each nation as an economic *super-model*. And it is a mistake, a common mistake, when economists and other observers talk about Europe as if it is a single, homogeneous society, even now with the existence of the European Union.

**Figure 21. Economic power of thirty-four European nations in 2010.
(Circle size represents GDP.)**

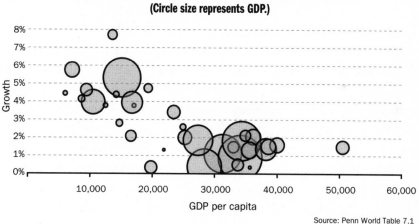

Source: Penn World Table 7.1

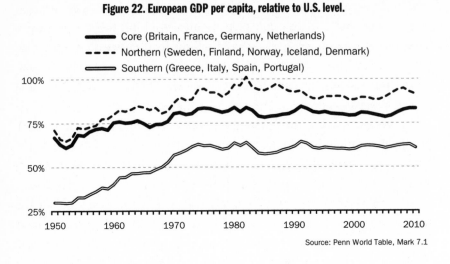

Figure 22. European GDP per capita, relative to U.S. level.

Source: Penn World Table, Mark 7.1

It is more instructive to recognize that there are roughly three economic supermodels in Europe (though each nation is unique in one way or another): core, Nordic, and southern. The core nations include four of the largest economies: Germany, the United Kingdom, France, and the Netherlands. The Nordic (or northern) countries include Sweden, Finland, Norway, Denmark, and Iceland, which are ethnically and culturally distinct, though their economic policies tend to be similar to the core. Southern European economies are generally poorer than those in the north, though they converged from the 25 percent level in the 1950s to the 60 percent level in the 1970s. Italy grew stronger than its southern peers and looked more like a core country in the 1990s, but it has an identical productivity level with Spain and Greece, at the 67 percent level. The different economic performance of the three western supermodels is evident in Figure 22, which shows how steady the average productivity levels have been for the past four decades.

There is a fourth cohort of economies in Eastern Europe, comprising the former Soviet satellites such as Estonia, Ukraine, Poland, and the Balkan states, but post-1991 reforms have been so diverse that it isn't clear what the common institutions among them are. Estonia, for example, borders Russia but is now a member of the European Union as well as NATO, and uses the euro as its national currency, whereas Belarus remains more of a command economy than Russia.

This relative growth experience is one of the most profound stylized facts in international economics, and it remains unappreciated by policymakers and scholars alike. Growth is too often treated as a commodity, as if 2 percent growth in Italy is equivalent to the same growth rate in Germany. Our framework for interpreting growth starts with the observation that all nations are not created equal; rather, they have a diverse mixture of institutions that determine its convergence productivity level. This framework was described as "barriers to riches" by economists Stephen Parente and Edward Prescott (recipient of the Nobel Prize in 2004). The barriers mindset assumes that all nations have the potential to be equal but their failure to achieve equality traces to governments' establishing suboptimal policies that hinder private sector development. Parente and Prescott explain that differences in relative income levels "are the primary result of country-specific policies that result in constraints on work practices and on the application of better production methods at the firm level."[3] Thus an economy with below-average GDP per capita should have an above-average growth rate, but for its barriers. Parente and Prescott witness double-digit growth rates in China not as miraculous, but as expected. What is unnatural is a 2 percent growth rate in South Africa, where such a low rate is a tragedy, unlike the same 2 percent rate in much wealthier Italy, where the rate is appropriate.

EUROZONE PROS, CONS, AND INTEREST RATES

Unfortunately, celebrating supermodel diversity and learning about the productivity frontier is not what the European leaders have been emphasizing in recent decades. Instead, perhaps haunted by the violence of World War II and the nuclear threat of the Cold War, Europeans have pushed for greater unification and harmony. To the extent there was a recognition of income differentials between Europe and North America, explanations focused on the advantages of scale enjoyed by the United States. If Europe could integrate all of its markets for goods, services, people, and capital the way the United States did, average incomes would catch up to, and possibly surpass, the American level.

The Treaty of Rome in 1957 established the first building block, with a common market among member states, which meant reduced barriers on trade, labor, and capital. The founders were Belgium, France, Germany, Italy, Luxembourg, and the Netherlands. In 1973, this European Economic Community welcomed Denmark, Ireland, and the United Kingdom. Soon after the Berlin Wall fell, the peaceful gravity toward further integration took hold. The Maastricht Treaty in 1992 laid the foundation for a true European Union, including a central bank, central parliament (with limited authority), and a common currency called the "euro." The Eurozone was initially established in 1999, when participating states fixed their exchange rates, and euro coins and bills entered circulation in 2002. Only 17 of the 27 states of the European Union participate in the Eurozone, as some powerful economies such as Norway and the United Kingdom voted in referendums to maintain independent currencies.

The logic driving the economic integration of Europe was that less diversity would lead to a lasting pacification of the "eternal war" among its member states. If the 2012 Nobel Peace Prize—awarded to the European Union—is appropriate, that goal has been achieved. The economic logic was that integration would lead to growth thanks to scale. These benefits have not worked out as well as expected, though the euro's first few years seemed to go smoothly. It was probably too smooth. As riots of disgruntled and unemployed youth across the continent have raged since the 2008 global recession, the question remains whether this price of peace was too steep.

Some critics, such as Paul Krugman, warned from the beginning that the common euro currency was ill-fated, but even Krugman acknowledges that the theory is appealing. He summarized all this in a recent address to macroeconomists: "The advantages of a common currency are obvious, if hard to quantify: reduced transaction costs, elimination of currency risk, greater transparency and possibly greater competition because prices are easier to compare."[4] Indeed, many proponents of a common currency point to the golden years after World War II when exchange rates were largely fixed across the globe among noncommunist powers, based on the gold standard. With fixed exchange rates, trade frictions and uncertainties disappeared, which led to an explosion of

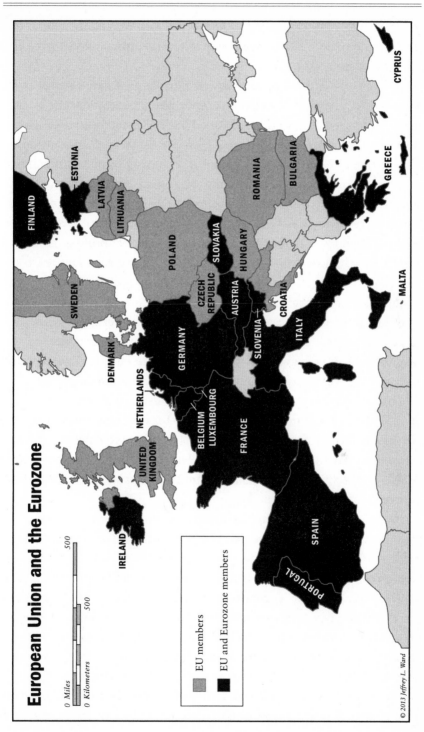

European Union and the Eurozone

0 Miles 500
0 Kilometers 500

EU members

EU and Eurozone members

FINLAND

ESTONIA

LATVIA

LITHUANIA

SWEDEN

POLAND

DENMARK

NETHERLANDS

GERMANY

CZECH REPUBLIC

SLOVAKIA

AUSTRIA

HUNGARY

ROMANIA

BULGARIA

GREECE

CYPRUS

MALTA

SLOVENIA

CROATIA

ITALY

BELGIUM

LUXEMBOURG

FRANCE

UNITED KINGDOM

IRELAND

SPAIN

PORTUGAL

© 2013 Jeffrey L. Ward

international trade flows. After that "Bretton Woods" system broke down in the early 1970s, there was a global growth slowdown. The conclusion seemed obvious.

Of course, there are advantages to *flexible* exchange rates as well. Number one among them is the independence of monetary policy by each sovereign nation. A country that found itself at a competitive disadvantage could adjust its currency to make its exports cheaper. Imagine the exchange rate of German marks for Italian lira going from 1:1 to 1:2. Not only would one thousand marks now be able to buy two thousand lira, but it could buy twice as many bottles of Chianti. There is a downside of a sovereign monetary system that overshadows smaller economies. The potential to manipulate one's currency—literally printing money to pay off government debts—makes it difficult for smaller countries to sell debt in the first place. Imperial Spain taught the world that lending to any country is risky. Global investors demand higher interest rates to compensate for that risk. Sovereign debt tends to have higher interest rates for smaller economies as a result, particularly when investors expect the rate of inflation will be higher there. The allure of the euro for investors and nations alike was a low, safe interest rate on government debt.

That assumption of a common interest rate was a fundamental error that led to the Eurozone's present crisis. Low interest rates created a perverse incentive for member states to borrow excessively, especially when local inflation made real interest rates negative. These low interest rates also precipitated the real estate bubble in Spain. Restoring the low rates cannot be a long-term solution.

Investors should not have assumed that Italian debt or Greek debt was just as safe as German debt, simply because they shared a common currency. But many made that assumption. Greece, Spain, Italy, and Portugal enjoyed interest rates identical to German and Dutch rates during 2002–2008. Inflation had indeed been subordinated to the European Central Bank, but it was a major error to assume that inflation was the sole risk factor in the quality of sovereign debt. Figure 23 reveals the dramatic convergence of interest rates for sovereign debt in the years before 2008, and the equally dramatic divergence afterward. One recent study from OECD economists describes the largest factor driving the renewed interest rate differential as "greater government indebtedness."[5]

In early 2012, the yield differential on ten-year bonds was nearly 500 basis points higher for Spanish bonds over Germany's, and 450 points for Italian bonds. Just stop borrowing, says common sense. That would be hard enough for national governments with perennial budget deficits, but the need to roll over old debts with new bond issues means the higher rates are unavoidable.

Figure 23. Interest rate differential disappears and reappears.

(Long term sovereign debt, percent interest rate.)

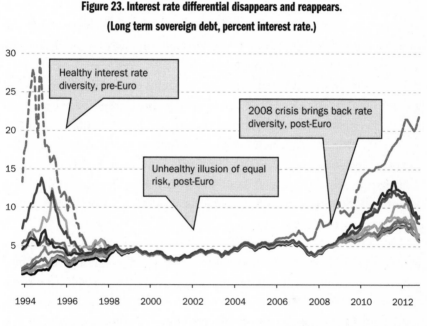

Source: European Central Bank (2012)

From the U.S. perspective, the convergence of European sovereign rates never made sense. America comprises 50 sovereign states, and each of them issues debt in the municipal bond market, where, rest assured, the credit ratings and interest rates are not harmonized. Those states with weak balance sheets have higher risk ratings, notably California and Illinois. So when the European debt divergence happened, it seemed to us to be a natural and necessary step in the Eurozone's evolution. It had to happen, but fortunately it only had to happen once. The Eurozone honeymoon may be over, but that doesn't mean the family needs to break up.

IS THE EUROZONE CRISIS A EURO CRISIS?

At the risk of dating this book, let us touch on what is being called the "Grexit"—that is, the pending or potential exit of Greece from the Eurozone. Greece has been in chaos for half a decade. Some say the survival of the euro currency is in doubt. Whatever happens, the debate over what caused the crisis will rage for decades. Analysts from the left and the right seem to agree that the existence of the euro itself is at fault. We think these analysts are overreaching, and believe that the monetary policy of Europe is being wrongly blamed for the disastrous fiscal policies of some of its members.

Ironically, *crisis* is a word with Greek origins (*krisis*), just like the origins of the looming depression. A research report prepared for the U.S. Congress explains that the "current Eurozone crisis has been unfolding since late 2009, when a new Greek government revealed that previous Greek governments had been underreporting the budget deficit. The crisis subsequently spread to Ireland and Portugal, while raising concerns about Italy, Spain, the European banking system, and more fundamental imbalances within the Eurozone."[6]

The Maastricht Treaty obligates Eurozone members to maintain sound fiscal policies, with total debt limited to 60 percent of GDP and annual deficits no greater than 3 percent of GDP. Not only did Greece exceed the 3 percent rule every year that it was part of the Eurozone, but it hid the true extent of its deficits from investors, including fellow EU nations. The misrepresentation was exposed in early 2010, and sparked a panic when the 2009 deficit was revised from 5 percent of GDP to the shocking truth of 12.7 percent of GDP. After investigations, European statistical agencies revised the figure to 15.6 percent of GDP.

By 2010, Greek debt had been rated as junk status. Private investors essentially refused to make new loans to Greece. The only option was a bailout from some higher power: its neighbor states in the European Union, the European Central Bank, or the International Monetary Fund. European Central Bank loans to Greece would probably never have happened if so much European money were not already invested. If existing Greek debt defaulted in a disorderly fashion (an "orderly" default implies a negotiation of new terms that reduces the value of the bonds to some value above zero), banks in France, Germany, and elsewhere would have been devastated. According to an explanation of the crisis by the British Broadcasting Corporation (BBC), total Greek debt exceeds $400 billion, and France owns a tenth of it,[7] implying that any Greek default also threatens to begin a contagious panic. Although contagion is possible, nobody knows its likelihood. The interest rate spreads since 2009 indicate that nervous investors will shift into safe European bonds. Contagion has its limits. Nevertheless, the idea that the Eurozone is only as strong as its weakest link is what analysts call a *systemic* risk. Few are willing to test how fantastical the theory might be.

Consequently, in May 2010, the European Union and International Monetary Fund bailed out Greece with 110 billion euros of direct loans to roll over its debts, conditional on a fiscal austerity package of reforms. Riots in Athens were the puzzling response to this offer of below-market rescue funds. After two years of wrangling, threats, conferences, more riots, and Greek elections, a second bailout of 130 billion euros was granted in 2012. An orderly default kept Greece in the Eurozone. The Greek people resented the austerity program, which curtails public pensions and public wages (some of the most generous in the world). They almost elected a government that promised to default on their austerity commitments, but 80 percent of Greeks also favor staying in the euro.

Greek resentment is understandable. A nation in recession for half a decade, losing GDP in huge chunks, is a nation at the breaking point. *Financial Times* columnist Martin Wolf describes the country as being stuck in "a doom loop. Unemployment soared from 7 per cent of the labor force in May 2008 to 22 per cent in January 2012, while the unemployment rate of people aged under 25 jumped from 21 per cent to 51 per cent."[8] Hard as it was to face, this loop was not just the bursting of a bubble, but the collapse of an illusion. The illusion, one enjoyed by most Europeans, was that there was a pan-European prosperity, as if European productivity levels were near or approaching the global frontier. In fact, the southern European supermodel was far below the frontier (as we show in Figure 22), and even the core European supermodel was 20 percent below the U.S. frontier. Nearly all members of the European Union have used fiscal deficits to bridge that illusion with unaffordable transfer, pension, and public employment programs. For those Greeks who thought this recession would be followed by a normal recovery, the shock has been difficult and maybe impossible to digest.

As much sympathy as we have for Greek citizens, the angry blame directed at reluctant creditors has been unfair. "The chief culprit is Germany," said an editorial in the *Economist* on April 29, 2010.[9] This sentiment has been echoed ad nauseam in the years since, calling for action, action, and more action, but only if the decisiveness meant endless bailouts from German taxpayers. Not only is this impractical advice for Angela Merkel, the chancellor, who has her own voters to represent, but it crosses two philosophical lines. First, Germany, above all other members of the European Union, has upheld its obligations to restrain self-serving fiscal programs and should not be expected to pay for foreign pensions that are more generous than Germany's own people receive. Second, the bailout solution—including the 2012 package—represents a second kind of systemic risk to the Eurozone. Greece establishes a precedent, and that precedent will create "moral hazard." Not only will other Eurozone states see the bailout of Greece as a new benchmark for the worst possible outcome (a generous deal, on balance), but it creates incentives for global investors as well to treat European Union member debt as, partially, German debt. The picture of sovereign interest rate differentials has been muddied when it actually needs to be cleared.

TAKING MEASURE OF INSTITUTIONS

The heated debate about the causes and cures of Europe's sovereign debt crisis—which spread to Spain, Portugal, Ireland, and Italy—settled for a while into a disagreement between deficit hawks and deficit doves. Fiscal doves argue that budget deficits are appropriate during recessions, whereas hawks believe that any deficit-fueled stimulus is ineffective, especially over the long term. At some point, successive deficits are not countering a recessionary lull in GDP; they are artificially propping it up rather than allowing it to find its natural equilibrium. Harvard economist Alberto Alesina made a further distinction between two kinds of deficit-fighting tools. Austerity can be achieved by cutting expenditures or by raising taxes or through a mix of the two.

Should a weakened state like Greece continue its austerity program? That depends on the kind of austerity. Alesina's research with numerous coauthors into the performance of dozens of countries in recent decades has revealed time and again that expenditure-cutting austerity does not hinder growth, but tax-raising does. Spending austerity, can in fact, encourage private sector investment.

When liberal economists attacked Alesina's research on austerity, he noted that he was not the first to make this claim. In his blog, Paul Krugman went so far as to say the research is irrelevant because fiscal policy is meaningless unless an economy has exhausted its monetary ammunition and is facing a "zero lower bound" in interest rates. This position seems desperate, and quite at odds with mainstream economists who are sympathetic to fiscal stimuli during recessions. Former Treasury secretary Lawrence Summers and University of California, Berkeley economist Bradford DeLong made a veiled criticism of Alesina in an academic paper for a Brookings Institution conference in the spring of 2012 that claimed "fiscal expansions may actually be self-financing,"[10] which reminded some readers of the exaggerated claim that "tax cuts pay for themselves," long attributed to right-wing straw men. An invited commenter on the paper, economist Valerie Ramey from the University of California, San Diego, delivered a devastating review, citing a "lack of rigor" in the theoretical part of the paper and a complete absence of empirical evidence. Historical data for the United States "suggest that the effect of government spending on output lasts only as long as the government spending," explained Ramey. She further punctured the theory that fiscal expenditures were more effective during a recession and/or when monetary policy was accommodative. Increasingly, this view of austerity is being embraced by finance ministers across Europe.

Perhaps the most contentious disagreement in the European Union is about the role of the central bank, specifically the European Central Bank, in resolving member states' fiscal dilemmas. "German policymakers and ECB executives consistently highlight the importance of upholding the bank's foundational principles: political independence; and a narrow mandate to maintain price stability," reported the Congressional

Research Service. "French leaders, on the other hand, have long en-visioned a more activist ECB that would play the role of a 'lender of last resort,' akin to the U.S. Federal Reserve."[11] The motive of French officials is to nudge the ECB far beyond monetary policy, though, into bailing out member states. This approach confuses the role of a central bank. Its role is to be a lender to the banking system, not shore up gov-ernments. While the ECB can ease liquidity concerns in the near term, it lacks tools to address structural fiscal problems in some countries. Remember that the Marshall Plan, which helped rebuild Europe after World War II with U.S. aid, focused on loans to businesses, not grants to governments.

That brings us, at last, to the frequently voiced criticism that the Eurozone cannot succeed as a monetary union unless it forms a fiscal union—with transfers across member states, too. Critics of the current structure point to the U.S. Congress, which has a far-reaching fiscal authority, unlike the European Parliament. The logic is that interstate trade imbalances in a mere currency union can only be resolved by capi-tal imbalances in the opposite direction, whereas a fiscal union would enable rebalancing through redistributive transfers, with countries in recessions, for example, receiving monetary transfers from better-performing countries. It is easy to sympathize with this argument, which is essentially a call for greater centralization, scale, growth, and so on. But it oversimplifies the difference between America's complex mix of institutions and the theory of a centralized superpower. For instance, left unexplained is why the United States thrived for 150 years without substantial fiscal redistribution. And while there are large fiscal transfers across U.S. states today, state government budgets face important local constraints. Transfers to rebalance interstate trade has never been U.S. government policy.

It's fair to say that the Eurozone trade imbalances between the core and periphery created an unsustainable dynamic, but we tend to think fiscal union by itself may be too easy an answer. One difference between European and American integration is much more fundamental, yet it has received little attention. Let's step back and consider the many ways that a federal organization can unify its member states, from least to most intrusive:

1. **Trade:** common market.
2. **Monetary:** currency union.
3. **Labor:** immigration between member states. No control over national migration.
4. **Regulation:** harmonized rules on business, manufacturing, labor, and environmental protection.
5. **Banking:** individual property is secured centrally and states do not have sovereign authority over assets.
6. **Fiscal:** states are subordinate in fiscal matters and can only set tax rates, expenditures, and debt issuance with central approval.

Reflecting on the U.S. federal-state policy mix, it is not correct that Washington, D.C., controls all six components. True, American states do surrender sovereign authority on components 1–4, as do European Union states. But American states do not subordinate their fiscal powers to Washington. Rather, the key distinction is component 5, banking freedom. The bank account of a citizen in Lansing, Michigan, is not threatened by confiscation by or default of the Michigan statehouse. That same security does not comfort the bank accounts of the people of Athens. Perhaps this distinction in banking freedom is the weak link in Eurozone affairs. Member states there retain the power to confiscate their citizens' financial assets and potentially convert them to an independent currency overnight. We suspect the attraction of nationalizing private wealth to address fiscal imbalances is an important reason that leaving the euro is at all attractive to highly indebted Eurozone members.

Institutional diversity among member states may have fueled long-term growth in Europe since 1500. Maintaining that diversity in the European Union is the best way to generate the real growth its member states need to resolve their debts. The first step is to stanch the bleeding with real gradual austerity in public spending. Whatever happens next with Greece and the other indebted nations, we are confident that the supermodels of the European Union will return to a focus on competitiveness, which means the Parente-Prescott framework of removing institutional barriers. Fortunately for Europe, this is the golden age for this kind of race toward higher productivity.

In the 1990s, a handful of new supermodel metrics were developed.

As we noted earlier in the book, the Heritage Foundation began publishing a worldwide index of economic freedom, in partnership with the *Wall Street Journal*. The most free European economy according to the 2012 Heritage index was Switzerland, which was measured as 81 percent free, which is an average of ten component freedoms that include measures of labor, taxes, trade, and business regulation. The economy of France, by contrast, was measured as 63 percent free. Interestingly, France has a business freedom score slightly higher than Switzerland (84 to 78 percent, respectively), but the French labor market is measured to be much less free than the Swiss labor market.

TABLE 7. ECONOMIC AND INSTITUTIONAL MEASURES OF SUPERMODEL ECONOMIES

COUNTRY	GDP per capita ($)	Growth (10-yr. Avg.)	GDP ($B)	Power (relative to U.S.)	Economic Freedom 2012 score	Doing Business 2013 rank
Core						
France	31,299	1.1%	2,027	10.8%	63.2	34
Germany	34,089	0.9%	2,783	14.4%	71.0	20
Netherlands	38,191	1.4%	641	4.6%	73.3	31
United Kingdom	34,268	1.8%	2,137	15.9%	74.1	7
Nordic						
Denmark	33,705	0.5%	186	0.7%	76.2	5
Finland	32,989	1.5%	173	1.1%	72.3	11
Iceland	35,612	0.4%	11	0.0%	70.9	14
Norway	50,488	1.5%	236	2.3%	68.8	6
Sweden	36,132	2.1%	328	2.7%	71.7	13
Southern						
Greece	25,216	2.0%	271	1.6%	55.4	78
Italy	28,377	0.4%	1,724	4.9%	58.8	73
Portugal	19,782	0.4%	212	0.4%	63.0	30
Spain	27,331	1.9%	1,271	7.6%	69.1	44
United States	41,365	1.4%	12,833	100%	76.3	4

Table is constructed with data from Penn World Table, Mark 7.1, Heritage Foundation's 2012 Index of Economic Freedom, and the World Bank Doing Business Report for 2013.

Some critics, such as Columbia economist Jeffrey Sachs, dislike the institutional explanation for macro performance. Sachs took the Heritage index to task in his bestselling book *The End of Poverty*. But the theories of development that Sachs favored, which stressed "big push" investment and aid, have failed to generate much real growth. International agencies like the World Bank began looking at alternatives. As we noted earlier in the book, the World Bank's *Doing Business* report includes indicators, each measuring some aspect of the regulatory environment for a small or medium-sized business. As described in the latest edition, *Doing Business* "provides quantitative measures of regulations for starting a business, dealing with construction permits, getting electricity, registering property, getting credit, protecting investors, paying taxes, trading across borders, enforcing contracts and resolving insolvency. *Doing Business* also looks at regulations on employing workers." [12] Now with the authority of the World Bank, the competitiveness of 188 supermodels is visible for all to see.

THE GHOST OF CHRISTMAS YET TO COME

The great English novelist Charles Dickens published his famous story *A Christmas Carol* in 1843. The selfish, wealthy Ebenezer Scrooge is visited on Christmas Eve by three spirits, who reveal to him the harsh truth about his life. Most disturbing of all is the ghost who shows him the future about to unfold unless Scrooge mends his course. It is a graveyard where an innocent boy, Tiny Tim, lies buried young, and also where there is an untended gravestone under which an unloved old man lies. The name etched in that gravestone is none other than that of Scrooge himself.

This parable of the "shadows of what may be" is apt for Americans who look across the Atlantic at the fate of highly indebted nations in Europe. For half a century, the United States has adopted increasingly generous features of the welfare state that mimic those in Europe. But now, for the first time, we are seeing a vicious cycle in which the unsustainable debts of the future can no longer be rolled over to the next generation. Europe is in more danger of failing than America, but both should know better. As Scrooge changed, so, too, can the world's great democracies.

SUMMARY OF DECLINE

Great Power:	European Union
Turning point:	2010?
Economic imbalance:	Fiscal
Political roots:	Unconstrained budget deficits and easy debt; moral hazard by semi-sovereign states
Behavioral dysfunction:	Limited time horizons of elected officials; loss aversion; heuristic of cultural superiority

11

CALIFORNIA DREAMING

"Gold is the corpse of value," says Goto Dengo. . . . "The General didn't care about the gold. He understood that the real gold is here," he points to his head, "in the intelligence of the people, and here," he holds out his hands, "in the work that they do. Getting rid of our gold was the best thing that ever happened to Nippon. It made us rich."

— Neal Stephenson, *Cryptonomicon*

O nly a few places in the world have perfect weather, formally known by the Köppen climate classification as *Csa* and informally known as *Mediterranean*. If you have a chance to look over a climate map of the earth, you'll see that roughly 90 percent of the land with this climate categorization lies in the dry, warm, coastal nations surrounding the Mediterranean Sea, such as northern Africa, Spain, Italy, Greece, Turkey, Syria, and Israel. Few other places enjoy the same mix of coastal breezes, dry summers, and warm winters. Perth, Australia, is one. Small areas on the cape of South Africa and the coast of Chile are two more. But the only major landmass with Mediterranean features *not* in the Mediterranean is a place Americans call the golden state: *California*.

When California joined the United States as a state in 1850, we might speculate that immigrants referred to it favorably as the "Greece of the Americas." The main difference back then was gold. Discovery of gold nuggets, literally found strewn along the ground in California's northern mountains, led to the "gold rush" and the nickname of "49ers" to the people who moved to the state that year. These people voted with their feet.

San Francisco, a sleepy village of 200 people in the early 1840s, added a population of 35,000 in two years, and the state's non–Native American population grew from 14,000 in 1848 to 250,000 in 1852.[1] But the state was home to more than fast riches. Immigrants stayed to farm the rich central valley and to fish the rich oceans. They built new towns and cities: Los Angeles, Eureka, Sonoma, La Jolla, Monterrey, San Diego.

All around the country during the first decade of the twentieth century, the growing popularity of "nickelodeons," which showed early black-and-white moving pictures, created demand for a new kind of industry—the film industry—which for production reasons established itself in the Csa climate of Southern California. In 1911, the first movie studio in California was established on Sunset Boulevard in Los Angeles. The world-famous HOLLYWOOD sign was erected in 1923. Today the film industry generates tens of billions of dollars in revenues and employs hundreds of thousands of people.

Fashion designers and department stores were a by-product of the potential that Hollywood held. They came clamoring to the stars for endorsements. Apparel and textile manufacture soon followed, and by the close of the twentieth century, California could claim a one-fifth share of jobs in apparel manufacturing.[2]

The defense industry also played a crucial role in the story of California's growth. That Csa climate made the state an ideal location for training troops, and its shores represented the first line of defense against a landed attack from Pacific threats. Howard Hughes and other aviation pioneers established early airplane factories there. The nation's entry into World War II sparked a further defense industry boom. Government expenditures in the state rose from $190 million in 1930 to $8.5 billion in 1945, as shipyards, naval and air bases, and military depots took root in the Golden State. The industrialist Henry Kaiser established four of his seven shipbuilding yards in the San Francisco Bay area alone.

The defense industry's concentration led to another lucky accident. Early development of the electronics industry, notably the semiconductor and microprocessor, happened in California. Hewlett-Packard was established in 1939 in one of the founder's garages, near Stanford University. The chipmaker Intel was established in 1968 in Mountain View, California. And as most everyone knows, Apple was founded by Steve Jobs and Steve Wozniak in the late 1970s in Cupertino. Thanks to what economists call *agglomeration effect*—the natural clustering of human capital in one location—Silicon Valley maintains a global competitive advantage as the source of innovations in information technology.

The growth of manufacturing and then high-technology clusters in San Diego, Orange County, and San Jose led to more waves of migration. Indeed, the top-line population of California is a big part of the story. As of this writing, the Census Bureau estimates a state population of 37,691,912 in 2011. In 1900, it was 1.49 million, then one-fifth of New York's 7.3 million residents. By 1920, both states had just over 10 million residents each, a shocking catch-up in any era. After that, the two states grew at the same pace decade after decade after decade. Then came the 1970s. During that decade, New York lost 1 million people. California gained 4 million. Not only was the national labor force transitioning from industrial to technological, and east to west, but the financial frontier changed, too. Big banks on Wall Street made room for new field of private equity known as venture capital, the kind of firms that helped launch Apple and Google with early-stage investments. California gained another 6.1 million people by 1990, and 4 million more by 2000. This is the equivalent of adding a midsized midwestern state like Wisconsin (population 5.7 million) every decade.

Another way to think about California's size is that it currently has fifty-three congressional districts. The apportionment of seats in the U.S. House of Representatives is reset every ten years based on shifts in the population and the fixed number (435) of seats. Never before in American history has a state had such a large number of seats as California does today. One in nine congressmen represent this single state. That also means the state has fifty-five electoral votes it casts in the presidential election—as a single block in our winner-take-all system—which is alone one-fifth of the total needed for a candidate to win the White House.

California's votes were reliably Republican ever since the Republican Party erupted as a national force in the form of Abraham Lincoln in 1860. There were exceptions, such as its support for the 1916 victory of Woodrow Wilson and the four landslide elections of FDR. But the state was also one of the few to vote for Teddy Roosevelt's third-party Bull Moose candidacy in 1912. Its conservative leanings were well established when it voted for native son Nixon rather than Kennedy in 1960, and later when it went for Ford rather than Carter in 1976.

A tectonic shift in its politics happened in 1992, when California's voters preferred Bill Clinton over George H. W. Bush. It was seen as a swing state, but the underlying demographics kept shifting left. It hasn't voted for a Republican presidential candidate in two decades, and nobody anticipates it will in the foreseeable future. Democrats in the state now outnumber Republicans among registered, nonindependent voters, 43 to 30 percent.[3] Nationally, those numbers are 31–27 percent. To understand how heavily Democratic California has become, consider states that have an inverse ratio of Democratic to Republican vote percentages: Georgia (32–44), South Carolina (33–44), and Kansas (27–44). Political pundits have written those states off as permanently "red" states, as if they always had been and always will be. This conclusion is odd, because the southern states shifted from bedrock Democratic to bedrock Republican during the 1970s and 1980s, just when California was shifting the other way. Why is California's shift characterized as the radical one? The difference is that the southern states were *conservative* the whole time, regardless of the partisan label. California, by contrast, experienced something more profound. There was an *ideological* shift from conservative to liberal underneath the superficial change in partisan labels. The makeup of the voters became more and more liberal, partly reflecting shifting cultural attitudes within the electorate and partly reflecting a migration of voters. New migrants into the state—from other countries and other states—tended to be more liberal, but there was an outmigration of conservatives to nearby states as well.

With their sudden ideological advantage, Democrats in the state capital made up for lost time by adopting liberal economic institutions based on what had been pioneered elsewhere: the most progressive taxes, one of the highest minimum wages, the most generous welfare programs, and the thorniest regulatory system.[4] At best, the institutional regime has had mixed results, but there is no doubt that today California's economy suffered more than others during the Great Recession. The rate of unemployment is above 9.8 percent as we write, while the total outstanding state debt stands over $100 billion. And that's just counting the formal debt. Meanwhile, the debt that is off the books—future obligations for the pensions of government employees, for example—is $612 billion, or roughly $18,000 per person according to *Governing* magazine.[5] When pundits refer to California as "America's Greece," it is no longer a compliment.

EMPIRE OF LIBERTY, UNION OF STATES

Is California a Great Power? We think yes, for a couple of reasons. First, if it were a country, California would rank in the top ten in terms of raw GDP. It has world-leading industries (Hollywood and Silicon Valley) and ample military firepower. The military bases in San Diego County alone (Miramar, Coronado, and Pendleton) rival most other nations. Second, the categorization of "state" power gets at the nature of the United States, which is more a federal union than a nation.

States are also an interesting topic for the larger theme of this book. The federalist structure of the United States is an excellent institutional arrangement for economic growth. Federalism allows internal competition among the fifty states in two ways. First, there is the competition among state policymakers to see which policies work best. Some people, even President Obama, characterize this kind of competition as a "race to the top." But even when leaders are not paying attention or using the right metrics, regular citizens can migrate between states to find the best mix of low taxes and ample public goods.

As for stature, California has a land area of 164,000 square miles, comparable to Japan's 145,000. And with 38 million residents, it is larger than most sovereign members of the United Nations.

TABLE 8. GDP RANKING IN 2010 (2005 $BILLION AND PERCENT OF WORLD TOTAL)

United States	12,833	16.5%
China	10,303	13.2%
India	4,079	5.2%
Japan	3,988	5.1%
Germany	2,783	3.6%
United Kingdom	2,137	2.7%
Russia	2,100	2.7%
France	2,027	2.6%
Italy	1,724	2.2%
California	1,702	2.2%
Brazil	1,674	2.2%
Mexico	1,343	1.7%
Korea	1,294	1.7%
Spain	1,271	1.6%
Canada	1,253	1.6%
Indonesia	964	1.2%
Australia	885	1.1%
Turkey	812	1.0%

Table is constructed with data from Penn World Table, Mark 7.1, and the U.S. Bureau of Economic Analysis.

If it were a nation, California would have the tenth-largest GDP in the world, behind Brazil and just ahead of Italy. The U.S. Bureau of Economic Analysis (a part of the Commerce Department that compiles official GDP figures) reports that the state GDP in 2011 was $1.7 trillion in 2005 dollars, adjusted for inflation.[6] Think of it this way: the United States and South Korea negotiated one of its largest free-trade deals ever, agreed to in 2007 under President George W. Bush and finally approved by the Senate under President Obama in 2011. It was a big deal, to be sure, but Korea's economy is a third smaller than California's. The same logic applies to the NAFTA trade deal among Canada, Mexico, and the United States, as each of those nations has a GDP of around $1.3 trillion. It is beneficial for the other forty-nine states to have relatively free trade with those countries, but not nearly as beneficial as the free trade they have with California.

In terms of economic power—which we defined earlier as a composite of GDP, productivity, and growth—California ranks third behind the United States and China, and ahead of every sovereign nation in Europe. Despite its troubles, California enjoyed an average annual growth rate of 3.7 percent during the first years of this century, and its GDP per capita is five thousand dollars higher than the "frontier" set by the United States (see Table 9). We express those three variables in Figure 24 as well, in which the circumference of the circle representing each country is the size of its GDP relative to the United States. Notice how the European economies as well as Japan are clustered in the low-growth, upper-middle-income zone. California looks different, but this appearance is deceiving.

TABLE 9. ECONOMIC POWER RANKING IN 2010 (2005 $)

	GDP per capita ($)	Growth	GDP ($T)	Power
United States	41,365	1.4%	12,833	100%
China	7,746	9.9%	10,303	40%
California	45,946	3.7%	1,700	24%
United Kingdom	34,268	1.8%	2,137	16%
Japan	31,447	0.5%	3,988	15%
Germany	34,089	0.9%	2,783	14%
Russia	15,068	5.3%	2,100	12%
Korea	26,609	4.0%	1,294	11%
France	31,299	1.1%	2,027	11%
Spain	27,331	1.9%	1,271	8%

Table is constructed with data from Penn World Table, Mark 7.1, and the U.S. Bureau of Economic Analysis.

The concentration of innovation capacity in this one region at this one time in history is profound and unparalleled, but it has also blinded many to the weakness of the state's fiscal situation. The past century of constant progress and prosperity bred a hubris, and along with it an ever-larger state government. In truth, California has been crumbling for decades. As for being the *tenth*-largest economy in the world? Just a few years ago, it was *fifth*.

It may just be that California's decline is a result of its losing top talent. In a seminal academic paper published in 1956, Charles Tiebout introduced the idea of citizens "voting with their feet" for the mix of programs and taxes that they preferred. A young person may not know a thing about policy, but he will move for a better job. In a way, the Tiebout hypothesis establishes migration as the bedrock human right, but he more importantly described the engine of interstate competition. States are not trying to "win" in the zero-sum sense, such as when one army defeats another, or Columbia beats Fordham in basketball. Indeed, most economists tend to scoff at the popular claim that nations compete when it comes to international trade or investment.

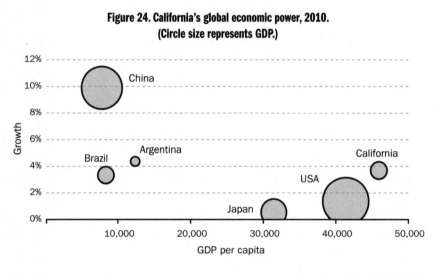

**Figure 24. California's global economic power, 2010.
(Circle size represents GDP.)**

Source: Penn World Table 7.1

No nation wins or loses when it comes to international trade. Here is a point where economists across the political spectrum nearly all agree, from Paul Krugman to Deirdre McCloskey. Yet it is a lost cause to explain comparative advantage to each new generation of business journalists, who reflexively cast a trade deficit as a malady. Cheap foreign imports are much more beneficial to domestic consumers than harmful to domestic producers. We could review the evidence about Japan's massive, incessant trade surplus with the United States, its manipulated currency, and the missing evidence that this has helped Japan or hurt America. But let's instead affirm the simple and profound empirical fact that countries more open to trade tend to grow faster and enrich their poorest citizens. The exceptional matter of unfair trade is not about imports, exports, tariffs, or quotas, but about theft of intellectual property. Nations that allow their domestic companies to steal the designs and patented technology of foreign companies are giving safe harbor to pirates. Unfortunately, the biggest costs are not to bottom lines of aggrieved companies, but in the diminished incentive for other companies to innovate in the future. A globalized world economy that cannot protect intellectual property cannot sustain growth at the technology frontier.

The right way to think about governmental competition is to see governments as suppliers of public services. Taxpayers consume those public services. By competing for freely migrating taxpayer-consumer-laborers, not to mention capital, governments are in a natural and unavoidable competition to discover new institutional mixtures. Tiebout's insight about "voting with one's feet" added a new dimension to an old idea.

GOVERNMENT BONDAGE (MUNIS AND PENSIONS)

The first cracks in the Golden State became publicly visible in 1994 when Orange County, the beautiful southern neighbor of Los Angeles, declared itself bankrupt. Longtime county treasurer Robert L. Citron, an official who had been reelected six times, was caught running a highly risky investment scheme that lost $1.64 billion. Citron had used excessive leverage to increase the county's investments. It was a gamble that paid off so long as interest rates on county debt stayed low. When rates rose in 1994, the county could no longer roll over its debt and so had no choice but to declare bankruptcy. Citron pled guilty to six felonies, though he never went to jail (he died in 2013). But thousands of county employees were laid off and public services were slashed.

Life went on. Orange County sold $880 million in bonds in 1996 to help cover its losses, and by June 1996, the county had emerged from bankruptcy. Its credit rating went from the lowest to the highest. In February of the following year, Fitch gave the county's investment pools its highest AAA rating. Overall, it was a quick turnaround for a county that many had thought lost.

Service cutbacks were severe, however, as author Mike Anton noted ten years later.[7] Reductions in routine cleaning and preventative maintenance led to dirtier government offices, uglier parks, and utilities that, when they break, require big investments to fix. Roads are resurfaced once every seven years as opposed to five, and landfills fill as the county takes on trash from Los Angeles and San Diego.

What looked like an anomaly in Orange County proved to be a cautionary tale. There were other cities throughout the state with budgets out of control. Just north of Silicon Valley, the town of Vallejo (population 116,000) declared bankruptcy in May 2008. Four years later, Stockton (300,000) and San Bernardino (200,000) declared bankruptcy as well. Poised to follow them off the fiscal cliff is San Jose (1,000,000), sitting at the heart of Silicon Valley.

One might think that of all places in the modern world, none could be as prosperous as Silicon Valley and its surrounding towns. Even as the Great Recession raged, the high-tech firms of this region prospered. Google is headquartered nearby, as are Facebook, Oracle, Yahoo!, Cisco, Netflix, Twitter, and YouTube. Apple, now in a tight race for the most highly valued corporation on earth, is planning to construct a 2.8 million square foot architectural wonder for its new headquarters in Cupertino, supplanting the Pentagon as the most impressive headquarters in the country. The irony of the presence of all of these start-up successes is that other states have tried to create the "next Silicon Valley" as have other nations. None have been successful. Boston has a fair claim as a rival, but the relocation of Mark Zuckerberg and his company from Harvard to the Valley is the norm. Talent of the hacker type will continue to be drawn to the state of California so long as it remains the center of gravity for technology companies, but it would be a mistake to think that status is permanent. Consider Vallejo, described here by Michael Lewis in a *Vanity Fair* article:

> Weeds surround abandoned businesses, and all traffic lights are set to permanently blink, which is a formality, as there are no longer any cops to police the streets. Vallejo is the one city in the Bay Area where you can park anywhere and not worry about getting a ticket, because there are no meter maids either. . . . The lobby of city hall is completely empty. There's

a receptionist's desk but no receptionist. Instead, there's a sign: *To fore-closure auctioneers and foreclosure bidders: Please do not conduct business in the city hall lobby....* Eighty percent of the city's budget—and the lion's share of the claims that had thrown it into bankruptcy—were wrapped up in the pay and benefits of public-safety workers.[8]

What happened in Vallejo in 2008 preceded the Great Recession and proved to be a small portion of the underlying problem. Cheap credit inflated housing values earlier in the decade, and that housing boom brought ample property tax revenues, which effectively hid deep-seated shortcomings in the city's economy. It also enabled unsustainable raises and bonuses for public officials and city workers. "After one year of service, public employees could get health care coverage for life, and so could their families," reported Hannah Dreier of the Associated Press.[9] The city began spending $3–4 million above annual revenues in 2005. Those were the good times.

Once the housing bubble popped, weak fiscal balance sheets were exposed in cities up and down the state. Unlike what happened in Orange County two decades ago, these fiscal shenanigans weren't felonies. Massive debt had become the new normal in California politics. Critics like economist John Cogan at Stanford's Hoover Institution have been sounding the debt alarm for years, and they were vindicated in 2009 when the long term became the short term.

Let's back up a bit, though, and think about what it means for a government to go bankrupt. Bankruptcy is something that people and companies do, but a city? It has taxes and fees that provide revenues, and then it spends those funds through expenditures: roads, schools, and emergency responders. Of course, paying for government workers is a big piece of the expenditure pie. If that's all governments did, bankruptcy would make no sense. Lacking revenues, it would have to cut expenditures down to size.

Not so fast. Governments often need to make investments in public goods such as highways and airports that are more expensive than any one year's revenues can cover. The logical thing to do is to borrow funds, issuing bonds that can be repaid over a decade or three. Wall Street has an active market worth $3 trillion for municipal bonds, and most cities have AAA credit ratings because they have ample capacity to raise taxes if necessary. And investors who purchase "muni" bonds—which includes bonds issued by a state, county, city, town, or village—get a tax advantage from the Internal Revenue Service. Investment income earned from holding those bonds is tax-free, unlike gains from investing in companies or other kinds of bonds.

Considered to be relatively safe, even boring, the muni bond market got a shock in December 2010. One Sunday night before the holidays, the CBS program *60 Minutes* aired an interview with Wall Street analyst Meredith Whitney. She wasn't a muni bond expert, but she had earned credibility because of her contrarian, and accurate, assessment of the subprime-mortgage exposure of big banks in 2007. Now Whitney was saying this: "There's not a doubt in my mind that you will see a spate of municipal bond defaults." When pressed, she predicted, "Fifty to 100 sizeable defaults. More. This will amount to hundreds of billions of dollars' worth of defaults."[10]

Her interview, while its claims were exaggerated, caused a small panic in munis the next day, but her core question had little to do with bonds. She had sensed a misalignment in America's federal structure. She had been motivated to dig into the muni market by an innocent question that had been nagging her. "How can GDP estimates be so high when the states that outperformed the U.S. economy during the boom were now underperforming the U.S. economy—and they were 22 percent of that economy?" she asked Michael Lewis during a 2011 interview.[11]

BREAKING THE TENSION

In states and cities across the country, there is a constant fiscal tension between spending and taxing. On the one hand, some economists believe that politicians want to increase expenditures by the government because doing so enhances their power, rewards the interests that support their election, and pleases voters. On the other hand, politicians dislike raising taxes, because voters dislike them even more. Fiscal tension is the crux of democracy's instinct for dysfunction: the incentive for politicians is to spend more than they tax.

Spending pressures are different at each level of government. Cities are traditionally responsible for public safety, particularly police and firefighters. States tend to be responsible for prisons, higher education, and health care (particularly under Medicaid). They share responsibility for primary education and roads. All kinds of governments resolve the spend-tax tension by paying their workforces with *future* revenue. Hence bonds.

The biggest source of red ink that cities face may be labor, and the big item within labor costs is pensions; these retirement programs don't require cash outlays when first given, but they are then increasingly costly once the number of retirees grows. In San Diego, pension payments will grow from $229 million in 2010 to an estimated $318 million in 2015. By 2025, this figure is projected to hit $512 million.[12] The San Diego story is hardly unique, but it is illuminating. In the mid-1990s, the local pension board, with approval of the city council, gave increased benefits to city employees but lowered funding levels. Whistleblowers later revealed this fact. In any case, the city was unable to find buyers for its new bonds in 2004, and the whole of city government faced a budget crisis. The issue has haunted local politics ever since, leading recent mayor Jerry Sanders to propose in 2010 ending pensions for future hires.

The manner in which some of the pension formulas were changed challenges the imagination. One proposal was approved in 2001 by Orange County supervisors (all Republicans) that retroactively increased the pension formula for sheriff's deputies by 50 percent. An even more generous pension program was extended to fourteen thousand public employees countywide a few years late. Why were these pensions boosts applied retroactively? The answer seems to be: because they could be. There was no underlying policy rationale, just raw payoff politics.

Statewide, the pension obligations are immense. One study finds the total unfunded state (not municipal) liability to be half a trillion dollars, or 30 percent of the state's gross annual product. The number isn't firm because the government can pretend it can cover future obligations by investing its savings really, really well. A common tactic is to use unrealistic discount rates. The CalSTRS state fund for K–12 educational workers uses a discount rate of 8 percent, whereas a more realistic 3.8 percent rate implies an unfunded liability six times larger.[13] Public

pensions loom large because they are designed as defined benefits, paying out the same large monthly amount to a retiree until death. Because
government owes so much money to retirees, they can hardly afford to
hire current workers. Chuck Reed, the mayor of San Jose, has cut the
city staff from 7,450 workers to 5,400 and suggests it could go all the
way to 1,600. "Our police and firefighters will earn more in retirement
than they did when they were working," he laments.[14]

It's clear that pensions are a budget problem, but changing them
appears impossible, a typical behavioral dysfunction of time preference and loss aversion in the extreme. The dilemma begs the question:
why did local governments start using pensions in the first place? A
century ago, employees were paid wages and salaries. The lucky few
had contracts that committed the employer to them for long terms.
Fringe benefits such as health insurance and retirement matching programs were rare or nonexistent before World War II. Indeed, we don't
think of employer-provided health care as a *fringe* benefit but as a new
kind of entitlement. The explosion of compensation through benefits
instead of higher salaries makes little sense. According to the U.S. Department of Labor's monthly index of total compensation, wages and
salaries make up only 70 percent of the total.[15] The remaining 30 percent represents the sum value of fringe benefits. It's hard to imagine that
Americans understand how much income they are losing. If offered a
50 percent pay raise, how many workers would keep their benefits instead?

The reason companies began to compensate this way is the tax code.
The IRS does not count benefits as taxable income, a policy change
made in another accident of history. Employers began offering beefed-up
benefits to circumvent wage and price controls set during World War II.
When challenged, the IRS ruled these benefits not to be taxable income,
which fueled their expansion in the decades after. Pensions were another
way to offer untaxed compensation, though governments were careful
to regulate private companies to prevent underfunding. In the public
sector, such safeguards were lacking. Who watches the watchmen?

The growth of public sector benefits is all too predictable in hindsight. Historically, the law did not grant public servants in the United
States the right to unionize. Franklin Roosevelt as president argued that

such a structure made no sense. "It is impossible to bargain collectively with the government," declared labor leader George Meany in 1955. Nevertheless, starting in 1959, Wisconsin allowed its state workers to bargain collectively. California and most other states caved to the pressure, though not all. Texas, for example, does not allow public sector unions. Nor does it have a fiscal crisis.

It remains to be seen if California can balance its budget in the years ahead, which by law it is required to do. This year has brought better short-term budget news, but severe long-term problems remain. Many cities around the state have turned to bankruptcy law as the only recourse, meaning that they restructure their obligations. Unions, naturally, want the law to make it harder for cities to escape their obligations to retired workers, but in many cases there is nobody left to pay. And voters have a say. Many taxpayers are fed up with the deals that have been made with public sector workers, and the state is in no condition to bail out cities on the verge of bankruptcy. The looming question is whether the federal government should bail out the state if it proves unable to square its expenditures and debts with revenues. Should the taxpayers of Ohio be on the hook for California's fiscal imbalance?

A STATE OF DENIAL (TAXES, DEFICITS, RAIL)

In May 2012, California's governor had a surprise announcement. In a video posted on YouTube, Governor Jerry Brown explained that the state's budget deficit was actually $16 billion, not the $9.2 billion estimated four months prior. Revenues were $3.5 billion lower than expected, mainly because the income tax receipts in April hadn't surged as hoped. Spending was also $2.1 billion more than budgeted.[16] How would he bridge the gap? No more borrowing from future lottery earnings. Years of accounting gimmicks had exhausted the state's ability to do anything but go to the bond markets again. The deficit peaked at $42 billion in 2009, but threatens to rebound in the future as pension and health-care costs rise.

In a 2009 report on the fiscal health of states, the nonpartisan Pew Center on the States remarked: "California's financial problems are in a league of their own."[17] The report used California as a benchmark (30 on its scale of 30) to measure the severity of fiscal problems in the other states. Even worse for the future, the state has developed institutions that are "barriers to growth," in the words of economists Edward Prescott and Stephen Parente. California ranked 47th out of the 50 states in terms of economic freedom in a 2008 study put out by the Pacific Research Institute. The Tax Foundation, another nonpartisan research institution in Washington, ranked California 48th out of 50 in its 2012 State Business Tax Climate Index, and 50th out of 50 for its individual income tax system, because it punishes business formation and employment.[18]

Many people complain that California's fiscal problems exist only because of unreasonable limitations on tax revenues. They point to Proposition 13, which caps the growth of property taxes paid by homeowners. But Prop 13 passed back in 1978 and remained popular for a long time; a November 2012 initiative allowed for an income tax increase, though the other complaint is that the state legislature can only increase taxes with a supermajority vote that includes two-thirds of its members, in both the state senate and the assembly. As Joe Matthews and Mark Paul explain in their recent book, *California Crackup*, the supermajority requirement is "uniquely undemocratic" because it effectively empowers a superminority, also known as the Republican Party, that can veto any tax hike. The authors provide some good suggestions, but on this score their heated criticism falls flat. True, spending could grow without supermajority approval, but taxes cannot, a distinct imbalance that effectively begs for deficits. That hardly excuses the dominant party, which has increased state spending with full knowledge that it was not paid for. Responsibility for that spending rests on the Democrats' shoulders alone. However, California has had some version of the two-thirds majority rule since 1935; still, it was only in recent decades that it became fiscally delinquent.

What distinguishes the state income tax in California from other states is not its size, but its shape. To our knowledge California is the only state that has a special tax bracket for millionaires (by income), who pay the top rate of 13.3 percent of their annual incomes to the state. This is arguably the most progressive tax in the nation, technically. The effect of such steep rates is a boom-and-bust cycle in state revenues. When the economy is strong, more people realize high annual incomes, and income tax payments are high. The state then perversely treats those revenue levels as normal. When the business cycle ebbs, the ranks of millionaires declines along with their incomes, and tax revenues fall even more sharply under the progressive rate structure. Already in deficit during the boom years, California's fiscal deficit has become unsustainable during the recession.

Oddly, Governor Brown plans to increase both taxes and spending. The top personal income tax rate under his agenda rose by 3 percentage points, to 13.3 percent in 2013—a temporary surcharge that would be set for the next *seven* years. On the spending side, the legislature rejected his recommendations in the spring of 2012. Brown did negotiate a 5 percent pay cut with public-employee unions to great fanfare during the summer of 2012, which Stanford economist Michael Boskin noted was coupled with a 5 percent reduction in work hours, yielding a meager 1.6 percent pay cut.[19] The governor punted the real fight over pensions until later, which as we write has ended with Brown caving in to superficial changes.

The economic crisis involves more than fiscal deficits, unfortunately, and reveals the political foundations of imbalance. Public workers have such a strong grip on elected officials that they have been able to get the legislatures and city councils to establish generous work rules. "It takes twice as many firefighters to put out half as many fires as it did 30 years ago," explained Holman Jenkins in a 2012 *Wall Street Journal* column. When fire crews are dispatched in Orange County, "only 2% of responses involve fires."[20] Regulations mandate this artificial demand for public services that are extraordinarily lucrative to suppliers, the firefighters union, a classic case of one special interest trumping the public interest while disguised in the name of "public safety." In some cities, regulations require five firefighters per truck, per the insistence of the National Fire Protection Association, regardless of the nature of the call.

Padding the public workforce is everywhere. Jenkins notes that the University of California system, ten campuses in all from Berkeley to Merced, has grown its senior administrative staff four times faster than its teaching staff since 1993. The ratio is now 1:1. Meanwhile, prisons in California were declared inhumane by the U.S. Supreme Court in 2011, with twice as many inmates as the design capacity of 80,000. The state is planning to push 30,000 of the overage into county jails. Yet analyst Jeff Tyler remarked on the radio program *Marketplace:* "Over the last decade, spending on California prisons has jumped from 5 percent of the state's general fund budget to around 11 percent."[21] How did this happen? The prison guards are soaking up the money, with increasingly generous contracts between their union and the sitting governor. Then-governor Gray Davis "agreed to a contract that gave guards a 34 percent pay increase between 2003 and 2008."[22] When did Davis cut the deal? It was done just days before the election that recalled him from office in 2003.

Despite its massive fiscal problems, the state continues to pursue fantastic and expensive projects, notably the high-speed rail line designed to connect the San Francisco Bay area and Los Angeles. The plan has little support among the electorate, sensing that its estimated cost having doubled to $100 billion will crowd out other infrastructure spending on roads and highways. Even liberal columnist Kevin Drum ridiculed the consulting study used to justify the project, noting in *Mother Jones* its assumptions that the rail line would serve trains with 1,000 passengers running both north and south every five minutes, 19 hours a day and 365 days a year.[23] The study further assumes the trains would be 70 percent full on average. Why then does Governor Brown back the rail program so dogmatically? The logical explanation is that it's his political support from the construction workers' union, which explanation is not at all politically irrational once we realize that public sector unions have taken over state government.

MEET THE NEW PRAETORIANS

Economically, the implacable fiscal crisis of California may resemble modern Greece, but politically the parallel is thousands of years older. The Roman army usurped control over imperial succession in the third century A.D. "An emperor would be chosen by a gang and would rule only so long as he pleased the assassins," explained historian Charles Van Doren.[24] The Roman Senate had no control. The emperor himself had no control. All power during Rome's political crisis was in the hands of a self-serving Praetorian Guard. Could interest groups in Sacramento be a temporary Praetorian Guard?

The largest and most powerful of the public sector unions is the California Teachers Association (CTA). K–12 expenditures take up 40 percent of the state's general fund. With 300,000 members paying dues to the CTA of $170 per year, the union has $50 million per year to spend, and much of it to influence politicians. Not only is it effectively shaping compensation, but it also promotes solidarity by protecting its members in the most outrageous circumstances. As the *Wall Street Journal* reported in an interview with Gloria Romero, a former Democratic state senator, the CTA "torpedoed a bill (introduced by Senator Alex Padilla) that would have made it easier for districts to fire teachers who molest students. Same for legislation to strip pensions from teachers who have sexual relationships with students."[25] After eight years as majority leader in Sacramento from 2001–2008, the pro-labor Romero realized that the unions "owned" the state. Now she wants to see their distortionary effect on elections curtailed by ending the use of union dues for political purposes without member consent. "They will be brought down; they must be brought down," she said. These are powerful words, but, sadly, Romero is no longer a legislator. The unions she crossed did not defeat her at the ballot box, though. Romero was term-limited in 2010.

TERM LIMITS AND TIME PREFERENCES

Forty-nine of every fifty members of the U.S. House of Representatives who ran for reelection in 1986 won, according to the Center for Responsive Politics.[26] The same percentage won again in 1988. In 1990, the reelection rate dropped from 98 percent to 96 percent. All the while, public approval of the U.S. Congress was low. A national wave of frustration with the status quo led to many statewide initiatives to limit the number of years any one legislator could hold office, known as term limits.

A natural question arises: if term limits are good enough for the president, why not for state and federal legislators? The U.S. Constitution allowed presidents to serve two terms in the White House, a norm set by George Washington that became a legal restriction after FDR passed away during his fourth term. The logic is that a permanent politician, to use the pejorative term, is more likely to abuse his or her position of

power. The public became frustrated with politicians who seemed un-
accountable in the 1980s, whipped up by media attention, and so was
born a reform movement to change the rules. This is civic engagement
at the locus of the political *rules of the game* that we are calling for in
this book. Unfortunately, term limits are a terrible way to fix a broken
political system, akin to taking the engine out of a car because it isn't
running smoothly and replacing it with a new engine.

Nevertheless, the concept of term limits remains popular. Pollster
Scott Rasmussen found in a 2011 telephone survey that 71 percent of
likely U.S. voters favor establishing term limits for all members of Congress, compared to 14 percent opposed.[27] Americans were split on legislative term limits from the 1940s to the 1970s, but Gallup found a surge
of support in 1981 that rose and peaked over the decade. That support
has remained strong ever since. The issue was placed on the ballot in
twenty-four states, starting in 1990, and became law in eight states.
House Republicans embraced the idea in the 1994 "Contract with
America," but the Supreme Court ruled state limits on *federal* legislators
to be unconstitutional. The ruling left limits on *state* legislators in place.

Currently, fifteen states limit the terms of state legislators, including Florida, Ohio, Michigan, and California. Most states limit terms
to a maximum of eight years each in the lower and upper chamber. In
Louisiana, the limit is twelve years. But in California, the term limit for
the assembly is shorter than anywhere else, at just six years. Six years
to master the ways of the capitol, build coalitions, propose legislation,
and try to get it passed. Only two other states have limits as strict—
Arkansas and Michigan.[28]

The theory of term limits does not make sense from an economic way
of thinking. Such limits are at odds with the economic theory of *time
preference*. We should think of the behavior and incentives of individuals in the public sector, specifically in political leadership, no differently
than we do those in private sector. Politicians, like merchants and farmers, are self-interested. But instead of maximizing profits, they maximize
power. Imagine if a farmer had a fixed term to work the land, say six
years. How would his incentives to preserve the land change?

A typical farmer with a fixed amount of time would exploit the land
in the short term to extract the maximum yield. Without ownership,

there is no concern for the long-term health of the soil, no investment in improvements to the land. By limiting the horizon of concern with a fixed tenure, the law guarantees that farmers will underinvest and make the land poorer, since they will not reap the consequences. Term-limited legislators have the same truncated consequence horizon.

In 1998, 64 of Michigan's 110 state legislators were unable to run for reelection. What kind of signals did that send? To be sure, there were sixty-four fresh faces in Lansing during the next legislative session, but they knew their days were numbered, and so did all the other people in state government. How much accountability can there be for state bureaucrats managed by representatives who won't be around for long? And what is the signal to potential candidates for office? Sure, there will be some citizens willing to take a temporary job, but there are many more who have ruled out running for office, once the option of a political career became impossible. Think of it this way: how many college students would be attracted to a job as a teacher if the law limited classroom time to eight years? A final effect is that term limits warp the behavior of the policymakers who win elections. It's not as if they stopped thinking about the long term. But with term limits on their time in the legislature, the focus of their long-term thoughts become less about policy and more about the office (or lobbying job) they might get next.

Economic reasoning suggests that term limits will lower the quality and potential effectiveness of elected officials. Idaho and Utah repealed their term limits for these reasons. The real-world experience did not generate better government. One reason is that the amount of operational power in state government did not simply go away. The new rules had the intended effect of limiting the power of elected officials, who were at least accountable to the public, but that didn't improve accountability. The main outcome was that the power of unelected staffers, lobbyists, and bureaucrats rose. A chief of staff might have to change horses every few years, but she stayed in Sacramento and knew how to run the government. The value of permanent staffers to rookie members rose after the reform.

Californians recognized that their initial limits were too harsh, after a decade of mismanagement by a group of legislators that nobody seemed to know. Who was the Speaker? In June 2012, a proposition to change the law passed decisively by a 2:1 ratio.[29] It extends the limit to twelve years in either chamber, not as long as we would recommend, but long enough to give the next generation of Gloria Romeros time to see their reforms stick.

POLARIZATION BY DESIGN

An even bigger problem for California is one that voters had nothing to do with. Because of its large and shifting demography, the state is required to conduct a significant redistricting after every decennial census. This happens on year-two elections (1982, 1992, 2002, and 2012) because the national census and reapportionment of seats is done at the turn of the decade (1980, 1990, 2000, and 2010). California was assigned seven new seats in the U.S. House of Representatives in 1990, a total of 52. Where to cut the new district lines? There is no set process to conduct redistricting, though the U.S. Supreme Court has issued various decisions to promote fairness over the years.

One of the principles the Court laid down early in America's history was that gerrymandering is unconstitutional. The definition of a gerrymandered district is one that has had its boundary lines cut in a way to favor one group over others, resulting in a telltale map with distorted contours. For example, imagine a small state with an evenly split population of Tories and Whigs. However, the ruling party cuts a map of five districts in such a way that four districts slightly favor Whigs, with 55 percent of registered voters in each, while the last district is packed full of Tories, with 90 percent of its voters being registered Tories. Despite having half of the state's voters, the Tories would only have one-fifth of its representatives in Congress.

Gerrymandering is more than a political theory, and it has a long history. In 1788, the Anti-Federalist Patrick Henry schemed to create a district map that would be impossible for Federalist James Madison to win election to the Virginia House of Delegates. Racial gerrymandering came under federal scrutiny after the passage of the Voting Rights Act in 1965, which scrutiny is laudable, but it led to the perverse outcome of sanctioned gerrymandering that *favored* minorities, on the theory it would ensure ethnic diversity among legislators. It worked, but over time morphed into a partisan gerrymander where both parties enjoyed "safe" seats and arguably segregated racial minorities in American politics. Consequently, most incumbents were unchallenged in their party's primary election and were then invincible in the general election thanks to the imbalanced advantage in voter registration. A safe seat, for example, would have a registration advantage of 10 points (55 percent of affiliated voters identifying with one party, 45 percent or fewer with the other). Many seats enjoyed partisan advantages of 20 or even 30 points.

What happened in California in the 2002 redistricting was as ingenious as it was unprecedented. The 1992 map yielded 52 congressional districts that had a smooth mix of competitive and partisan seats, drawn up when Republican Pete Wilson was governor and Democrats controlled the legislature. When it came time to redraw the districts in 2002, however, Democrats had complete control of the state government. They produced a new district map of 53 seats. It protected not only the 32 incumbent Democrats but also all 20 incumbent Republicans. In the words of the *Los Angeles Times*, the new map "eliminated the handful of moderate, 'swing' districts that, in the 2000 elections, helped make California a key battleground."[30] Worse, each incumbent Democrat had paid the consultant tasked with drawing up the map to guarantee them a safe seat. Newspapers joked that democracy had been turned upside down. Voters no longer chose representatives; instead the representatives chose their voters. The decimation of moderate seats led to a decimation of moderate votes. Incumbents were safe in the general election but shifted toward ideological extremes to prevent an intraparty primary challenge. The same thing happened to districts for state assembly and state senate. Polarization turned poisonous for the next decade.

BANKRUPT INCENTIVES

In hindsight, one can see how the elements of the Greek tragedy in California were set in place decades ago. Gerrymandered legislative districts locked polarized politics into place. Shortsighted time preferences also were locked into place with term limits for legislators. Budget deficits were cemented with votes on expenditures that had a lower threshold for passage than tax votes. All of those stars aligned during the 1990s and exerted their ill effect during the past decade.

Fortunately, Californians have started to make structural changes. Many of the fixes were put in place thanks to diligent citizens and in no small part due to the dogged effort of Governor Arnold Schwarzenegger. He fought for redistricting reform as a statewide ballot issue, Proposition 20. Approved by 61 percent of voters in November 2010, that reform passed before the once-every-decade redistricting that set up new boundaries for the 2012 elections. And in those elections, another surprising result occurred: a supermajority of Democrats was elected to the state legislature, meaning that Republicans can no longer stop the balancing of taxes and spending in whatever way the Democrats deem best. This outcome is a mixed blessing for the Democrats, who cannot blame intransigence of an opposition that no longer exists.

In a surprising twist, Governor Jerry Brown had a very different budget announcement in January 2013 compared to the dire situation a half year prior. Brown declared that his proposed budget for the new year was balanced. Well-respected independent analyst Mac Taylor remarked that Brown was more or less correct, largely due to the $5 billion tax hike approved by voters in November 2012 as well as the governor's insistence on spending cuts. Taylor also warned that this balance neglects off-budget pension liabilities.[31] Time will tell if the tax dynamics hold as projected, and if so, whether a tax-heavy model will generate the kind of growth California needs to retain its status or instead leads to an outmigration of talented taxpayers.

At the least, the structural reforms give California a chance, but the question is whether real leadership will take advantage of the opportunity. Despite Brown's exclamations, California has the worst credit rating of any state. When it raises money from the bond markets, it has to pay more interest than other states. Just like how Greece pays more than any other Eurozone member. And if creditors stop buying, what then? Technically, a state cannot declare bankruptcy, unlike a city. During the Great Depression, Congress made an allowance for local governments to declare a "Chapter 9" bankruptcy due to insolvency, but not states. A state can default on its debt payments, however, even without bankruptcy, though this action has not been taken in the United States since the 1840s. Some observers thought such a default was likely again after the housing bubble and financial crisis in 2008.

In 2009, the state controller of California issued IOUs instead of cash, not only to vendors, but also to local governments and taxpayers due a refund on their income tax returns.[32] If this substitution of IOUs for cash happens again, and if the credit markets freeze, should the federal government step in and guarantee a loan to the state? If that happens, the backbone of American federalism will have been broken. Perhaps not irreparably, but it would signal another step toward the centralization of authority. The incentives for states to control spending will erode, and the likely fiscal behavior of states will make "too big to fail" on Wall Street look like little league. This bad behavior is moral hazard at work. As one economist quipped: "Capitalism without failure is like religion without sin—it doesn't work."[33]

Contagion is the danger that motivates some policymakers to do bailouts. If the credit markets freeze up for California's debt, will that spread to other states' municipal bonds? Will interest rates skyrocket for all municipal obligations? This pattern is what's known as a systemic risk. But there is another side to systemic risk. If the federal government does backstop California, all of the anxiety about California bonds shifts to U.S. Treasuries. Investors will understand that the primary check on state budgets has been removed. How will they assess federal commitments? Right now, the sum total of all state debts is estimated to be $4 trillion or more, which is one-fourth of federal debt. After a bailout, that number would grow much faster than otherwise. It would be wise, then, for the federal government to make its intentions known.

Federalism is an important institution. For it to work, governments must be allowed to experiment and even fail. Trial and error doesn't work without error, after all. Still, we should not forget that the national government had a hand in creating the bad incentives, by letting municipal bonds enjoy federal tax benefits. This benefit creates excess demand for municipal bonds over other kinds of investments, which in theory seems difficult to justify. While revoking the tax advantage would probably cause unfair losses and an unnecessary financial shock, Congress should consider making the tax benefits conditional on some changes.

Specifically, municipal bonds could be given differential tax treatment by the Congress in the future. One smart reform would make the tax benefits of newly issued bonds conditional on the fiscal and regulatory strength of the local government. States and cities that met all conditions would receive full tax exemptions, while states in violation of those conditions would not have tax-free status. Conditions might include maximum debt-to-GDP ratios and minimum pension funding levels. And to limit turmoil, the rule could be enacted to apply only to newly issued bonds. Issuers would have to apply for a tax-free certification from the U.S. Treasury. It only makes sense for the federal government to get out of the bubble-subsidizing business wherever possible. Underfunded state and city pension liabilities offer a good place to start.

California shows how poorly structured political institutions can lead to a death spiral of economic mismanagement. The state has suffered political polarization just when it needed commonsense compromises. The polarization can be traced back to two structural decisions—term limits for state legislators that are the shortest of the fifty states, and extreme gerrymandering of its representative districts after the 2000 census. With term limits, no legislators have an incentive to worry or even consider long-term consequences. And because of gerrymandering, every legislator has only one possibility of not being reelected—defeat by a challenger in the primary if the incumbent legislator exhibits moderation or independence. These political institutions are poorly adapted to facing long-term budget challenges responsibly.

SUMMARY OF DECLINE

Great Power:	California
Turning point:	1992–present
Economic imbalance:	Fiscal
Political roots:	Partisan polarization from gerrymandering and term limits; extremely progressive tax rates and strong public-sector unions
Behavioral dysfunction:	Limited time horizons of elected officials; collective action problem of special interests

12

UNITED STATES BEYOND THE CONSEQUENCE HORIZON

Things fall apart; the center cannot hold;
Mere anarchy is loosed upon the world,
The blood-dimmed tide is loosed, and everywhere
The ceremony of innocence is drowned;
The best lack all conviction, while the worst
Are full of passionate intensity.

— William Butler Yeats, "The Second Coming," 1919

fter reflecting on the common patterns of decline in the Great Powers of the past, the question we face now is this one: *Can the United States survive?* Will it be doomed to repeat the cycle of historical decline: centralization of authority, weakening of individual liberty, and strengthening of rent-seeking groups that hinder creative destruction? Will the economic power of the United States fade as its relative, or worse, absolute growth slows? Will an expansive government crowd out private markets and devour more of the taxpayers' labor and capital? Will globalization encourage people to vote with their feet and leave?

We've tried to put this question in perspective by analyzing the declinist bell, one rung all too often. Our questions, we hope, are different. We are not warning about a bogeyman challenger that is a trope in this line of inquiry (Russia! Japan! China!). The challenges facing America originate from within. And yes, there are troubling signs that sober thinkers have been discussing for decades. The most obvious signs are fiscal—a rising tide of budget deficits since the 1970s, outpacing the rising tide of federal taxation. The math adds up to future fiscal commitments beyond the consequence horizon of policymakers. If that were all, America would have what amounts to a multi-trillion-dollar math problem. Unfortunately, the United States is cursed with behavioral dysfunction in the political system that makes the math problem look easy. In late 2011, Bloomberg columnist Clive Crook presented the standard diagnosis:

> Let's not reject the obvious reason just because it's obvious. The polarization of American politics is the proximate cause [of the ongoing budget deficit], at least. . . . Lately the ideological center in Congress has thinned, and the distance between the parties has widened. Compromise has come to be seen as surrender—and the U.S. government has all but come to a halt.[1]

This chapter examines the dangerous trends in both our economic and political institutions. The federal budget faces enormous long-term obligations from unfunded future entitlements, essentially guaranteeing that the center will be spending more every year in the future. This trajectory is unsustainable. As for politics, polarization by both main political parties worsened in recent decades, although not in the way that most reporters describe it. In what we hope is a surprise, we will explain how the political stagnation is being turned around. *There's a good reason to believe the United States will avoid the Great Power curse.*

THE CENTER HOLDS

A century ago, the poet W. B. Yeats described an apocalyptic social collapse in words that have echoed many times: "Things fall apart; the center cannot hold." These are ironic words in the view of history. The precursor to anarchy is almost never a center that cannot hold, but instead a center that holds too tightly. Republics give way to autocrats, autocrats to tyrants.

The Founding Fathers understood this danger, which is why they designed the Constitution with every care to preserve democratic rule by *the people* against the encroachment of *national* power. When Virginia governor Edmund Randolph disdained a "merely federal" structure at the Constitutional Convention in 1787, his call for a national structure was met with silence, "complete and ominous."[2] Instead the Framers delivered a carefully balanced social contract, described often as a negative constraint on government power in defense of natural human rights. The Constitution does not include the word *nation*. The three branches—legislative, executive, and judicial—were given neatly divided roles and powers. And when the completed draft of the Constitution was presented to the states, many refused to ratify the new document until an additional ten amendments were added, a *Bill of Rights* that guaranteed individual and *state* freedom against growth of federal authority.

The first amendment among those ten was the most important, affirming the absoluteness of three freedoms that would remain explicitly beyond federal authority—religion, speech, and assembly. The Constitution has been amended many times in the centuries since its adoption, but never have those core freedoms been modified. What makes the First Amendment so resolute is not any kind of creation or guarantee by the government of the three freedoms, routinely miscast as positive "rights." The Framers did not believe the government had the authority to grant rights. Those rights are natural. Instead, they recognized that governments incessantly tried to curb freedoms, which is why the text is written as an ironclad ban on federal authority: "Congress shall make no law respecting an establishment of religion . . . abridging the freedom of speech . . . the right of the people peaceably to assemble, and to petition the Government." For hundreds of years, this ban on federal control of free speech held strong, even when it annoyed some early political leaders. Thomas Jefferson's second inaugural lamented that the "artillery of the press has been leveled against us, charged with whatsoever its licentiousness could devise or dare," and urged state and local governments to do what he could not to limit the press.

The design of the government itself was conspicuously hostile to centralized power. The states were sovereign entities, not mere administrative provinces. Governors were to be elected locally, not appointed by the president. States were allowed their own militias. Moreover, the journey of any proposal from its birth as an idea to its realization as law was designed with checks and balances meant to hinder it: two legislatures, the executive veto, and judicial review. The Tenth Amendment reserved all powers to the states, or to the people, that were not explicitly granted to United States. The only prohibitions on states were tariffs on commerce across their borders or abolishment of their republican forms of local government.

Another limit on federal centralization was the power to tax. Only the most democratic institution, the lower-legislative House of Representatives, was given the constitutional power of the "the purse" to initiate bills for raising revenue. Further, the types of revenue were limited—duties, imposts, and excises that "shall be uniform throughout the United States."

This book is being published in the year 2013, the hundred-year anniversary of the creation of the federal income tax in the United States. In 1912, such a tax was unconstitutional—the "center" held the fifty states lightly then. Instead, the U.S. Treasury raised revenues primarily through international tariffs, excise taxes, or indirect taxes on the states (applied proportionally based on population). Then, in 1913, the United States adopted the Sixteenth Amendment, which allowed for "direct" taxation, and Congress immediately passed an income tax. It had a top rate of 7 percent applied to incomes above $11 million and no tax on incomes below $450,000 (these figures are in 2011 dollars).[3] Just this year, the top rate rose to almost 40 percent, not including income surtaxes included in the Affordable Care Act. The Treasury also collects numerous other taxes such as those on corporate incomes, payrolls, and estates.

The size of Leviathan and the strength of its grip are increasing. America's modern political culture tends to cast all arguments about the size of government as favoring absolute high-tax statism (taxing 100 percent) or no-tax laissez-faire. But that contrast is cartoonish. Most liberals recognize the vitality of the private sector, not the state, as the foundation of prosperity. And most conservatives believe in the modern federal role in our economy—for the central bank's authority, for programs that fight poverty at the federal level, for national security, and even for social security. What frustrates conservatives is the poor design of such programs, particularly when the programs are oblivious to incentives to work, save, or invest. There is little reason to think the current level of government is *that* detrimental to growth. The budget proposal crafted by 2012 Republican presidential candidate Mitt Romney and his running mate Paul Ryan, on whose campaign we worked, for example, envisions a federal level of expenditures equal to one-fifth of GDP. That spending level is not far from the level under President Obama of about one-fourth of GDP.

No one can deny that the scope of the federal government has increased during the past century. Both tax rates and tax complexity have risen. Congressional power of the purse has been challenged by what some call an imperial presidency. And federalism has eroded. (Supreme Court justice Sandra Day O'Connor once lamented from the bench that the Tenth Amendment had been effectively repealed.) Can the growth rate of government itself be slowed in the coming decades and, more subtly, will the nature of the Leviathan keep evolving toward social entitlement and away from protecting individual liberties and property?

A more sympathetic reading of Yeats's warning is that the center at risk of cracking is not the government's power, but its moderation. The *political* center has frayed. "The best lack all conviction, while the worst / Are full of passionate intensity." Intensified polarization was Crook's point as well, and one that we agree must be considered as a proximate cause to begin our search for the mysterious ultimate cause of our broken politics.

A FIRST LOOK AT POLARIZATION

Like most Americans, we dream of political leaders who make decisions beyond the narrow boundaries of their tribe, party, or what James Madison called "faction." The Constitution does not mention political parties, precisely because it was largely designed to prevent partisanship from overwhelming the union.

George Washington was the first, and last, nonpartisan president. At the end of his second four-year term, the country witnessed a full eruption of partisan fighting between the Federalist candidate, John Adams, and the Republican-Democrat candidate, Thomas Jefferson. There were scurrilous accusations made against both men (including the lingering but controversial rumor that Jefferson fathered a child with one of his slaves).[4] No politician, especially a candidate for the presidency, has been spared the ugly accusations and slander of the campaign trail. Even Abraham Lincoln was mocked ruthlessly for his looks, manners, and accent.

What is new and frustrating is that the center in American politics has melted away. Polarization has gotten measurably worse during our lifetimes, a trend that can be traced to the 1970s. Simultaneously, public respect for Congress has set record low after record low, and cannot go much further before hitting zero percent approval.

In the 1960s, a few legislators identified themselves with the extreme right or the extreme left. Most were measurably centrist. Indeed, General Dwight D. Eisenhower was offered the presidential nomination by both the Republican and Democratic parties, an almost inconceivable notion in today's politics. An analysis of voting patterns in the 1960s shows a large percentage of elected Democrats were more conservative than the norm in their voting patterns and that a large percentage of Republicans were liberal. While the center may well have moved to the right, voting patterns have shifted so that almost no member of Congress now occupies the middle ground.

These patterns are documented in the recent, and aptly named, book *It's Even Worse Than It Looks,* by Thomas Mann and Norman Ornstein (which we discussed earlier). The authors are well-respected political scientists who work at think tanks in Washington, D.C. (Mann at the Brookings Institution and Ornstein at the American Enterprise Institute), and their book blamed Republicans for the ills of modern politics.

Using a metric that determines the relative partisan voting pattern of legislators, DW-NOMINATE, the authors show that party extremism increased dramatically since the mid-1970s. Mann and Ornstein did not create this data series, a workhorse of scholarly research developed initially by political scientists Keith T. Poole and Howard Rosenthal in the early 1980s. In fact, the DW-NOMINATE scores can be assessed all the way back to the first Congress in 1789. Clearly, the conservative and liberal ideologies evolved dramatically over the centuries. For example, Republicans were the antislavery party in the 1860s, and more Republicans were in favor of full voting rights for minorities in the 1960s than were Democrats, yet relative scaling systems such as this one do not attempt to distinguish the ideological content of partisanship. The point is that DW-NOMINATE is a *relative* measure of partisanship and party unity—it cannot say which party is more or less extreme in philosophical terms.

What the data can tell us is that moderation is no longer a political virtue. Keith Poole maintains a series of updated charts of the data on the VoteView website and blog.[5] Polarization is evident in the disappearing overlap of congressional voting between parties. Figure 25 shows the evolution of partisan voting behavior between the 92nd Congress in 1971–72 to the 112th Congress in 2011–12.[6] The left-right vote pattern of party members looks like a bell curve, with the Democratic bell toward the left side of the spectrum, naturally. The important feature of the 1960s is that the bells overlapped so much that the extreme inner tail of each curve went past the center of the other party, roughly 25 percent overlap. By the 1980s, the tails overlapped only slightly, with 10 percent of each inner tail crossing the other, but by 2007, the overlap was almost gone. Using a similar rating of legislators based on their voting record, *National Journal*[7] has been tracking House and Senate members for more than thirty years. In 2011, for the first time, there was no overlap: not a single Democrat was more conservative than the most liberal Republican in Congress.

Scholars can calculate the degree of partisan separation even more exactly than our "eyeball" assessment of the bell curves. The DW-NOMINATE scale goes from negative 1.0 to positive 1.0, so a fair measure of partisanship is the distance between the average score of each party's members. For half a century after 1930, that distance in the House of Representatives was around 0.5, but it began to rise significantly in the late 1970s, crossing 0.8 in 1995 and growing larger every following cycle. See Figure 26 for the partisan distance in both the Senate and the House of Representatives. Both chambers did experience intense partisanship for more than thirty years at the turn of the twentieth century, but not quite as bad as today.

Figure 25. Ideological polarization in U.S. politics.

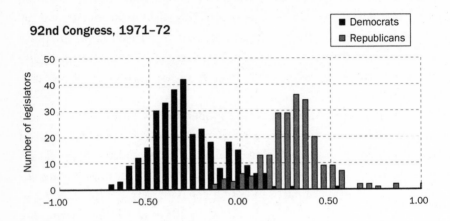

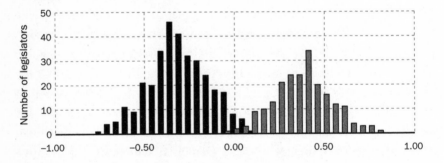

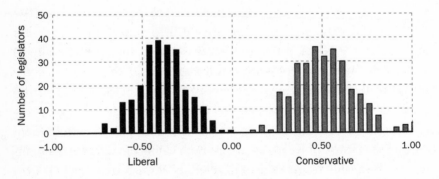

Source: Lewis, Poole, and Rosenthal, http://www.voteview.com (2013)

Figure 26. Party polarization in the United States Congress, 1901–2011.

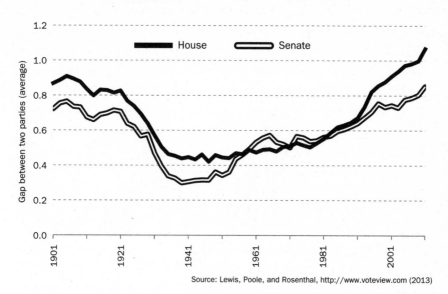

Source: Lewis, Poole, and Rosenthal, http://www.voteview.com (2013)

Today's conventional wisdom holds that the presidency of George W. Bush established a hyperpartisan approach to governing that left scars on Washington, D.C., and that distort his party still. That's not a fair representation of the decades-old erosion of bipartisanship in the capital; witness the previous disagreement between President Bill Clinton and Speaker Newt Gingrich. Unlike most presidents, Bush was inaugurated after a rare split between the popular vote and the Electoral College vote, and a particularly nasty court fight over the fate of the outcome in the swing state of Florida.

This starting point is where Mann and Ornstein entered, blaming the Republican Party for the gridlock: "an insurgent outlier—ideologically extreme; contemptuous of the inherited social and economic policy regime; scornful of compromise; unpersuaded by conventional understanding of facts, evidence and science; and dismissive of the legitimacy of its political opposition."

Laying blame is almost certainly more complicated. For example, the respected economist Bill Galston points to the shifting electorate and the counterintuitive rise of independent voters.[8] Sean Trende, an analyst at RealClearPolitics.com, described the Mann-Ornstein claims as a "misapplication" of DW-NOMINATE, to which the authors referred only tangentially without ever showing the time series we showed earlier in Figure 26. Because the scale is defined relative to the issues voted in the contemporary Congress: "One simply cannot say that Republicans are the most conservative they've been since the 1880s, because the DW-NOMINATE scores are created without any fixed meaning." [9] Perhaps Republicans are becoming more conservative, but that depends entirely on what *conservative* means. Some extreme libertarian conservatives want to legalize drugs. Is that conservative? Unfortunately, that is not the kind of nuance Mann and Ornstein are interested in. The *Economist* summed up their book as "committing the very sin they decry. That is to say, they question the legitimacy of a party with which they happen to disagree." [10]

A second assertion is that the polarization of politicians reflects the polarization of the American people. The existence of a "radical" Tea Party and a "radical" Occupy protest movement give weight to that narrative, but survey data do not. The Pew Research Center published a study in mid-2012 claiming increased polarization among the American public along political party lines, but it rested on a flexible definition of *who* counts as polarized. The underlying data seem much less certain. Consider the study's summary paragraph alone:

> Americans' values and basic beliefs are more polarized along partisan lines than at any point in the past 25 years. Party has now become the single largest fissure in American society, with the values gap between Republicans and Democrats greater than gender, age, race or class divides. The parties also have become smaller and more ideologically homogeneous over this period.

Pew found a growing gap between citizens who identified with a party, but a smaller percentage of the public are actually doing just that—identifying with a party. Because party identification is voluntary (unlike gender, age, race), declaring a growing ideological gap among shrinking self-declared ideological groups is circular logic. Let's set aside the headline and appreciate that the Pew study contains a treasure trove of insights:

1. A growing number of Americans are nonpartisan. The share of independents has grown from 29 percent in 1990 to 38 percent in 2012. Democrat affiliation is steady (33 to 32), while Republican has dropped from 31 to 24. Interestingly, the shift is entirely driven by males—4 percent left the GOP and 6 percent left the Democratic Party.

2. Americans of all ideologies distrust centralized government. Limiting federal powers in line with the Tenth Amendment—long since abandoned in practice— was supported by 75 percent of those surveyed people in 1987 and still by 69 percent today. Independents' views are unchanged, Republican attitudes have hardened slightly (to 84 percent), but Democratic attitudes changed more, with only a narrow majority of 54 percent distrusting centralization.

3. Americans continue to support compromise. Contrary to the headlines, the percentage of Republican voters—even the shrinking, more ideological cohort—that support compromise remains unchanged from 1987 to 2012, nearly 70 percent. Democrat support for compromise has risen from 77 to 90 percent. Eight in ten Americans agree with this statement "I like political leaders who are willing to make compromises in order to get the job done."

What explains the rise of the Tea Party is not so much a change in the American people as a change in the electioneering rules that stopped repression of this group's point of view. When the Tea Party freshmen in the Republican House caucus refused to authorize a higher debt ceiling during the summer of 2011, the traditional forces of so-called moderation went ballistic. One of the checks on excessive government spending is the power of the purse in the House of Representatives, because that body can limit the executive branch's ability to spend money that does not exist. Think of the official debt limit in terms of a parent's limit on her child's credit card. What is calmly celebrated as our system of "checks and balances" in high schools across the country is described as hostage-taking when one's preferred policies are checked!

Now let's consider the extremism of recent presidents. If we look at the signature laws passed during the George W. Bush presidency

compared to the Obama presidency—the roll call votes in particular—
the difference is surprising. In education policy, No Child Left Behind
(NCLB) passed both chambers in 2001, with 46 Senate votes from
Democrats in the Senate and 197 votes from Democrats in the House.
The Obama administration's first-term record contains much less evi-
dence of bipartisan support.

**TABLE 10. PARTISAN VOTING PATTERNS FOR MAJOR LEGISLATION DURING
THE FIRST PRESIDENTIAL TERMS OF GEORGE W. BUSH AND BARACK OBAMA**

LEGISLATION	Nay— President's party (Senate)	Yea— opposing party (Senate)	Nay— President's party (House)	Yea— opposing party (House)
EGGTRA 2001	2	12	0	28
NCLB 2001	6	46	34	197
PATRIOT Act 2001	0	47	3	145
Iraq resolution 2002	1	29	6	82
MMA 2003	8	11	25	16
Fair Pay Act 2009	0	4	5	3
Stimulus 2009	0	2	11	0
PPACA 2009	0	0	33	0
Dodd-Frank 2010	1	2	19	3
DADT repeal 2010	0	6	15	15
Bush	17	145	68	468
Obama	1	14	83	21

Source: Authors' analysis of congressional records.

The above chart expands the comparison to five signature laws from
each president, George W. Bush and Barack Obama. It includes the Bush
tax cuts of 2001 (formally known as EGGTRA), the Iraq use-of-force
resolution, the PATRIOT Act, NCLB, and the Medicare Modernization
Act of 2003. Republicans in the Senate voted against Bush's education reform, but 46 Democrats voted for it. Compare the Bush bills
to Obama's legislation—Lilly Ledbetter Fair Pay Act, the stimulus, the
Patient Protection and Affordable Care Act, the Dodd-Frank Act, and
the repeal of Don't Ask, Don't Tell (DADT). The total number of opposition votes Obama attracted for all five signature laws was just 14 in

the Senate and 21 in the House. The comparable numbers for Bush are 145 votes in the Senate and 468 in the House. More House Democrats voted for the Bush's tax cuts than House Republicans voted for all five Obama bills combined. Whether this pattern will change in President Obama's second term remains to be seen.

Of course, an alternative interpretation of the difference in bipartisanship between the Bush and Obama legislative record is a rise in congressional brinksmanship after the election in 2008. But there is a bigger point: it would be far smarter to step back from the blame game and think a little bit more carefully about underlying institutions that create the perverse incentives for politicians to play the game this way in the first place.

Lastly, we need to be careful not to confuse partisan polarization with ideological fervor. Partisans, in our understanding, care more about their party than underlying principles, which is unproductive for the greater good. While ideological extremists—think of the abolitionist Republicans as described in Steven Spielberg's movie *Lincoln*—can be corrosive to the public debate, they are not always corrosive to good policy. Likewise, the Founding Fathers were extremists, risking life and property for principle. What seems to have gone wrong with modern American politics, by contrast, is a dilution of ideological principles with empty partisanship.

As Haynes Johnson and David Broder described the scene in their 1996 book, *The System,* written a few years before either George W. Bush or Barack Obama was on the political radar: "The Democratic Party is far more motivated to gain or keep political jobs than to deliver essential programs for its constituents. And the people who pay the party's bills, the contributors, care much more about keeping their friends in office than they do about fulfilling what the party claims to be its policy objectives."[11] This assessment was harsh in 1996 when the book was published, one the authors leveled just as harshly at both parties. Since then, those institutional pressures have worsened. The self-centered orientation of the modern political party renders a politics that avoids hard choices, exemplified most alarmingly by the refusal to address the crisis of health-care costs and entitlement spending on Social Security and Medicare.

THE HISTORY AND FUTURE OF DEBT

For nearly half a century, economists have been warning about the long-term fiscal imbalances of the federal government's increasingly generous entitlement expenditures. The warnings, coupled with countless plans to fix the budget, have been ignored while larger deficits piled up, each new wave surprisingly large relative to the last. The public has become desensitized to these events and warnings. In 2011, the U.S. debt held by the public broke the $10 trillion threshold for the first time in history. It is projected under the CBO's "alternative" (read: realistic) scenario to surpass the peak debt-to-GDP ratio when it rises above the World War II era level of 109 percent. That is likely to happen sometime around 2025.[12] What the CBO calls the "explosive path of federal debt" will add 3 percent of GDP to the national debt each year this decade, followed by 4–5 percent per year next decade.[13]

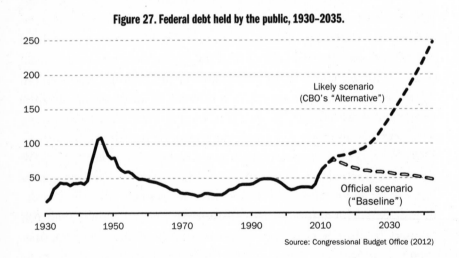

Figure 27. Federal debt held by the public, 1930–2035.

Source: Congressional Budget Office (2012)

When viewed in historical perspective, this tide of red ink seems less daunting to some. The federal government has resolved six major debt episodes in its 235-year history, as we show in Figure 27, which was published originally by the CBO. Why worry now?[14] The answer is that the five previous debt recoveries were qualitatively different from what the nation now faces. Every major debt spike before this one was driven by war—the Revolutionary War (1789 debts upon founding), War of 1812, Civil War (1861–65), World War I (1914–18), and World War II (1941–45). The only caveat is that the Great Depression preceded the World War II debt spike. In all five cases, once the wars stopped, so did the building of debt relative to GDP. Today's debt, in contrast, has been building for many decades and cannot be pinned on a singular event, and certainly not a war.

Blaming the modern deficits on high military spending is a common refrain without much basis in fact. In the ten years since 2001, the year of Al Qaeda's worst terror attacks, the United States has spent a cumulative total of $1.3 trillion on war outlays, according to a recent report from the Congressional Research Service, including budgetary costs of operations in the Middle East as well as "diplomatic operations, and medical care for Iraq and Afghan war veterans."[15] Although veterans' medical care and retirement could double that number in coming decades, the combined total would still be only 20 percent of present GDP. The Civil War by comparison added roughly 35 percentage points to the national debt in just a handful of years, World War I added about 30 percent and World War II added 75 percent. To put the war cost in perspective, consider that contemporary entitlements are five to ten times larger. For comparison, the cost of war operations in Iraq over the past decade was $100 billion per year, roughly equivalent to one year's outlay for the disability insurance component of Social Security.

As for the Pentagon overall, defense spending as a percentage of GDP has been cut in half since 1970. Table 11 shows the large shift in spending on different categories. In the 1950s, defense spending was 10 percent of GDP, compared to Social Security outlays that were one-tenth the size. In the 1960s, two relatively small federal health care entitlements were enacted, Medicare and Medicaid. In the 1970s, expenditures on those three entitlements were roughly equal to defense, but after the 1990s, entitlement spending was larger by a 2:1 ratio. In a real sense, the overall size of government expenditures looks relatively stable based on the bottom line, but that stability is an illusion. Relative to the size of the economy, defense spending has been whittled incessantly and those dollars shifted to mandatory social welfare programs. The only way to right the spending ship with defense spending cuts would be to bring Pentagon spending from its current level of 4 percent of GDP all the way to zero.

TABLE 11. OUTLAYS BY FEDERAL CATEGORY

	Defense	Social Security	Medicare	Health (Medicaid)
1940s	17.0	0.1		0.1
1950s	10.4	1.1		0.1
1960s	8.7	2.6	0.4	0.3
1970s	5.9	3.8	0.9	0.4
1980s	5.8	4.5	1.6	0.6
1990s	4.1	4.4	2.2	1.1
2000s	3.8	4.3	2.7	1.4

Table is constructed with data from the Office of Management and Budget for 1941–70, then CBO data from Congressional Budget Office for 1971–2010. The Office of Management and Budget data had a lower estimate for entitlement spending, up to half a percentage point lower for Medicare.

"ENTITLEMENTS" PRIMER

When Social Security was signed into law in 1935, during Franklin Roosevelt's presidency, it was a modest program to fight destitution among the elderly. The relatively small income supplement (the first monthly payment went to Ida Fuller on January 31, 1940, for $23) has evolved into a major retirement pension, with average monthly payouts of $1,100. Demographics are pushing the system toward bankruptcy, primarily the increase of American life expectancy from 62 years in 1935 to 75.4 years in 1990. Life expectancy is 78.7 years today. The addition of three decades of life expectancy for the average American during the twentieth century is wonderful for those people living lives (adding $1.2 million of value per life, according to one scholarly estimate) and for the economy (the same study estimated that gains since 1970 added $3.2 trillion per year to GDP), but it puts a strain on entitlements.[16] The programs are not sustainable if life expectancy continues to rise. A report from the International Monetary Fund in 2012 noted that across the Western world, government actuaries have underestimated longevity gains by three years, and warns that if longevity in 2050 turns out to be three years longer than expected, the costs will be enormous for pension plans, public and private.[17]

Today, more than 50 million people, one-sixth of the U.S. population, receive Social Security benefits. Relative to the working population, this number of retirees is much larger than that for which the system's framers planned, and increasing longevity is accelerating the popular program's fiscal day of reckoning. Trustees of the program reported in 2012 that so-called trust fund—the accounting summary of accumulated tax revenue over expenses—will be exhausted in 2033, three years faster than projected even in 2011. We say "so-called" because Congress has not saved their balances; it has spent them. The trust funds hold IOUs from the Treasury. Roughly one-fifth of recipients are not even retirees. Rather, they qualify under the disability insurance program, which has grown far more dramatically than trends in observed workplace disability.

The Social Security program worked in accomplishing its primary objective. No longer do we see senior citizens who are homeless on the streets. As former president Bill Clinton likes to say, this program should be mended, not ended. One key feature that makes Social Security effective is that it does not use what is known as "means-testing" to assess benefits; quite the opposite. Workers with higher incomes pay more into the program; it was designed to reflect personal effort (and not simply redistribution). Those workers also get larger benefits from the program once they begin receiving payments, which is normally after the age of sixty-five. A means-tested program would deny or sharply reduce payments to individuals who have more personal wealth or income. Economic logic tells us that if Social Security were means-tested, elderly citizens would have the incentive to spend all of their savings before retirement, or worse, hide it in overseas bank accounts or cash. A reform to Social Security that might make sense is to equalize payments for all seniors, so that every elderly citizen receives the same amount each month. Ironically, some reform advocates think equal treatment, advocated in one form by an investment company executive named Robert Pozen, is a radical idea, but that means-testing is moderate.

Social Security is the easy nut to crack, just in terms of math. It is a simple transfer program. It is popular. It has been reformed before. And the commonsense outlines of how to craft an efficient retirement system have been tested and refined in the private sector. Most readers probably know about the major shift of private pensions from defined benefit to defined contribution plans like 401(k)s. It is hard to imagine Congress avoiding some kind of compromise when, as we expect, biotechnologies of the twenty-first century expand human longevity.

Time has revealed the tendency of an entitlement promise to expand beyond the obligation assumptions of its creators. We might call these bubbles. The rise in longevity is one. Another bubble in Social Security is inflation, or rather overinflation. Inflation is a boon to most debtors, but Social Security payments are indexed to rise along with inflation. In addition, each new group of retirees has its payments indexed to the existing wage rate, which rises *faster* than price inflation. On the one hand, this promise means that each new cohort of retirees gets a better deal than the last. On the other hand, the promise requires ever more tax revenue from future generations, which are less likely to get anything in return.

The introduction of Medicare and Medicaid in 1965 by Congress introduced what has become a hard nut to crack. Congress made binding expenditure commitments into the long-term future, beyond the horizon of political consequences. While Social Security made similar binding commitments beyond the consequence horizon, its commitments were slower to grow and fundamentally simple. The health-care entitlements, innocently intended to "fill the gaps" in medical insurance, have instead driven an ever-growing wedge that has left tens of millions uninsured by distorting the idea of what health insurance is and how the American medical market operates. The future is now.

Medicare provides medical insurance for roughly 50 million Americans, mostly citizens over the age of sixty-five and also those qualified as disabled. Its sister program, Medicaid, is a federal-state program that offers similar insurance to low-income people and supports up to 50 million people, mostly poor children, every year. Both programs displace private insurance. And, unlike Social Security, these programs generate perverse incentives in the larger health-care market by cleaving consumption behavior from the normal demand function, what is known as the third-party-payer problem. Medicare recipients can demand substantial medical care without having to pay much of the bill directly, leading to overconsumption as well as price inflation. In this respect, the programs amplify problems existing in private insurance.

In 1975, the year we peg as the turning point of American imbalance, Medicare outlays were $14.1 billion. In 2010, they were $520.4 billion. The third-party-payer distortion explains in part the spiraling costs, but as the late Milton Friedman explained in 2001, it also hurts patients by elevating the bureaucracy over the caregiver in rationing care. Promises of escalating future payments yielded obvious political payoffs as these programs grew in the 1960s, 1970s, 1980s, and early 2000s.[18] But now that the fiscal train is heading for a cliff, it seems impossible to stop. If we amend the outlays table presented earlier with CBO's best projections for entitlement growth, it looks like this:

TABLE 12. OUTLAYS BY FEDERAL CATEGORY (ANNUAL AVERAGE AS PERCENTAGE OF GDP)

	Defense	Social Security	Medicare	Health (Medicaid CHIP, and Exchange Subsidies)
1940s	17.0	0.1	—	0.1
1950s	10.4	1.1	—	0.1
1960s	8.7	2.6	0.4	0.3
1970s	5.9	3.8	0.9	0.4
1980s	5.8	4.5	1.6	0.6
1990s	4.1	4.4	2.2	1.1
2000s	3.8	4.3	2.7	1.4
2010s*	—	5.1	3.8	2.3
2020s*	—	5.7	4.8	3.1
2030s*	—	6.1	6.3	3.6
2040s*	—	6.1	7.6	4.0

Table is constructed with data from the Office of Management and Budget for 1941–70, then data from the Congressional Budget Office for 1971–2010.

Entitlement outlays are on track to double from 8.7 percent of GDP in the 2000s to 17.9 in the 2040s. Unfortunately, there are no answers in America's historical experience. In the five historical cases of explosive national debt spikes, the debt as a percentage of GDP was gradually reduced to nearly zero by a combination of two basic policies. First, the numerator (debt) held steady, thanks to Congresses that stopped running budget deficits. Second, the denominator (GDP) grew dramatically. Will high modern growth save America from making hard choices? No. Even if the economy grows at 2 or 3 percent per year, it will be outpaced by automatic "cost of living" entitlement growth, an aging population (with fewer children per adult), a longer-living population, rising health-care costs, and, possibly, galloping interest payments on the existing debt.

Modern deficits are unprecedented not just in scale but in nature. Outlays are outpacing GDP growth and tax revenues because our political institutions have difficulties adjusting to today's spending categories. This viewpoint helps us see that getting the federal budget "under control" is impossible *given the current rules of the political game*. It also clarifies the Obama administration's typical approach during the past three budget cycles: deferring action on the deficit until the economy gets "back on track." That logic might have made sense in 2009 during the Great Recession's worst plunge, and even in 2010, but now, after three years without any budget passing the United States Senate, one wonders whether U.S. political institutions are merely weak or in fact downright shattered.

BREAKING A POLITICAL PRISONERS' DILEMMA

Jonathan Rauch, one of the most respected political observers of our time, analyzed "why Washington stopped working," the subtitle of his 1999 book, *Government's End*. As a student of the economist Mancur Olson, he was savvy enough to discard the standard reasons for broken politics: bad leadership, public cynicism, money in politics, split-party government, and corporate lobbying. In his book he dispatches each of those answers in turn, observing that all of the consensus explanations been around since America's beginnings. Rauch believes that "the problem must be of a sort that it is not transparent to the people within the system." Now he's speaking our language, or rather, the language of larger behavioral-economic forces that shape agents in a system even when their behaviors are not advantageous in the long run.

The prisoners' dilemma is a famous lesson from game theory, which shows how two criminals can be motivated to confess when isolated from one another. It originated in the work of RAND scholars in the 1950s. The game gets its name from the problem faced by two suspects the police arrest for a crime. If the police lack other evidence, they may separate the suspects and offer each a reduced prison sentence in exchange for confessing to the crime and testifying against his accomplice. Isolated from one another, what should the prisoners do? It seems irrational for either prisoner to confess, but not when one considers the individual incentives in a payoff matrix. No matter what one accomplice chooses, the other one is better off confessing (see Figure 28). The insight is that a stable equilibrium emerges that involves self-destructive behavior. Both prisoners will rationally confess and serve a three-month prison sentence.

Figure 28. Prisoners' dilemma.

		PRISONER A CHOICES	
		Stay Silent	Confess and Betray
PRISONER B CHOICES	Stay Silent	Each serves one month in jail	Prisoner A goes free Prisoner B serves full year in jail
	Confess and Betray	Prisoner A serves full year in jail Prisoner B goes free	Each serves three months in jail

America today faces such a dilemma, with two parties that have the wrong incentives. It may seem irrational for conservatives to push ever harder for lowering taxes while liberals advocate larger expenditures, but electoral incentives are pulling them away from a budget solution for the nation's entitlement spending promises and pushing the country toward economic imbalance. Consider the following matrix, in which both Republicans and Democrats in Congress have two policy choices. Republicans always promise lower taxes, so their choice is between two spending levels: cut spending or maintain high spending levels? Democrats, in contrast, generally want to keep spending high, so their choice is about taxes: raise taxes or keep taxes low?

Figure 29. Political prisoners' dilemma.

		DEMOCRATIC CHOICES	
		Raise Taxes	Keep Taxes Low
REPUBLICAN CHOICES	Cut Spending	Compromise Fiscal balance	Democratic political advantage Fiscal imbalance
	Keep Spending High	Republican political advantage Fiscal imbalance	Political stalemate Fiscal imbalance

A close look at the matrix in Figure 29 shows that it is *politically* rational for the Republicans to maintain higher spending, regardless of the fiscal behavior of Democrats. If the Republicans legislate spending cuts, their opponents attack them and they tend to lose seats. Advantage Democrats. Likewise, whether Republicans cut or maintain spending, Democrats are better off politically to maintain low taxes. This explains why, despite President Obama's lofty rhetoric about raising taxes on the rich and cutting the deficit in half, he and other Democrats balked on walking the walk when they controlled both chambers of Congress in 2009 and 2010.

To be sure, politicians in both parties make noises about good economic choices (from their perspective) that balance the budget, but their actual behavior is what matters. President George W. Bush oversaw the *expansion* of spending on entitlements, as well as on defense, education, and other discretionary programs. "The American electorate has dug in against both major tax increases and major spending cuts," explained economist Tyler Cowen recently.[19] Politicians may know what is best for the long term, but they have no real choice to change their behavior in the modern polarized political climate. Political punishment is the payoff for the party that deviates toward budget balance.

Fiscal imbalance is an *institutional* failure. For most of the nation's history, the rules of the budget game worked, but they no longer do. America is becoming unbalanced in a way that echoes the fiscal rent-seeking of the Roman and Ottoman empires. Fortunately, the nation has time to focus on the problem and institute new rules to regain our balance.

A SECOND LOOK AT POLARIZATION

Unlike so many of the Great Powers described in this book, the United States is a democracy. Most would agree that the quality of democracy practiced in the United States is as transparent and fair as has ever been. The American experiment started by the Founding Fathers in 1776, then radically recast with the effective adoption of the Constitution in 1789, has proved a success. But the pressures of special interests and rent-seekers are no different in our more perfect union than in dictatorships of empires past. This role for rent-seeking isn't a surprise, especially if you believe that *homo economicus* represents universal instincts.

Democracies are usually organized around the institution of ideological political parties. Outside the United States, votes are cast in the typical democratic election for a party, not for an individual candidate. This orientation is the system of "proportional representation." In Canada, for example, votes are routinely split between three main parties—Conservative, Liberal, and New Democrat. In Germany, there are six or seven main parties at present, including the Christian Democrats, Social Democrats, Free Democrats, the Left, Alliance Greens, and the Christian Social Union. Rarely can a single party muster a majority of votes, so coalition government is the norm. A combination of parties, led by the one that received the most votes, will form a government of the majority in parliament and from their ranks will select a prime minister to lead the executive branch. By contrast, the United States has legislative districts based on geography rather than ideology. The way we elect the president is also bizarre to most non-Americans, which is totally separate from the legislative majority but also based on the fifty-state Electoral College. Those who believe in strong, ideologically coherent government dislike the American system, while others believe its nonideological hue stands as James Madison's greatest achievement.

Writing as one of the three anonymous authors of the Federalist Papers, which were circulated in the late 1780s to promote adoption of the Constitution by the states, Madison explained that ideological political factions—"the mortal diseases under which popular governments have everywhere perished"—could only be broken and controlled by a well-constructed union, never eliminated. Madison defined factions as "a number of citizens, whether amounting to a majority or a minority of the whole, who are united and actuated by some common impulse of passion, or of interest, adversed to the rights of other citizens, or to the permanent and aggregate interests of the community." This description matches the modern economic description of a *special interest* and predicts their rent-seeking behavior. But Madison wisely cautioned that factions were natural. Their emergence represents the right of assembly.

The Madisonian design of American democracy explains why political parties here emerged as they did. Under the Constitution, congressional candidates compete in geographic districts, where individual victors represent the interest of their constituents back home. Further, votes are cast in winner-take-all elections, which generate a mathematically stable equilibrium for only two parties. A third party that gets 5 percent or even 15 percent of support nationally will tend to get zero seats in the Congress. And because this "two-party" equilibrium encompasses such diverse factions, the parties tended to be ideologically moderate. The two parties weren't polarized for most of American history. As recently as the 1970s there was a "liberal" wing in the Grand Old Party (GOP), called "Rockefeller Republicans" after Vice President Nelson Rockefeller. Likewise, there were plenty of conservative Democrats, and not just the southern "Dixiecrats." Pro-defense Democratic legislators such as Henry "Scoop" Jackson, from Washington State, remain widely admired, if not emulated.

What makes U.S. politics so exciting is that coalitions are formed informally, before elections. In European proportional-representation systems, coalitions are formed formally, after elections. The two dominant U.S. parties, starting with the Federalists versus the Republican-Democrats in the 1790s, tend to be informal coalitions that mix ethnic factions, regional factions, religious factions, economic factions, and ideological factions. A party might be cobbled together with support from westerners, laborers, Catholics, Asians, veterans, and so on.

For two centuries, factions were well controlled within the constitutional system. Free to flourish, they balanced one another out. Even so, these outside factions that we now think of as "special interests" were never popular in the public imagination. A recurring theme of political campaigns was to decry the special interests, even though nothing seemed to change decade after decade. President Harry Truman railed against "moneyed special interests" in his fiery 1948 speech at the Democratic National Convention. President Dwight Eisenhower warned against the "military-industrial complex" in his 1961 farewell address. President Bill Clinton made a solemn promise on the night of his election victory in 1992 to "reform the political system, to reduce the influence of special interests." Why has nothing really changed?

Something big did change, and it changed in 1974. It launched the partisanship gap in the DW-NOMINATE scores that trended higher for the next four decades. The growing partisan polarization has roots, ironically, in reforms meant to fix politics: campaign finance reform.

The concern of political commentators in the 1970s was that Republican and Democratic parties were too *weak*, which made them unable to stand up to the unruly mass of unregulated factions. A young David Broder lamented the impotence of politics in an influential essay in the *Atlantic,* published in March 1972.[20] He cited a 1951 report by the American Political Science Association that warned about the ineffectiveness of the U.S. party system. Other countries in Europe and Asia had a purposeful direction as a consequence of the philosophical clarity of their party structure and the unified capabilities of their governments. Broder and other intellectuals thought more partisanship— strengthening the role and ideological clarity of the two major political parties—would diminish the polarized discourse of informal groups. Take a careful look at what he wrote in 1972:

Is there not a better way to resolve our differences, to move ahead on our common problems? I believe there is. The instrument available to us is responsible party government. The alternative to making policy in the streets is to make it in the voting booth. But if that proposition is to be more than a cliché, there must be real choices presented at election time—choices involving more than a selection between two sincere-sounding, photogenic graduates of some campaign consultant's academy of political and dramatic arts.

. . . we have not seen responsible party government in this country—in Washington or in most states and cities—in the sixteen years I have been covering national politics. Instead, we have fractured, irresponsible nonparty government, and we have paid a fearful price for it.

... The habit of partisanship, once lost, may be very difficult to regain. ... More minor-party or independent candidates may find their way into Congress, weakening the existing party structure there.[21]

After a lengthy and touching essay about the chaos of the 1970s, Broder next offered a dozen proposed reforms (including direct election of the president), all aimed at strengthening the two parties. This paragraph stands out:

Most important of all the structural reforms, we need to follow through on the recent congressional effort to discipline the use of money in politics, by setting realistic limits on campaign spending, limiting and publicizing individual and organizational gifts and *channeling much more of the money (including, in my view, all general election spending) through the respective party committees* rather than through individual candidates' treasuries.[22] (emphasis added)

Broder closed his essay with a scolding of the public for splitting the ticket, that is, voting for candidates of different parties (conservative John for Senate, liberal Jim for Congress). "It seems to me that we should ask, before splitting a ticket, what it is we hope to accomplish by dividing between the parties the responsibility for government of our country, our state, or our community. Do we think there is no difference between the parties?" Today, these arguments read as shockingly naïve. Broder imagined that creativity and energy rest with the big organization, not the entrepreneurial individual. Did he or other reformers ever look back on the 1974 campaign finance reforms, which did precisely what they hoped, and realize that giving the two parties monopoly power over money in politics had backfired?

In the wake of the Watergate scandal, Congress amended the 1971 Federal Election Campaign Act to place severe new limits on campaign finances. The 1974 law crossed one First Amendment line by limiting the speech of individuals and groups. It limited indirect speech as well, by establishing dollar limits on the contributions an individual could make to a political campaign. According to the law, it was illegal for an individual to publish a book or place advertisements on television.

Immediately challenged, the most egregious parts of the law were pared back by the Supreme Court in the controversial 1976 case, *Buckley v. Valeo*. The court declared any restrictions on individual independent expenditures a violation of free speech, but it let stand the new, effectively monopoly powers of the two parties over campaign dollars. Candidates were barred from coordinated campaigns with independent expenditures by individuals, which basically drove such expenditures to extinction. The newly created Federal Election Commission threatened to penalize any citizen who spoke or assembled in violation of the arcane law. The law was modified repeatedly in subsequent years, supposedly to control the flow of corrupting money, but each new iteration led to more party control over the flow of electioneering funds. Direct fund-raising by candidates was limited, while "soft money" donated to national party offices was not.

Polarization got worse as a result of campaign finance reform in the 1970s. The parties became more ideologically rigid, decade after decade. And instead of more action-oriented, responsible government, the public saw more gridlock. When the public grew frustrated and clamored for changes, reformers devised even more elaborate campaign finance restrictions.[23] They helped staffers in the Congress draft the McCain-Feingold Act, which passed in 2002. The new law addressed the loophole of so-called issue advocacy, which skirted the electioneering rules by pretending to be educational (hypothetically, "Abortions in the third trimester are murder, and, by the way, Senator Smith is for them"). The revised Federal Election Commission under McCain-Feingold also was instructed to penalize corporations and unions that tried to participate in campaigns in unapproved ways. Bans on corporate speech limited most nonprofit organizations. For example, the National Rifle Association, the American Civil Liberties Union, the local plumbers' unions, the Sierra Club, Columbia University, and the National Association for the Advancement of Colored People were so affected—but not the two organizations that stood to gain the most: the Democratic Party and the Republican Party. They had license to spend however much money they wanted, anytime and anywhere.

This unequal treatment led to the monumental Supreme Court case in 2010 known as *Citizens United v. Federal Election Commission*. The nonprofit organization called Citizens United had produced a documentary film about then-presidential candidate Hillary Clinton but was barred from showing the film on cable television, even on pay-per-view, during the Democratic primaries in 2007 and 2008. When the case was brought before the Supreme Court on March 24, 2009, the Court's questioning was pointed.[24]

Chief Justice John Roberts asked a hypothetical question of the administration's deputy solicitor general, Malcolm Stewart. "It's a 500-page book, and at the end it says, 'And so vote for X.' The government could ban that?"

"We could prohibit the publication of the book," Stewart agreed. He tried to hedge that it would only apply to books produced with money from an organization's "treasury" rather than its political arm, and the hypothetical book ban only applied during the sixty days before an election. But those are intractable when free speech emanates from non-profit corporations that exist expressly for advocacy. Stewart further argued that the government could ban a union from hiring an author to write a political book. "That's pretty incredible," said a stunned Justice Samuel Alito when Stewart argued that the government's censorship role applied to books as well as movies and television commercials.

The initial decision rendered by the Court was deemed too narrow, especially in light of the inherent conflicts that had arisen between the government's growing censorship powers and the chilling effect that had even on legitimate speech (such as independent expenditures). Roberts called for a reargument on the memorable date of 9/9/2009. In its ultimate decision, the Court struck down restrictions on all independent expenditures for political speech. The majority opinion, penned by Justice Anthony Kennedy, said: "If the First Amendment has any force, it prohibits Congress from fining or jailing citizens, or associations of citizens, for simply engaging in political speech."

Unfortunately, some critics of the decision have misrepresented the outcome, claiming that contribution limits and disclosure requirements on candidate campaigns were rescinded (they were not) and that foreign corporations were now free to contribute in U.S. elections (also untrue). Those critics also warned that a flood of for-profit corporate cash would take over the republic. And the media parroted the idea that big donors like Sheldon Adelson and George Soros had been given new license to take over politics, when in fact that right of individual independent expenditures had been upheld since the 1970s. What changed in 2010 is that individuals were allowed once again to create coordinating organizations for political activity, known historically as the freedom of assembly.

Unleashing competitive political speech is important in battling the polarization we noted earlier. Polarization locked in the worst quadrant of budget deficits in the "prisoners' dilemma" and let elected officials focus on short-term battles rather than long-term compromises. In essence, polarization is just another limit on the consequence horizon. Good government requires political agents with the longest possible consequence horizon.

Properly understood, *Citizens United* ends the repression of independent political voices for the first time in four decades. Granting monopoly (or duopoly) power over any market will almost always end badly, even if it is what some commentators believe to be a morally superior market. But the history of the past four bitter decades of hyperpartisanship has taught us that campaign finance reform failed to make politics less polarized. Instead it made it far worse. If instead, America is governed through truly free elections, we believe the new political coalitions will be able to remedy the fiscal crisis, born of short consequence horizons. We anticipate a third party that stands for something radical, like the abolitionists of the 1860s did, and a fourth party, a fifth party, and most important of all, truly independent legislators.

SUMMARY OF DECLINE	
Great Power:	America
Turning point:	1975
Economic imbalance:	Fiscal
Political roots:	Partisan polarization
Behavioral dysfunction:	Loss aversion by political parties at the expense of entrepreneurial policymakers; collective action problem of special interests

13

AMENDING AMERICA

The preservation of the sacred fire of liberty, and the destiny of the republican model of government, are justly considered as deeply, perhaps as finally, staked on the experiment entrusted to the hands of the American people.

— George Washington, First Inaugural Address, April 30, 1798

As the old joke goes, economics is the painful elaboration of the obvious. So, after a world (history) tour of economic tragedies and imperial failures, have we learned what America should do to save itself from the Great Power curse? We could write out equations with Greek-lettered parameters and the arcane symbols of econometrics, but common sense reaches the same conclusions. When it comes to avoiding the Great Power curse, the common sense of the American people is right on target: the explosion of national debt is destroying our future.

It would be nice if all we had to do as economists is offer some consensus reforms for the *economic* challenges facing the United States. Plenty of fine books do that. Unfortunately, when we set about working on this project, we realized that this approach is unsatisfactory. It makes the classic mistake of this old joke:

A physicist, a chemist, and an economist are stranded on an island, with nothing to eat. A can of soup washes ashore. The physicist says, "Let's smash the can open with a rock." The chemist says, "Let's build a fire and heat the can until it bursts open." Recognizing the messiness of those solutions, the economist says, "Let's assume a can-opener. . . ."

Fixing America's economic mess begins by recognizing that we cannot "assume a good government." On the contrary, the first lesson of history is that governments of men and women are not pure-hearted leaders above the human condition. We need to turn our economic toolkit loose on the political paradox of what Jonathan Rauch calls "demosclerosis." There is a natural tendency for states to atrophy, just as capital equipment depreciates over time. Set up a rule to channel the baser tendencies of human nature, and human nature will find a way to subvert those rules. We have seen it happen. In the late twentieth century, America's ironclad guarantee of free political speech from any government control somehow became an elaborate government-managed duopoly over political speech. And although the Supreme Court moved to restore some of those freedoms with its *Citizen United* decision, the forces of Leviathan are already pushing to reassert centralized control.

This final chapter summarizes some of major lessons of Great Power history. We will also consider—assuming a can opener—some of the economic reforms that would get America back on a path of economic growth and broadly shared prosperity. Finally, we offer an economic defense of democracy, capped by a handful of recommended institutional reforms for U.S. politics. Logically, our suggestions won't permanently guard against the Great Power curse. Human frailty is eternal. The real lesson is that economic prosperity will always rely on political reform. As Thomas Jefferson put it, "The price of liberty is eternal vigilance."

THE LESSONS OF GREAT POWER HISTORY

Our American polity descends from the wisdom of Moses, through the ancient Greek democracies, through the Roman laws, through the kingdoms of Europe and the particular French and British intellectual rebellions against them. But most of all, our polity is rooted in Greek rationality.

So it is with no little irony that the architecture of the U.S. Capitol and the monuments in Washington are based on Greek forms, yet in defiance of Greek philosophers. Skeptics of the American way of life quote Plato and Aristotle, ancient Greek scholars who believed that democracy was doomed to collapse into mob violence and anarchy. For more than two centuries, the American experiment has been proving Plato and Aristotle wrong. The United States expanded freedom—first by emancipating slaves, second by recognizing the equality of women, and always by emphasizing the merit of every citizen over the fiction of noble blood. Here any American can achieve success in the free market. Rational thought concludes that democracy need not be doomed. Instead, governments can and do learn from the past. Following our tour of Great Power history, here then are seven lessons we draw.

1. Nothing is inevitable.

At any moment in time, no great power is destined to succeed or to fail. Long-lived states such as Rome or Ottoman Turkey did not appreciate the reality of their own demise. However, we should not assume that America's demise is inevitable. Many contemporaries fretted about Britain's decline. Great Powers have long cycles of prosperity and decline, with hundreds of decisive points.

America should take inspiration from the states that have transformed themselves successfully, reforming not only their economies but also the nature of their institutions. In modern times, Sweden stands out. A Swedish ambassador to the United States joked that nobody in America believes him when he says his country isn't socialist anymore. Liberals still refer to it as a role model, conservatives as a cautionary tale, but it is neither. As the late Johnny Munkhammar, a Swedish member of Parliament who died tragically young of cancer, wrote in 2011: "Decisive economic liberalizations, and not socialism, are what laid the foundations for Sweden's success over the past 15 years. . . . Today, the state's total tax take comes to 45% of GDP, from 56% ten years ago."[1]

2. People are people.

There was never such a thing as "Jewish physics." That is, however, how many nationalist Germans in the early twentieth century characterized the research of their countryman Albert Einstein. In the same vein, we are typical of economists who reject the idea of ethnic economics. Supply and demand curves operate the same way in Beijing, Munich, Boston, and Mumbai. Growth will accelerate in any country that establishes superior institutions with incentives for commerce, entrepreneurship, and technological change.

The historical record of Great Powers affirms this lesson. The same inconsistent tendencies arise. In imperial China, for example, the stereotype of "Chinese isolationism" is only true in some periods, but the deeper truth is that the Chinese court within the Ming Dynasty alone varied between isolationism under one emperor to openness under the next, then back again, then forth again, and back for good. It is an error to think that the Chinese character is innately isolationist, or more nationalistic.

A great power will wisely embrace its cultural strengths, but, even more wisely, it will not allow backwardness-commanding cultural weaknesses to bind it. As an example, we would highlight the wisdom of the late Ottoman sultanate's efforts to throw off the conservative elements within Islam. More often than not, religious edicts are pretexts for economic rent-seeking, as we saw with the Janissary Corps.

3. The existential threat is internal.
In every case study, we saw Great Powers decline internally centuries before external threats toppled them. The decline in Rome was economic, from the rampant inflation and excessive taxation of the third century to the central-planning tragedy of Diocletian.

Although economic imbalances can develop in many ways—trade, innovation, and money, to name a few—we see fiscal imbalance take center stage in case study after case study. California is the latest example, unable to match its fiscal appetites with its evaporating tax base. Nothing external caused California's crisis. There are no barbarians at the borders, just a parade of technology entrepreneurs leaving for better economic climates.

4. Ignorance is the ultimate bind.

Time and again, Great Powers decline because their wise and brave rulers do not know something essential about their economy. However, as we observed throughout our text, nobody else alive knew it, either. The Romans did not know anything about monetary economics and so were unprepared to fight inflation. Remedies proposed were draconian and ineffectual, notably the elimination of flexibility in the labor market. The Chinese did not appreciate the importance of trade, particularly imports. The Spanish never fathomed productivity, believing that the wealth of nations was simply its liquid wealth, with no clue about human capital.

The modern world is armed with a much richer stock of economic knowledge, one that allows prosperity while also helping our leaders avoid shocks and sudden declines. No doubt modern economies will make fresh errors due to our own blinders. This curse is one of bounded rationality on a national level. What could be the danger ahead that we cannot see? In our analysis, three dangers stand out, though we submit that the real lesson from thinking about bounded rationality is to accept one's limits with humility and to stay alert.

Nevertheless, some weaknesses seem to be threatening our long-term prospects already. One obvious blind spot is the overreliance on monetary policy to cover for destructive fiscal policy. To conduct countercyclical monetary policy in recent decades, the Federal Reserve has reacted aggressively to stimulate aggregate demand with lower interest rates. This practice is noncontroversial, but there is a question of whether rates have been allowed to remain too low for too long, a potential ingredient in creating bubbles in real estate (in the mid 2000s) and technology stock market values (in the late 1990s). The Federal Reserve's ability to stimulate the economy is much cleaner, in a sense, than that of the Congress, which faces inherent structural limitations. It is difficult to fine-tune expenditures to counteract the business cycle in a timely fashion. And as we know now, there is rarely a fiscal stimulus expenditure that remains "temporary."

Another blind spot may be in our economic models, which emphasize mathematical precision and quantifiable components. Early models of growth, for example, including Nobel laureate Robert Solow's seminal contribution,[2] did not consider intangibles such as human capital and institutional quality. One consequence in the policy arena is that elected officials may not appreciate the fundamental importance of intangible institutions. The rule of law comes to mind. The policymakers trampled the rights of bondholders during the General Motors bankruptcy in 2009 in favor of the United Auto Workers, which move profoundly damaged trust among investors in the rule of law. But the damage is difficult to measure directly. Instead we are left with an economy that seems to have shifted gears with higher uncertainty and less trust.

The drop-off in the ratio of the population that is employed (which is arguably a better measure of labor capacity utilization than the official unemployment rate) and its stagnation after 2009 has stunned many economists. This ratio was above 63 percent before the recession. During the recession, it dropped more than 4 percentage points and has remained stubbornly at the lower level for three years and counting. "In another very real sense, that gap cannot be exploited in the short run by reflationary policy," wrote Tyler Cowen at MarginalRevolution.com. "Once again, it requires a reestablishment of trust. Trust is more easily broken than repaired." [3]

5. Governments are the most dangerous "faction."

Every country has a diverse population, though outside observers often miss this fact, as they are prone to generalizations. Even supposedly homogeneous ethnic nations such as Japan, Israel, or Nigeria have, in reality, sharp internal divisions. It is impossible to impose unity or to outlaw diversity in politics. Factions of minority interests are natural, and they deserve and desire a voice in how the government is run.

The task of a well-run democracy is to balance the interests of these inevitable factions, an outcome aided by freedom of expression. However, one faction threatens to destabilize a democracy and is much more dangerous than any other. That faction is the government itself. When the people who control the levers of government are able to enrich themselves at taxpayer expense, and when such centralized rent-seeking is unchecked, the situation can deteriorate toward fiscal ruin.

6. Loss aversion threatens innovation.

In most cases of imperial decline, there was some faction that controlled the government and insisted on preservation of the status quo. When such a faction, like the Janissaries, for example, inserts itself into the economy, tolerance for economic innovation disappears.

Behavioral economics, particularly prospect theory, tells us that people are more sensitive to economic losses than to gains, and that people are most sensitive to immediate losses. Because innovation routinely threatens traditional production methods (and profits), resistance to economic innovation is common among all growing economies, as for example with nineteenth-century Luddites' resistance to the substitution of mechanical devices for artisans' labor or the contemporary resistance of some office workers to information technologies that substitute for them. This protectionist instinct is a shortsighted one, based on a shallow understanding of the economy, while an understanding of the centrality of dynamism and productivity for wealth and prosperity gives a different view.

7. Understretch is a greater threat than overstretch.

Finally, as we reflect back on Paul Kennedy's book *The Rise and Fall of the Great Powers* and his argument that "imperial overstretch" led to imperial decline, it seems clear that the economic history of Great Powers does not support that thesis. As we noted earlier, critics in the late 1980s objected to the guns-or-butter perspective. The data collected and assembled in the quarter century since then provide more evidence to the contrary.

In Rome, the legions did indeed bust the budget, but lack of fiscal rectitude was a consequence more of rent-seeking graft than of overstretch. Indeed, Rome was *understretching* from A.D. 117 onward. And in China, a close inspection of Zheng He's treasure ship narrative reveals less a budget bust than a complicated account of booming trade undone by internal political squabbles. If it were true that Zhu Di's expansive foreign policies were ruinous, why did the mandarinate see the need to burn the imperial records of Zheng He's voyages? No matter, the subsequent experience of isolationism and decline is a case study in itself. Once the Chinese state turned inward, it stopped innovating, too, and the world passed it by. Finally, our look at Britain presents another caution of accidental understretch. Critics of British imperial decline emphasize that it was the epitome of free-trade openness, stretched thin with an overcommitted navy and expensive coaling stations all around the world's oceans. But critics ignore the fact that the United Kingdom was closed in much more important ways. Ambitious to colonize, it owned territories without peer in North America and India but failed to extend citizenship to the people there. John Bull never really declined. He just stopped growing.

The lesson for America is that understretch can happen even when critics are warning of the opposite. In an age of transformational globalization, we should wonder if the heuristic of wide-open America capitalism is a myth or a reality. International measures of economic freedom hint that the United States seems to be incrementally losing its vaunted free-market lead. Take, for example, our network of free-trade agreements.

After World War II, the United States. along with its European allies, advanced the cause of lower trade barriers. Tariff reductions were a priority, affirmed in multilateral and then bilateral agreements. As recently as 1993, President Bill Clinton affirmed the bipartisan consensus on trade by pushing for passage of the North American Free Trade Agreement (NAFTA) with Mexico and Canada. At the same time that China was brought into the World Trade Organization, the trade agenda largely stalled for multilaterals and has been slowing for new bilateral agreements. And even the notion of free trade is a bit of a misnomer, subject to an escalating set of conditional restrictions on labor standards, phytosanitary (yes, it's a real word—concerns the health of plants) standards, and so on. Are we truly as open as we should be for economic growth?

These seven lessons should serve as a reliable guide for the United States as it seeks to regain its balance in the years ahead.

BALANCE OF ECONOMICS

Two centuries ago, when the United States was a much weaker nation-
state than the European powers, George Washington warned against
"permanent Alliances," in his final speech as president, known as his
farewell address. Washington intended for his policy of nonalignment
and noninterventionism to protect America from any military entangle-
ments or worse, dependency, that would inhibit liberty. The relentlessly
shifting diplomatic game known as the balance of power in Europe
might have swallowed up the New World's republics if Washington had
not wisely steered clear. Less well-known are the following lines in the
farewell address, about economics. "Harmony, liberal intercourse with
all Nations, are recommended," Washington said, "by policy, humanity
and interest" (meaning self-interest). Commercial openness, he believed,
would ensure future economic growth.

When the American colossus emerged as a manufacturing power-
house in the late nineteenth century, the public realized that there was
little threat of dependency in foreign relations. Indeed, the United States'
devotion to the idea of liberty compelled an interest in supporting democracy and freedom in all countries, an idealism that drew America
into the European-sparked world wars in the first half of the twentieth
century. After 1945, the United States found itself as the main power,
balanced against communist power. Some called it a bipolar world, split
between the United States and the Soviet Union.

Our theory is that the *balance of power*—primarily defined by military strength at hand—masks a more influential *balance of economics*
between the leading states of the world at any given time. A classically
understood power balance only made sense in a stable world, not a
dynamic world. In other words, the "sleeping giant" did not fall from
the sky into Europe's calamity. It grew. And in the sixty years since
"Rosie the Riveter" appeared on the cover of *The Saturday Evening
Post,* American military strength has grown in absolute terms, even as
its military expenditures declined by 2 to 4 percentage points per decade
relative to U.S. GDP.

So, as we imagine the world of the coming century, let us ponder
what the balance of economics might be. China is growing rapidly,

following the robust Asian growth model pioneered by Japan and the other Asian "tigers." Other countries are growing and developing at a dramatically fast pace as well—Brazil, India, Chile, and Indonesia, for example. And prospects for economic growth in many emerging economies is bright, at least according to the assessment of experts at the World Bank.

Let's recall the economic power measure presented in Chapter 2. Table 13 and Figure 30 repeat the three-dimensional representation of GDP, GDP per capita, and growth for six different economies (United States; seventeen countries in Europe; China; Japan; India; and three countries in South America) in the year 2009.

TABLE 13. ECONOMIC POWER IN 2010 (RELATIVE TO THE UNITED STATES) [4]

	GDP per capita ($)	Growth	GDP ($B)	Econ. Power
USA	41,365	1.4%	12,833	100%
Europe	32,004	1.2%	12,875	73%
China	7,746	9.9%	10,303	40%
Japan	31,447	0.5%	3,988	15%
South America	9,236	3.6%	2,394	7%
India	3,477	7.7%	4,079	6%

Figure 30. Economic power in 2010 (relative to the United States).
(Circle size represents GDP.)

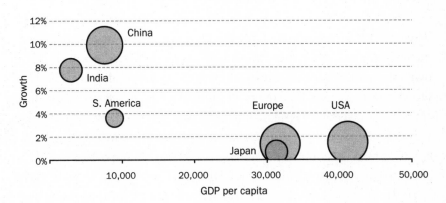

Source: Penn World Table 7.1

TABLE 14. ECONOMIC POWER IN 2030 (RELATIVE TO THE UNITED STATES)

	GDP per capita ($)	Growth	GDP ($B)	Econ. Power
USA	60,570	3.0%	23,894	100%
Europe	52,080	2.8%	23,042	80%
China	22,384	6.0%	35,025	77%
Japan	51,544	2.5%	6,727	22%
South America	24,877	6.3%	8,721	22%
India	13,802	8.7%	23,479	38%
USA*	76,462	4.0%	29,440	154%

Figure 31. Economic power in 2030, two scenarios projected.

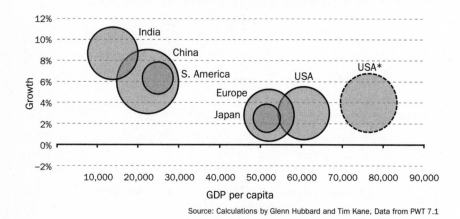

Source: Calculations by Glenn Hubbard and Tim Kane, Data from PWT 7.1

Table 14 and Figure 31 show a forecast scenario for the year 2030 based on the assumption that all countries converge toward the productivity frontier. Convergence means a growth rate that is proportionally faster for countries with initially lower productivity levels.[5] The U.S. rate of per capita GDP growth in this model equals 1.8 percent. Other countries' per capita GDP growth rates were 5.3 percent (China), 2.3 percent (Japan), 6.9 percent (India), and 2.4 percent (a weighted average of European countries). Assume a 1.1 percent growth rate in U.S. population per year yields a net GDP growth rate of 2.9 percent per year. We also assessed a scenario where the U.S. GDP per capita and

GDP growth rates were 3 and 4 percent, respectively, noted by * in Figure 31.

The contrast between Figures 30 and 31 reveals just how much relative economic power is shifting. Economies with larger GDP, such as Europe and the United States, dominated similar charts for 1970 and 1980, with Japan growing prominently. Now Japan is on its way to being a fifth wheel, with India, China, Europe, and the United States representing four clusters of economic power. Our convergence scenario forecasts that each of those four clusters will have a GDP in the $25 trillion range in real dollar terms (compared to the present U.S. GDP of around $16 trillion).

The alternative scenario is worth some serious reflection. If the United States can increase its productivity growth rate from the 1.83 percent in our baseline model (which happens to equal the average rate over the past four decades), it will accrue much more economic power. How much more? If the growth rate could be increased by just over 1 full percentage point to 3 percent, economic power by 2030 would be 61 percentage points higher, the nation's GDP in 2030 would be more than $6 trillion bigger, and per capita income would be $16,000 higher per year. Likewise, a slowdown in productivity growth, feared by some economists, will reduce U.S. economic power and living trends.

THE OPTIMAL ECONOMIC FUTURE

The word *balance* has taken on a modern meaning among Washington policymakers in a way that reminds us of the Old Testament account of Solomon's Judgment. Two women who shared a house in Israel, sisters-in-law, approached King Solomon, each claiming to be the mother of the same infant and calling the other a liar. "Fetch me a sword," Solomon said, and then: "Divide the living child in two, and give half to the one, and half to the other." One of the women, spiteful and bitter in the heat of the argument, agreed to the split. The other cried out and begged Solomon not to slay the child, but rather to give it wholly to the first woman. King Solomon gave the child to the woman who truly loved the infant, after his trick brought the truth into the open.

Today, Washington faces a similar dilemma. Instead of a baby, it fights over an ailing economy. Instead of two warring sisters-in-law, we have two political parties and two approaches to the trillion-dollar budget deficit. Not surprisingly, some political leaders call for a "balanced approach" to budget reform that would split the difference. As Solomon would understand, this notion of balance is a mistake.

A smarter fiscal balance is one that prioritizes outcomes—more jobs, faster growth, less poverty—not inputs. The goal of good fiscal policy is less about equating revenue with outlays and more about the fiscal mix that optimizes long-term prosperity. So, if we could simply "assume a good government," what balanced policies would it embrace to enhance its growth rate? We have already made our case that excessive spending coupled with excessive government debt is a dangerous path. But there are multiple ways to balance a budget, some with high spending and high taxes, others with low spending and low taxes. The optimal policy approach will be the one that generates the most economic growth, not one that treats a zero budget deficit as an end in itself.

Recall that there are three different types of economic growth: innovation, investment, and scale. All three types have been American strengths during the past century, though the globalization of the world economy—linking together rapidly developing countries with the advanced, older economies—is a double-edged sword. Globalization offers unprecedented scale opportunities, but it also exposes America to competition that can be disruptive. Embrace globalization naïvely and the United States could see foreign pirates of U.S. intellectual property undercut its innovation advantages. Alternatively, if isolationists have their way, the United States will miss out on global commercial scale and risk relative decline. Loss aversion is a major worry here, as special interests will push—as they do in all Great Powers—for protectionism of their jobs and traditional approaches.

We see three strategies that will accelerate American growth in each dimension during the twenty-first century. Some are old saws, but as true as ever, while some are original.

First, America desperately needs to reform its tax code to encourage investment-driven growth and innovation. The current code is not only an embarrassing bundle of loopholes and complexity, but it is also making American manufacturers, entrepreneurs, and other employers less competitive. "[T]he literature on fundamental tax reform suggests that a well-designed reform could deliver about a percent a year of extra growth over the next decade," says Kevin Hassett, an economist at the American Enterprise Institute.[6] Foreign countries have accepted that globalization makes capital more liquid than ever, which is why European nations have been in a virtual race to slash tax rates on corporate income. A few years ago, the United States had one of the highest tax rates on profits, set at 35 percent. As of 2012, this is the highest rate of any major trading partner, whereas other advanced economies cut their average from 22.2 percent in 2005 to 19.4 percent in 2012.[7]

Second, the United States needs to work to expand the scale of its economy. Usually, large scale implies external expansion or openness, but scale can also be enhanced by lowering barriers to trade and the flow of ideas among the fifty states. Interstate competition in the health insurance markets is one example that could increase the quality of care and reduce medical price inflation. External scale seems to many observers to be nearly maximized, due to the proliferation of trade agreements. America enjoys nineteen bilateral trade agreements in addition to membership in the World Trade Organization and other multilateral institutions. In actuality, there remains a large unexplored opportunity beyond just trade. There is an expanding flow of ideas, capital, and labor, in addition to goods—the four corners of globalization. We believe the United States should get ahead of the curve and promote "alliance agreements" that encompass all four corners. We should challenge ourselves to imagine a bond with our closest allies (perhaps the United Kingdom, Japan, and Canada, to name a few) that would lower restrictions on labor flexibility across borders and encourage a freer flow of direct equity investments in land and businesses.

Third, the United States needs to focus on arresting a decline in entrepreneurial business formation and job creation. New official data that account for the age of companies reveal that every year start-up companies create roughly three million net new jobs, compared to the loss of one million net jobs by the far larger group of non-start-ups. On a per capita basis, however, the rate of start-ups and start-up job creation has been eroding for decades. After stabilizing at 1.1 percent of the population joining a start-up per year under presidents from 1998 to 2008, the rate fell to 0.8 percent after that period, a sharper decline than in previous economic downturns.

Economic theory suggests that the modern economy offers an excellent environment for entrepreneurship. First, there is a wider technology frontier to explore. Second, a wealthier society enables more individuals to explore this frontier rather than merely work to survive. Third, the shift to economic activity in services requires less start-up capital than does manufacturing or agriculture. The downward trend in the rate of entrepreneurship should have rebounded decades ago. According to Dutch economist Sander Wennekers and colleagues, there is an empirically based U-shaped relationship between self-employment and economic development, meaning entrepreneurship rates should be trending up in the United States.[8]

Our potential reason for entrepreneurial decline is increased government regulation of business. In the fall of 2009, the IRS began cracking down on companies that hired American part-time workers without full-time employment benefits. The passage of the Patient Protection and Affordable Care Act of 2010 is a regulatory expansion that changes how employers engage their workforces, and it will be some time before those changes are understood. Already, roughly one-third of the average American worker's pay is not salary or wages, but benefits, especially employer-provided health insurance. The dilemma for U.S. policy is that an American entrepreneur has zero tax or regulatory burden when hiring a consultant/contractor who resides abroad. But that same employer is subject to paperwork, taxation, and possible IRS harassment if employing U.S.-based contractors. Finally, there has been a steady barrier erected against entrepreneurs at the local policy level. Brink Lindsey points out in his book *Human Capital* that the rise of occupational licensing is destroying start-up opportunities for lower- and middle-income Americans. Matt Yglesias pointed to one of the more ridiculous examples in a 2012 blog post: "Nevada, Louisiana, Florida, and the District of Columbia, for example, all require aspiring interior designers to undergo 2,190 hours of training and apprenticeship and pass an exam before practicing. In the other 47 states, meanwhile, there's no legal training requirement."[9]

This "new normal" tethers workers to their jobs and hinders labor flexibility, but it is a double hit to entrepreneurship. First, it discourages employees from venturing out with their own companies. Second, it discourages entrepreneurs from hiring American workers with all of the expensive benefits that are required. America can do better, and with the worldwide labor market opening, it will have to rethink insular labor regulations.

DEFENDING DEMOCRACY

Doubts about democracy are hardly new, extending back to ancient philosophers, but modern skeptics are surprisingly mainstream and increasingly frank. Joel Klein of *Time* magazine wrote that our "nation of dodos" is "too dumb to thrive," and Thomas Friedman of the *New York Times* repeatedly points to Chinese authoritarianism as a model of efficient policymaking for the new century. Many such pundits probably agree with us that our democracy has been dangerously AWOL in addressing the deficit imbalance, but we are skeptical of remedies of greater centralization or limiting public participation in our democracy.

Our critique of democracy and debt is that the crisis failure of American democracy is *behavioral*. The debt mess is a reflection of representative democracy's worst tendencies—the perverse incentives of politicians to pursue reelection and the bounded rationality of voters who are not required to consider long-term fiscal constraints.

More alarming is what happens when the behavioral dysfunction goes to extremes. In 2011, Greek pensioners, youths, and labor unions in Athens violently protested the austerity of their government. Fellow European states, under no obligation to lend money to Greece, offered a conditional bailout that the Greek public resents as foreign tyranny. Fresh riots erupted in February 2012 when the Greek government accepted rescue financing from the European Union along with further cuts in spending. There were at least 80,000 protesters, and the extremists among them vandalized more than 150 stores and burned 45 buildings beyond repair.[10] We are witnessing, in the birthplace of democracy no less, the failure of self-government to self-control its aggregated appetites. Similar riots in Spain and Italy, where in the latter a march by public-sector unions forced the closure of Rome's Colosseum, raise questions whether democratic self-correction is possible.

The present crisis of democracies would not surprise ancient Greek philosophers Plato and Aristotle. This intellectual skepticism has its champions today. In his book *The Myth of the Rational Voter,* Bryan Caplan uses public polls to reveal individuals' deeply held biases about basic economic principles. Caplan identifies popular biases against foreign trade, productivity, and markets in general. His conclusion is that democratic rule is bound to be economically incoherent.

The behavior of American politicians seems to validate Caplan's democratic skepticism, particularly the tendency for the minority party to demonize the majority when it proposes or passes substantive reforms. Congressman Paul Ryan's plan to reform Medicare with premium support was passed by the House of Representatives in mid-April by a vote of 235–193, with no support from Democrats. It was vilified by Democrats—famously so in an activist video of a grandmother being wheeled off a cliff, but more notably by the national Democratic Party chair, who called the proposal a "death trap." Likewise, the Democratic health-care law passed in 2010 includes an Independent Payment Advisory Board (IPAB) to control Medicare costs, which board was widely attacked by Republicans for instituting "death panels."

The inability to square the costs and benefits of Medicare is a perfect example of what economists call *fiscal illusion,* one of the root causes of budgetary dysfunction. The idea of fiscal illusion comes to us from research on public choice, primarily from work by the late Nobel laureate James Buchanan. Fiscal illusion obscures the costs of publicly provided goods because citizens think that the bonds they hold, and the entitlements they are promised, represent real wealth. They fail to consider that the future taxes they will owe to pay off debt and entitlement promises do not undercut their wealth.

In an influential 1977 book, Buchanan and Richard Wagner explained: "Debt financing reduces the perceived price of publicly provided goods and services. In response, citizen-taxpayers increase their demands for such goods and services." Citizens have the illusion that government-financed goods are less costly than the cost in taxes needed to provide them. Part of this illusion comes from the delay in timing of payments due to debt-financing; part is due to the complexity of the tax code, which obscures who pays for what; and part is due to a general decoupling of taxation and expenditure. On this last point, the late economist William Niskanen discovered that the conservative strategy of "starving the beast" was counterproductive, since lower tax rates are actually correlated with faster growth in federal outlays. He wrote in 2006: "Federal spending is better described as buying government services at a discount equal to the deficit, the costs of which will be borne by someone sometime in the future."

Empirical studies of fiscal illusion until recently have produced mixed results. Niskanen's 2006 paper was a bombshell inside conservative circles when it was released (he was a longtime senior economist at the libertarian Cato Institute). More recently, Christina Romer and David Romer found in a 2009 paper no evidence that tax cuts starve the beast. What's left in the hardened anti-tax stance of the Republicans is not a defense of limited government, but simply low taxes alongside rising debt.

Yet there seems to be an error in the thinking of democracy's skeptics. Voter beliefs may be biased, but they are all-important, particularly to voters themselves. In the end, votes are cast based on real-world results, not policy theory. A case in point is the reelection of President Bill Clinton in 1996. Despite his support for the unpopular North American Free Trade Agreement, which was and remains unpopular among non-economists, the experience of fast economic growth and low unemployment returned him to office in a near landslide.

How should we connect these dots? Does Bill Clinton's anti-populist, pro-growth economic policy mean that the weakness of democracy itself an illusion? No. That voters reward performance still skews policymaking, but not in the way a naïve reading of Caplan implies. Representatives face election-cycle incentives that favor short-term performance of the economy at the expense of long-term growth and solvency. The weakness of democracy is not voter irrationality, then, but incumbent *rationality*. Without hard budget constraints, politicians have no incentive to limit deficits. Thus the American and European experiences writ large validate the curse of fiscal illusion, not just in fact but in scope. We are witnessing political paralysis in the face of excessive state expenditure, and the current budget rules are designed to generate exactly this result.

Our challenge is to eliminate the political disconnect contained within the short-long policy trade-off. In other words, America needs new rules to constrain the "election attention deficit disorder."

THE REFORM ODYSSEY

The word *constraint* is part of the lingo of economics. The introductory microeconomic model of consumer equilibrium imagines an individual who can allot household income between two goods, say food and clothing, by spending all personal income on one or the other. Or the individual can divide his or her income proportionally anywhere along that line. The line representing those possible combinations is known as the "budget constraint."

Wouldn't it be nice if Congress had a budget constraint that was as powerful as that which binds the budgets of most households? Everywhere in the world, moms and dads make hard choices about how to allot their monthly incomes between heating bills, clothing for their children, and retirement savings. And they do it. So why can't Congress?

The simple answer is that Congress does not have to. Its temptation to do the wrong thing is unconstrained.

As usual, the early Greeks understood this basic human instinct and passed down a legend of temptation and constraint. Homer's epic poem *The Odyssey* describes a rocky island occupied by Sirens—beautiful creatures that would sing out to sailors and draw them in with their enchanting songs. Legend has it that during his sea voyage back to Greece after the Trojan War, Odysseus ordered his men to plug their ears with beeswax so that they could sail safely by, but also had them bind him to the mast with ropes so that he could hear their song while being constrained from jumping overboard.

The term "siren song" is understood still today as a fatal attraction nearly impossible to resist. "Tied to the mast" is a metaphor for being forced to resist temptation. George Mason University economist Robin Hanson thinks often about the idea of "pre-commitment," which he says the tale of Odysseus and the Sirens exemplifies. Hanson uses a painting of that scene by John William Waterhouse as the header for his blog, overcomingbias.com. We are not the first to apply the metaphor of constrained decision-making to economic problems. Indeed, *Tied to the Mast* is the title of a December 2011 report by the Peterson-Pew Commission on Budget Reform.

To date, the Peterson-Pew Commission has issued three major reports after working with nearly two dozen expert commissioners. These reports describe four basic types of fiscal rules: balanced budgets, targets for debt or deficits, limits on expenditures, and limits on revenues.

Activity in Congress has been admirably active on all these fronts in 2011 and 2012. The Congressional Research Service described five specific pieces of legislation, three of which the House of Representatives has already passed.[11] The House Budget Committee lists ten different pieces of legislation that it has proposed to tie itself to the mast. The first bill proposes to make the actual budget a piece of legislation subject to presidential veto. The committee has also advanced legislation that will give the president a line-item veto, meaning the White House could cut specific parts of the budget and thus police some of the pork-barreling in current all-or-nothing appropriations. Other bills would put all types of spending—mandatory "entitlements" for Social Security and Medicare, as well as discretionary outlays—on equal footing subject to an annual constraint, stripping away the automatic upward adjustment of the budget based on inflation estimates. As Alison Fraser, a budget expert at the Heritage Foundation, says: "The big three entitlement programs . . . are allowed to grow on autopilot."[12] Icarus comes to mind.

The details of budget process reform can get tedious awfully fast, but that tediousness is actually a weapon of special interests against the public. A more honest and transparent accounting of how the federal budget is made is essential to get the public more engaged. The Congressional Budget Office (CBO) has done good work in making the numbers accessible, even adding a director's blog to the cbo.gov website in recent years. Also to the CBO's credit is the publication since 1996 of the *Long-Term Budget Outlook,* which has now become an annual event that draws media scrutiny and cuts through the political spin. But there is some important accounting that CBO and Congress are not doing that they should be.

For starters, they should consider the dynamic effects of policy changes. The standard practice on Capitol Hill is to conduct *static scoring* of budget changes. For example, a 50 percent increase in tax rates is assumed to increase tax revenues by 50 percent. It makes far more sense to anticipate resulting changes in economic activity that will lead to less than a 50 percent increase in revenues, what is known as *dynamic scoring*. Academic economists use dynamic models that incorporate behavioral changes of agents all the time, even the simplest introductory micro models of supply, demand, and tax wedges. Implementing dynamic scores by the CBO—as a supplement to the static models, at least—should be uncontroversial.

Another accounting issue is that the federal government continues to use cash accounting rather than accrual accounting, which counts up the costs of new long-term obligations in the year the obligation is made, not the year in the distant future when they will be paid. Changes in the accrued liabilities of entitlement programs, in particular, should be assessed on-budget each year. While that sounds like a easy fix, it will be a political shock to the way Washington talks about its deficits. Unfunded obligations of Social Security are around $6.5 trillion, which is a kind of debt taxpayers owe in addition to the on-budget debt that is roughly $16 trillion as we write. The kicker is that the amount of newly accrued liabilities in Social Security each year reveals how big the off-budget deficits are.

The annual report of the Board of Trustees of the Social Security Trust Fund devotes a whole section to "Reasons for Change in Actuarial Balance from Last Report." In 2011, the actuarial gap between projected spending on benefits over projected revenue from payroll taxes over a 75-year horizon was 0.3 percent worse than in 2010, measured as a percentage of taxable payroll (which is about $5.5 trillion, or one-third the size of GDP). In 2012, the actual balance shifted again, this time by 0.44 percentage points. The overall actuarial balance totaled −2.67 percentage points, which led the trustees to report in 2012 that the combined trust funds will be exhausted in the year 2033, which is three years earlier than forecast in the 2011 report.

All of these rule changes would go a long way to fixing the imbalanced process of federal budgeting, but a doubt lingers. What kind of rule—or rope—should be used to bind the budget? The ideas above are changes in resolution and law, but as Federal Reserve chairman Ben Bernanke recently observed: "Clearly, a fiscal rule does not guarantee improved budget outcomes; after all, any rule imposed by a legislature can be revoked or circumvented by the same legislature." [13] Congress has tried internal reforms of the budget process before, which seemed to be effective at the time but broke down when the going got tough. In 1985, Congress enacted the Gramm-Rudman-Hollings Act as an annual deficit constraint that required the president to cut outlays if the deficits exceeded the target and established supermajority requirements for overrides. Congress supplanted this act in 1990 with the Budget Enforcement Act, which aimed to control spending instead of deficits. The act also introduced an effective pay-as-you-go rule, or PAYGO, which required every spending increase to be paid for with a reduction elsewhere. The rules were enforced through 2002, although the legislature watered them down significantly when, ironically, there were budget surpluses in the late 1990s.

Three decades of experience with fiscal rules has taught us what works and what doesn't. A nonideological rule is lesson one, as any ideological rule will tend to lack public support and be voted down. Such rules are proffered more as political signals of partisans than real reforms. Experience with enacted rules suggests that the best variable to constrain is expenditures, rather than debt, deficits, or revenue. International and state experience with fiscal rules also caution against murky accounting, particularly allowing some programs to be "off-budget." We have also learned that establishing a glide path toward balance, even if it is a relatively long period of ten years or more, is a necessary cushion against shocking the macroeconomy. Resolutions and laws decompose under pressure and time. Those lessons outline a clear agenda for real reform that can work.

THE TWENTY-EIGHTH AMENDMENT?

The most promising fiscal rules for the United States may be one or more amendments to the Constitution. There have been twenty-seven amendments approved in American history, averaging about one every eight years, though the last was ratified in 1992. Proposals for fiscal amendments have actually been around for more than two centuries. In a letter to a friend in 1798, Thomas Jefferson wished for a single additional amendment "taking from the Federal Government the power of borrowing." [14] At other times, notably in letters a decade earlier, he had recognized the importance of credit access for a nation in its self-defense, but he also argued against debt otherwise. He thought it immoral and existentially dangerous for debt to rise above a level payable within a generation (nineteen years was the time frame he used). The norms of Congress essentially respected the notion Jefferson favored—budgets were balanced during all times other than war—until the 1970s. This history may be why there has been renewed interest in fiscal amendments, starting with state petitions in 1975. The idea of a balanced budget amendment is favored by 65–70 percent of Americans, according to recent polls.

There are two ways such an amendment could be realized, as described in Article V of the Constitution. That article is both profound and brief, at a mere 143 words long. The entire document has just seven articles, describing in the barest terms how the new federal government would function. Article V showed the desire of the Framers to make their social contract a "living document," not through the interpretation of legislators, judges, or executives, nor through the interpretation of the people, but rather through the express modification of the text.

> The Congress, whenever two thirds of both Houses shall deem it necessary, shall propose Amendments to this Constitution, or, on the Application of the Legislatures of two thirds of the several States, shall call a Convention for proposing Amendments, which, in either Case, shall be valid to all Intents and Purposes, as Part of this Constitution, when ratified by the Legislatures of three fourths of the several States, or by Conventions in three fourths thereof, as the one or the other Mode of Ratification may be proposed by the Congress; Provided that no Amendment which may be made prior to the Year One thousand eight hundred and eight shall in any Manner affect the first and fourth Clauses in the Ninth Section of the first Article; and that no State, without its Consent, shall be deprived of its equal Suffrage in the Senate.

The twenty-seven amendments approved so far have all gone through the first path (approval by two-thirds of both chambers of Congress, then also by three-fourths of the state legislatures), and none by the second path (a petition of states for a convention). It should come as no surprise that Congress has resisted efforts to modify its fiscal powers, the equivalent of tying itself to the mast. In 1982, then again in 1995, and now in 2011, some version of the balanced budget amendment has passed one house of Congress but failed to pass both and move on to the states. In 1982, there were 69 votes in the Senate, and nearly two-thirds in the House. In 1995, two-thirds did pass the amendment in the House, but it fell a single vote shy of two-thirds in the Senate.

The second path has been active however, and is closer to realization than many people realize. Since 1975, thirty-two different state legislatures have petitioned Congress on this issue.[15] Although only seventeen of those states have kept the petitions active, getting just two more state legislatures to petition on this matter would make constitutional history. The required two-thirds majority will be met (34 out of 50 states), and Congress would then have to call a constitutional convention for the first time since 1787. The outcome of that convention will be a draft amendment—the twenty-eighth—that all 50 states will then consider. It will become law if 38 approve.

A balanced budget amendment has many critics, and the two of us agree with many of their points. In late 2010, economist Bruce Bartlett described the balanced budget act as a "phony solution."[16] His was an assessment of Republican motives, seeing the support for the balanced budget amendment as political posturing and nothing more. "Republicans also know that most Americans are opposed to cutting vital spending or raising taxes to close the deficit, so they don't dare offer any meaningful program for actually balancing the budget."[17] While we agree that votes for a balanced budget amendment are often cynical signaling, we disagree that an amendment is a substitute for real action. That line of attack presumes that the institution is solid and its members are simply weak, which illustrates ignorance of the prisoners' dilemma of modern politics.

Bartlett and other economists have raised two good objections to the way the proposed balanced budget amendments have been drafted. First, the proposed amendments allow an exception in times of war or other emergency, but Congress could exploit this loophole easily by declaring a perpetual state of ambiguous war, such as a "war on terror" or "war on poverty," to justify deficit spending. The second objection is the difficulty of enforcement. While many of the legal concerns are technocratic—surely the courts could clarify definitions of expenditure and revenue—the matter of timing is not. "As a legal matter, we would have no way of knowing that the budget was in fact unbalanced until the fiscal year had ended. Even a federal court can't make people give back federal funds that have already been paid out," Bartlett writes, thus the "amendment *of the sort* Republicans propose is effectively unenforceable" (emphasis added).

In 1997, when the balanced budget act (BBA) came to a vote in both houses of Congress, the Center on Budget and Policy Priorities presented an array of essays on the topic.[18] Commentators laid out a thorough case against the BBA under consideration, taking aim at the requirement for annual balance, which would amplify the business cycle. The stark annual requirement for balance within this time frame drives the recessionary risk of the balanced budget act in its entirety. Revenues from taxation fall and rise along with business cycles, and swings of 10 or even 20 percent per year are common. The critics are right that federal expenditure swings of such magnitude would be disastrous. Similar arguments against the balanced budget act are based on the risk to the banking system, particularly the recessionary need for deposit insurance payments. Again, this is rooted in the construction of the within-year balance constraint.

Unfortunately, the consensus balanced budget act that emerged from Senate Republicans in late March 2011 was considerably more restrictive than previous texts. Although it failed to pass, it seems to remain the focus of reform efforts. This outline requires the president to submit a balanced budget every year, requiring further that outlays not exceed 18 percent of GDP. It requires a two-third supermajority (67 votes in the Senate) for deficits in any given year; however, a simple majority is required during declared wars. The 2011 balanced budget act also adds a clause restricting congressional expenditures to 18 percent of GDP, with similar majority and supermajority rules. Additional clauses of this nature restrict taxes and increases in the debt limit. It bars the courts from raising taxes as a remedy.

This approach is no good. It is no doubt ideologically pure, but it is hostile to democracy. James Buchanan, who favored a budget amendment, warned against this kind of "prescriptive" approach. Buchanan recommended, and we concur, that a nonprescriptive rule would allow the will of the people to be expressed.

While a constitutional amendment is arguably the only fiscal rule that would correct the deficit dysfunction, it will fail to pass unless the text is politically neutral. A neutral text would require budgetary balance through whatever combination of taxes and spending Congress deemed appropriate and would embody trust in the voters to let their preferences be known. This route is not, as the *Wall Street Journal* editorial page suggests, an excuse to raise taxes. We have faith that the people will choose lower taxes and spending if given a real choice.

The other serious objection to the idea of a balanced budget amendment is the assumption that it must be an *annual* constraint. Not so. An amendment requiring annual fiscal balance is objectionable to almost all economists, including us, because it would amplify the business cycle. But economists, of all people, should be making the case that a *moving average* of federal revenues of five years or more would effectively cap spending without exacerbating the business cycles. Representative Justin Amash, a Republican from Michigan, proposed in 2011 just such an amendment, though it has received little support to date.

Some legal scholars have objected to the traditional balanced budget act because reconciling expenditures and revenues would be impossible in real time, forcing the judiciary to resolve the entire budget. This argument is either impractical, unconstitutional, or both. We agree, which is why what we recommend is actually a constitutional constraint on *expenditures,* not deficits. Alex Tabarrok, an economist at George Mason University, endorses this approach, calling it the "unbalanced" budget amendment. Tax revenues, as an example, rose gradually over the seven years from 1994 to 2000, from $1.26 trillion, or 18.0 percent of GDP, to $2.03 trillion, or 20.6 percent. The moving-average constraint would limit expenditures in 2001 to 19.3 percent of GDP. In fact, 2001 outlays equaled 18.2 percent of GDP. Revenues had surged with the business cycle in the late 1990s, so an expenditure cushion was already built in. What the rule would have prevented was *not* the countercyclical spending in 2001–2003, but the *procyclical* expansion of spending in 2005–2007, when spending peaked over 20 percent of GDP.

Congress, or the next constitutional convention, should reconsider a *nonpartisan* budget amendment. And we are not alone in reconsidering our previous reluctance. Edward Glaeser, an economist at Harvard University, described his shift toward favoring a fiscal amendment in a Bloomberg op-ed: "It would be far better if we could just count on Congress to live within its means, but the fiscal experience of the past decade has made such optimism untenable." [19] Here are four modifications that will enhance the traditional text, improve its odds of becoming law, and just maybe preempt the coming fiscal crisis:

1. The annual constraint on expenditure should be defined by the median federal inflation-adjusted revenues of the previous seven years, not the current year. Current-year revenues aren't knowable, and worse, will fluctuate with the business cycle. Conservatives tend to eschew fine-tuning federal spending when it is countercyclical, and they should oppose it when it amplifies the cycle, too.

2. Any amendment should be simple, focused only on fiscal balance. That balance should count accrued liabilities in entitlement programs, not just outlays. And the process should be neutral, not ideological. Limited government is a natural outcome of the process of balancing the budget, *if one trusts the voters*, but dictating that as the means only insures liberal opposition.

3. Any new rule or balanced budget amendment should use escalating supermajorities for exemptions that are universal. *Escalating* means that the Congress could allow higher expenditures in a given year with a supermajority vote that increases in successive years. For example, a three-fifths vote in both houses is required the first year of exemption, four-sixths the second year, five-sevenths the next, and so on. *Universal* means that exemptions are not predefined, such as wars or recessions. Or a natural catastrophe. Again, trusting future congresses to judge what is best for their time rather than prescribing specific outcomes is a way to help ratification and protect the nation.

4. The balanced budget act should provide a glide path to a lower debt-to-GDP ratio. For example, after the date of enactment, the average fiscal gap of the

preceding decade should be narrowed by one-seventh per year for seven years. That will avoid sudden, and some would say recessionary, shocks. Not only is this good policy, but it mitigates the objections of those who actually oppose fiscal balance with easy sound bites.

While many voices object to amending the Constitution, the public has a different view. When times change, or more specifically, the behavior of our elected leaders changes negatively with the times, the nation needs to change its rules. A better rule or balanced budget amendment will do exactly that.

AMERICAN REBIRTH

In the middle of September, as the Constitutional Convention came to a close in the year 1787, Benjamin Franklin confessed to a few of his fellow delegates that he had been thinking whimsically about the chair in which George Washington sat at the head of the proceedings as the debates raged. It was unclear whether the convention would be a success. Franklin noticed the chair had a carved sun in the wood across its back. It seemed a metaphor for his young country, particularly after a decade of imbalanced and weak government under the initial social contract known as the Articles of Confederation. Without a revamped federal document, most Founding Fathers worried that the American experiment was doomed. And so Franklin wondered about that carved sun: "Whether it was rising or setting; but now at length, I have the happiness to know that it is a rising and not a setting sun."

This book has surveyed dangers of decline, yet neither of us believes the United States is a nation in decline. Declinism as a topic smacks of both inevitability and failure. Neither adjective describes the United States or its economy. To economists, at best, that is a debate about whether other nations are converging toward a common level, usually defined in terms of income (or output) per capita. And we believe the United States has remained amazingly productive while innovating at the edge of potential economic growth. To put it in our own tribal language, America is advancing past the productivity frontier, thanks to the best set of economic institutions the world has ever seen.

What we also see, however, are the storm clouds of history. American political stagnation, and the stealthy erosion of those mighty economic institutions—constitutional rights, properly regulated markets, entrepreneurship, to name a few—concern us. The most alarming lesson of Great Power decline from A.D. 0 to today is how the tides of prosperity can change. Tipping points in history are real, and it is unwise for the United States to test how far it can push partisan and budgetary imbalances before falling.

The United States should right its politics first by returning to constitutional principles. Those are federalism, a limited central government, and unconditionally free speech and assembly. Honest budgeting is the second major step toward balance—with honest accounting of all future obligations and a hard constraint on expenditure commitments, which will force Congress to make difficult choices instead of deferring a mountain of difficulty to the future. The United States will be well poised for a rebirth of the kind of growth that propelled it to unrivaled economic power with global engagement, pioneering innovation, and ample jobs. History says that nothing lasts forever, but our own history says that American democracy has proven itself more powerful than all of the skeptics' and cynics' concerns.

It is still a rising sun.

APPENDIX

PROPOSED TEXT FOR A NONPARTISAN BALANCED BUDGET AMENDMENT

Section 1. Total outlays for a year shall not exceed the median annual revenue collected in the seven prior years. Total outlays shall include all outlays of the United States except those for payment of debt, and revenue shall include all revenue of the United States except that derived from borrowing.

Section 2. A three-fifths supermajority of the whole number of each House of Congress may by roll call vote declare a one-year emergency exemption and provide by law for specific outlays in excess of the limit in section 1. Additional exemptions may be approved by escalating votes in both Houses of four-sixths in the second year, five-sevenths in the third year, and so on.

Section 3. All revenue in excess of outlays shall be used to reduce the debt of the United States.

Section 4. The Congress shall have power to enforce and implement this article by appropriate legislation.

Section 5. This article shall take effect in the seventh year following ratification. During the transition, the total annual outlays shall be reduced by equal proportions each year, so that the deficit between median annual outlays and median annual revenue collected in the seven prior years is reduced by one-seventh each year.

REFERENCES

Abramowitz, Alan. *The Disappearing Center: Engaged Citizens, Polarization, and American Democracy*. New Haven: Yale University Press, 2010.

Acemoglu, Daron, and James Robinson. *Why Nations Fail: The Origins of Power, Posterity, and Poverty*. New York: Crown, 2012.

Akerlof, George, and Rachel Cranton. *Identity Economics*. Princeton: Princeton University Press, 2010.

Alesina, Alberto, and Silvia Ardagna. "Large Changes in Fiscal Policy: Taxes Versus Spending." in *Tax Policy and the Economy*, vol. 24, Cambridge, Mass.: MIT Press, 2010.

Alesina, Alberto, and Francesco Giavazzi. "The Austerity Questions: 'How' Is as Important as 'How Much.' " VOX, April 3, 2012. http://www.voxeu.org/article/austerity-question-how-important-how-much.

"All Prizes in Economic Sciences." Nobelprize.org. http://www.nobelprize.org/nobel_prizes/economics/laureates/, accessed July 23, 2012.

"Are the Republicans Mad?" *Economist*, April 28, 2012. http://www.economist.com/node/21553449.

Bakker, Gerben. "The Economic History of the International Film Industry," EH.net, February 2, 2010. http://eh.net/encyclopedia/article/bakker.film.

Barro, Robert J., and Xavier Sala-i-Martin. *Economic Growth*. Cambridge, Mass.: MIT Press, 1995.

Bartlett, Bruce. "Balanced Budget Amendment a 'Phony' Deficit Solution." *Fiscal Times*, August 27, 2010. http://www.thefiscaltimes.com/Columns/2010/08/27/Balanced-Budget-Amendment-a-Bad-Approach.aspx, accessed September 4, 2011.

————. "How Excessive Government Killed Ancient Rome," *Cato Journal* 14, no. 2 (Fall 1994): 287–303.

Belasco, Amy. "The Cost of Iraq, Afghanistan, and Other Global War on Terror Operations Since 9/11." Washington, D.C.: Congressional Research Service, RL33110, March 29, 2011.

Boards of Trustees, Federal Hospital Insurance and Federal Supplementary Medical Insurance Trust Funds. 2011 Annual Report of the Board of Trustees of the Federal Hospital Insurance and Federal Supplementary Medical Insurance Trust Funds. Washington, D.C., May 13, 2011, https://www.cms .gov/ReportsTrustFunds/downloads/tr2011.pdf, accessed August 29, 2012.

Bowen, Catherine Drinker. *Miracle at Philadelphia*. Boston: Little, Brown, 1986.

Broder, David. "The Party's Over." *Atlantic*, March 1972.

Broder, David, and Haynes Johnson. *The System: The American Way of Politics at the Breaking Point*. New York: Little, Brown, 1996.

Brown, Clifton. "3-Pointer Adds Dimension To N.B.A.," *New York Times*, February 5, 1990. http://www.nytimes.com/1990/02/05/sports/3-pointer-adds -dimension-to-nba.html?pagewanted=all&src=pm, accessed June 20, 2012.

Buchanan, James M. *Public Finance in Democratic Process: Fiscal Institutions and Individual Choice*. Chapel Hill: University of North Carolina Press, 1967.

Buchanan, James M., and Richard E. Wagner. *Democracy in Deficit: The Political Legacy of Lord Keynes*. Indianapolis: Liberty Fund, 1977.

Caplan, Bryan. *The Myth of the Rational Voter: Why Democracies Choose Bad Policies*. Princeton: Princeton University Press, 2007.

Carroll, Royce, Jeff Lewis, James Lo, Nolan McCarty, Keith Poole, and Howard Rosenthal. "Who Is More Liberal, Senator Obama or Senator Clinton?" Working Paper, VoteView, April 18, 2008, http://voteview.com/Clinton_and _Obama.htm, accessed October 11, 2012.

Center for Economic Studies, National Bureau of Economic Research. http:// webserver03.ces.census.gov/docs/bds/bds_paper_CAED_may2008_dec2.pdf, accessed May 18, 2010.

Center on Budget and Policy Priorities. "Special Report Series: The Balanced Budget Constitutional Amendment." http://www.cbpp.org/archiveSite/bba .htm, accessed August 22, 2011.

Chen, Duanjie, and Jack Mintz. "Corporate Tax Competitiveness Rankings for 2012." *Cato Institute Tax and Budget Bulletin* 65 (2012). http://www.cato .org/pubs/tbb/tbb_65.pdf, accessed August 22, 2011.

Chua, Amy. *Day of Empire: How Hyperpowers Rise to Global Dominance— and Why They Fall*. New York: Doubleday, 2007.

Cillizza, Chris. "Is Polarization Really All Republicans' Fault?" *Washington Post*, The Fix blog, April 30, 2012. http://www.washingtonpost.com/

blogs/the-fix/post/is-polarization-really-all-republicans-fault/2012/04/30/gIQAJXFAsT_blog.html, accessed October 11, 2012.

Colley, Linda. "Britishness and Otherness: An Argument." *Journal of British Studies* 31 (1992): 309–29.

Clark, Gregory. *A Farewell to Alms*. Princeton: Princeton University Press, 2007.

"Confucius." *Stanford Encyclopedia of Philosophy*. http://plato.stanford.edu/entries/confucius/, accessed August 20, 2012.

Congressional Budget Office. The Budget and Economic Outlook: Fiscal Years 2010 to 2020. Washington, D.C., 2011. Accessed August 29, 2012. http://www.cbo.gov/ftpdocs/108xx/doc10871/01-26-Outlook.pdf.

———. "CBO's 2011 Long-Term Budget Outlook." Washington, D.C., 2011. http://cbo.gov/ftpdocs/122xx/doc12212/2011_06_22_summary.pdf, accessed August 29, 2012.

———. "Federal Debt and the Risk of a Fiscal Crisis." Washington, D.C., 2010. http://www.cbo.gov/sites/default/files/cbofiles/ftpdocs/116xx/doc11659/07-27_debt_fiscalcrisis_brief.pdf, accessed October 11, 2012.

Cowen, Tyler. "Introduction to Symposium on U.S. Sovereign Debt Crisis: Tipping-Point Scenarios and Crash Dynamics." Symposium, Mercatus Center, George Mason University, Arlington, Va., January 23, 2012. http://mercatus.org/publication/us-sovereign-debt-crisis-tipping-point-scenarios-and-crash-dynamics/introduction, accessed August 29, 2012.

———. "Multiple Equilibria?" Marginal Revolution, October 10, 2012, http://marginalrevolution.com/marginalrevolution/2012/10/multiple-equilibria.html, accessed August 29, 2012.

Coy, Peter. "Keynes vs. Alesina. Alesina Who?" *Bloomberg Businessweek*, June 29, 2010. http://www.businessweek.com/stories/2010-06-29/keynes-vs-dot-alesina-dot-alesina-who.

Crook, Clive. "Paralysis in Congress Better Than Self-Destruction." Bloomberg, November 22, 2011, http://www.bloomberg.com/news/2011-11-23/paralyzed-congress-better-than-self-destruction-commentary-by-clive-crook.html, accessed October 11, 2012.

Davis, Steven J., John Haltiwanger, and Scott Schuh. *Job Creation and Destruction*. Cambridge, Mass.: MIT Press, 1996.

Devore, Veronica. "President Obama Ignites Debate Over Executive Powers." PBS, July 3, 2012, http://www.pbs.org/newshour/extra/features/us/jan-june12/executive_07-03.html, accessed August 29, 2012.

DiSalvo, Daniel. "Dues and Deep Pockets: Public-Sector Unions' Money Machine." Manhattan Institute for Policy Research, Civic Reports, No. 67, March 2012, http://www.manhattan-institute.org/html/cr_67.htm, accessed September 20, 2012.

———. "The Trouble with Public Sector Unions." *National Affairs*, Fall 2010, http://www.nationalaffairs.com/publications/detail/the-trouble-with-public -sector-unions.

Dollery, Brian, and Andrew Worthington. "The Empirical Analysis of Fiscal Illusion." *Journal of Economic Surveys* 10 (1996): 261–97.

Donadio, Rachel, and Niki Kitsantonis. "Greek Revolt on Bailout Vote May Oust Prime Minister." *New York Times*, November 1, 2011, http://www .nytimes.com/2011/11/02/world/europe/markets-tumble-as-greece-plans -referendum-on-latest-europe-aid-deal.html?scp=3&sq=greece&st=cse, accessed August 29, 2012.

Dreyer, Edward L. "The Poyang Campaign of 1363: Inland Naval Warfare in the Founding of the Ming Dynasty." In Frank A. Kierman and John K. Fairbank, eds., *Chinese Ways in Warfare*. Cambridge, Mass.: Harvard University Press, 1974.

Duncan, Mike. *The History of Rome*. Podcastshttp://thehistoryofrome.typepad .com/.

Durant, Will, and Ariel Durant. *The Lessons of History*. New York: Simon & Schuster, 1968.

Easterbrook, Gregg. *The Progress Paradox: How Life Gets Better While People Feel Worse*. New York: Random House, 2003.

Fackler, Martin. "Japan Goes from Dynamic to Disheartened." *New York Times*, October 16, 2010, http://www.nytimes.com/2010/10/17/world /asia/17japan.html?pagewanted=all.

———. "In Japan, Young Face Generational Roadblocks," *New York Times*, January 27, 2011. http://www.nytimes.com/2011/01/28/world /asia/28generation.html?ref=martinfackler.

Fallows, James M. *Looking at the Sun: The Rise of the New East Asian Economic and Political System*. New York: Pantheon Books, 1994.

Feldstein, Martin. "Japan's Savings Crisis." Project Syndicate, September 24, 2010. http://www.project-syndicate.org/commentary/japan-s-savings-crisis.

Ferguson, Niall. *Empire: The Rise and Demise of the British World Order and the Lessons for Global Power*. London: Allen Lane, 2002.

———. *The Ascent of Money: A Financial History of the World*. New York: Penguin Press, 2008.

Feulner, Edwin, et al. "2012 Index of Economic Freedom." The Heritage Foundation. 2012.

Flynn, Dennis O. "Fiscal Crisis and the Decline of Spain (Castile)." *Journal of Economic History* 42 (1982): 139.

Fraser, Alison Acosta. "The Broken Budget Process: Legislative Proposals." Testimony before the Committee on the Budget, United States House of Representatives, May 31, 2012.

Friedberg, Aaron. *The Weary Titan: Britain and the Experience of Relative Decline, 1895–1905.* Princeton: Princeton University Press, 1988.

Fukuyama, Francis. *The End of History and the Last Man.* New York: Free Press, 1992.

———. *The Origins of Political Order.* New York: Farrar, Straus & Giroux, 2011.

Gaston, William. "Why Republicans Aren't the Only Ones to Blame for Polarization." *New Republic,* May 18, 2012. http://www.tnr.com/article/the-vital-center/103394/polarization-norm-ornstein-republicans-democrats#, accessed October 11, 2012.

Gibbon, Edward and David Womersley. *The History of the Decline and Fall of the Roman Empire.* New York: Penguin Books, 2000.

Giddens, Anthony, Michael Mann, and Immanuel Wallerstein. "Comments on Paul Kennedy's *The Rise and Fall of the Great Powers.*" *British Journal of Sociology* 40 (June 1989): 328–40.

Gigerenzer, Gerd, and Reinhard Selten. *Bounded Rationality: The Adaptive Toolbox.* Cambridge: MIT Press, 2002.

Glaeser, Edward. "Balanced Budget Suddenly Looks More Appealing." Bloomberg, August 1, 2011, http://www.bloomberg.com/news/2011-08-02/balanced-budget-suddenly-looks-more-appealing-edward-glaeser.html, accessed August 4, 2011.

Grandoni, Dino. "Senate Gridlock Explained in One Chart." *Atlantic Wire,* March 8, 2012. http://www.theatlanticwire.com/national/2012/03/us-senate-now-completely-polarized/49641/, accessed October 11, 2012.

Grier, Robin M. "Colonial Legacies and Economic Growth." *Public Choice* 98 (1999): 317–35.

Haltiwanger, John, Ron S. Jarmin, and Javier Miranda. "Business Formation and Dynamics by Business Age: Results from the New Business Dynamics Statistics." CES preliminary paper, 2008. http://webserver03.ces.census.gov/docs/bds/bds_paper_CAED_may2008_dec2.pdf, downloaded May 18, 2010.

Hamilton, Earl J. "Revisions in Economic History: Viii—The Decline of Spain." *Economic History Review* 8 (1938): 168–79.

Hassett, Kevin A. Testimony Before the House Ways and Means Committee Regarding the Importance of Comprehensive Tax Reform, January 20, 2011. http://waysandmeans.house.gov/news/documentsingle.aspx?DocumentID=229436, accessed June 5, 2011.

Helpman, Elhanan. *The Mystery of Economic Growth.* Cambridge, Mass.: Belknap Press of Harvard University Press, 2004.

Heston, Alan, Robert Summers, and Bettina Aten. Penn World Table Version 7.0, Center for International Comparisons of Production, Income and Prices at the University of Pennsylvania, June 2011.

Hobson, Howard. *Scientific Basketball*. New York: Prentice-Hall, 1949.

Homer. *The Odyssey*. Translated by Robert Fagles. London: Penguin, 1996.

Hoover Institution. Eureka: California's Policy, Economics and Politics. http://www.advancingafreesociety.org/category/eureka/.

Hoshi, Takeo, and Takatoshi Ito. "Defying Gravity: How Long Will Japanese Government Bond Prices Remain High?" National Bureau of Economic Research Working Paper No. 18287, August 2012.

Howard, Michael. "Imperial Cycles: Bucks, Bullets and Bust." Review of *The Rise and Fall of the Great Powers*, by Paul Kennedy. *New York Times*, Sunday Book Review, January 10, 1988.

"Howard Hobson; Basketball Pioneer and Coach Was 87." *New York Times*, June 10, 1991. http://www.nytimes.com/1991/06/10/obituaries/howard-hobson-basketball-pioneer-and-coach-was-87.html, accessed January 9, 2012.

Hubbard, Glenn and Tim Kane. "How America Should Avoid Its Looming Fiscal Crisis." *Financial Times*. February 3, 2013. http://blogs.ft.com/the-a-list/2013/02/03/how-america-should-avert-its-looming-fiscal-crisis/?#axzz2O0lmxhAc.

———. "In Pursuit of a Balance Budget," *Politico*. July 28, 2011. http://www.politico.com/news/stories/0711/60103.html.

———. "Regaining America's Balance," *National Affairs*, no. 14 (Winter, 2013). http://www.nationalaffairs.com/publications/detail/regaining-americas-balance.

Hubbard, R. Glenn, and Anthony O'Brien. *Economics*. 4th ed. Boston: Pearson, 2013.

Hunt, Michael H. Review of *The Rise and Fall of the Great Powers: Economic Change and Military Conflict from 1500 to 2000*, by Paul Kennedy. *Journal of American History* 75 (March 1989): 1285–86.

Huntington, Samuel P. *The Clash of Civilizations and the Remaking of World Order*. New York: Simon & Schuster, 1996.

Ingham, Alan. Review of *The Rise and Fall of the Great Powers: Economic Change and Military Conflict from 1500 to 2000*, by Paul Kennedy. *Economic Journal* 99 (December 1989): 1221–22.

International Monetary Fund. "Global Financial Stability Report: The Quest for Lasting Stability." Washington, D.C., April, 2012. http://www.imf.org/external/pubs/ft/gfsr/2012/01/pdf/c4.pdf, accessed October 11, 2012.

Isaacson, Walter. "The Empire in the Mirror." *New York Times*, May 13, 2007. http://www.nytimes.com/2007/05/13/books/review/Isaacson-t.html?_r=0.

Jacobson, Gary C. "The President, the Tea Party, and Voting Behavior in 2010: Insights from the Cooperative Congressional Election Study." August 9, 2011. http://ssrn.com/abstract=1907251.

James, Harold. Review of *The Rise and Fall of the Great Powers: Economic Change and Military Conflict from 1500 to 2000*, by Paul Kennedy. *Political Science Quarterly* 103 (Autumn 1988): 549–50.

Jones, Garett. "The Bond Market Wins." *Econ Journal Watch* 9 (January 2012): 41–50.

"Jordan, Michael." *The Official NBA Encyclopedia*. Ed. Jan Hubbard. 3rd ed. New York: Doubleday, 2000.

Kamen, Henry. "Decline of Castile: The Last Crisis." *Economic History Review* (1964): 63–76.

———. "The Decline of Spain: A Historical Myth?" *Past and Present* 81 (1978): 24–50.

Kane, Tim. "The Collapse of Startups in Job Creation and Job Destruction," Hudson Institute Economic Policy Briefing Paper. September 2012. http://www.hudson.org/files/publications/Kane--TheCollapseofStartupsinJob Creation0912web.pdf.

———. "Debt and Democracy." *Economists' Voice* 9 (2012).

———. "The Importance of Startups in Job Creation and Job Destruction," Kauffman Foundation Research Series: Firm Formation and Economic Growth. July 2010. http://www.kauffman.org/uploadedFiles/firm_ formation_importance_of_startups.pdf.

———. "Who Is the Divisive President?" *Washington Examiner,* June 4, 2012. http://washingtonexaminer.com/article/686906.

Karp, Jeffrey A. "Explaining Public Support for Legislative Term Limits." *Public Opinion Quarterly* 59, no. 3 (1995): 373–91

Kellenbenz, Hermann. "The Impact of Growth on Government: The Example of Spain." *Journal of Economic History* 27, no. 3 (1967): 340.

Kennedy, Paul M. *The Rise and Fall of the Great Powers: Economic Change and Military Conflict from 1500 to 2000*. New York: Random House, 1987.

Keller, Morton. "Debt: The Shame of Cities and States." *Policy Review* 169 (October 1, 2011). http://www.hoover.org/publications/policy-review/article/93501.

Kitsantonis, Niki, and Rachel Donadio. "Athens Shaken by Riots after Vote for Austerity." *New York Times*, February 13, 2012. http://www.nytimes .com/2012/02/14/world/europe/athens-shaken-by-riots-after-vote-for-greek -austerity-plan.html, accessed August 22, 2012.

Krugman, Paul. "The Myth of Asia's Miracle," *Foreign Affairs* (November-December, 1994). http://www.foreignaffairs.com/articles/50550/paul-krug man/the-myth-of-asias-miracle).

Kupchan, Charles A. "Empire, Military Power, and Economic Decline." Review of *The Rise and Fall of the Great Powers*, by Paul Kennedy. *International Security* 13 (Spring 1989): 36–53.

Lachmann, Richard. "Elite Self-Interest and Economic Decline in Early Modern Europe." *American Sociological Review* 68, no. 3 (2003): 346–72.

Landes, David. *The Wealth and Poverty of Nations: Why Some Are So Rich and Some So Poor*. New York: W. W. Norton & Company, 1998.

Levathes, Louise. *When China Ruled the Seas: The Treasure Fleet of the Dragon Throne, 1405–1433*. Oxford: Oxford University Press, 1997.

Library of Economics and Liberty. "Keynesian Economics." http://www.econlib .org/library/Enc/KeynesianEconomics.html, accessed July 23, 2012.

Lin, Judy. "Analyst Agrees Brown's Calif. Budget In Balance." Associated Press, http://bigstory.ap.org/article/analyst-agrees-browns-calif-budget-balance, accessed February 12, 2013.

Lipscomb, Andrew A., and Albert Bergh, eds. *The Writings of Thomas Jefferson*. Memorial Edition. Washington, D.C.: Thomas Jefferson Memorial Association of the United States, 1903.

Luttwak, Edward. *The Grand Strategy of the Roman Empire from the First Century A.D. to the Third*. Baltimore: Johns Hopkins University Press, 1976.

Lynch, Megan Suzanne. "Budget Process Reform: Proposals and Legislative Actions in 2012." Washington, D.C.: Congressional Research Service, R42383, March 2, 2012.

Maddison, Angus. *The World Economy*. Paris: Organisation for Economic Cooperation and Development, 2006.

McCloskey, Deirdre. *Bourgeois Dignity: Why Economics Can't Explain the Modern World*. Chicago: University of Chicago Press, 2011.

McGraw-Hill. "S&P/Case-Shiller Home Price Indices." http://www.standardand poors.com/indices/sp-case-shiller-home-price-indices/en/us/?indexId=spusa -cashpidff—p-us—, accessed October 30, 2012.

McQuillan, Lawrence J., Michael T. Maloney, Eric Daniels, and Brent M. Eastwood. U.S. Economic Freedom Index: 2008 Report. San Francisco: Pacific Research Institute, 2008.

Miller, Terry, Kim R. Holmes, and Edwin J. Feulner. 2012 Index of Economic Freedom. Washington, D.C.: Heritage Foundation, 2012.

Mischel, Walter, Yuichi Shoda, and Philip K. Peake. "The Nature of Adolescent Competencies Predicted by Preschool Delay of Gratification." *Journal of Personality and Social Psychology* 54 (1988): 687–96.

Mokyr, Joel. *The Lever of Riches: Technological Creativity and Economic Progress*. Oxford: Oxford University Press, 1992.

Munkhammar, Johnny. "The Swedish Model: It's the Free-Market Reforms, Stupid." *Wall Street Journal*, January 26, 2011. http://online.wsj.com/article /SB10001424052748704698004576104023432243468.html, accessed February 10, 2011.

Murphy, Cullen. *Are We Rome? The Fall of an Empire and the Fate of America.* Boston: Houghton Mifflin, 2007.

Murphy, Kevin, and Robert Topel. "The Value of Health and Longevity." *Journal of Political Economy* 114 (2006): 871–904. http://www.dartmouth.edu /~jskinner/documents/MurphyTopelJPE.pdf, accessed October 11, 2012.

"New World Order? A Review of *On China*, by Henry Kissinger." Claremont Institute. http://www.claremont.org/publications/crb/id.1884/article_detail .asp, accessed November 5, 2012.

Niskanen, William. "Limiting Government: The Failure of 'Starve the Beast.' " *Cato Journal* 26 (2006): 553–58.

North, Douglass. *Understanding the Process of Economic Change.* Princeton: Princeton University Press, 2010.

North, Douglass C. *Structure and Change in Economic History.* New York: Norton, 1981.

Oertel, Friedrich. "The Economic Life of the Empire." In S. A. Cook, et al., eds., *The Imperial Crisis and Recovery*, 232–81. Vol. 12 of *The Cambridge Ancient History*. London: Cambridge University Press, 1939.

———. "The Economic Unification of the Mediterranean Region: Industry, Trade, and Commerce." In S. A. Cook, F. E. Adcock, and M. P. Charlesworth, eds., *The Augustan Empire, 44 B.C.–A.D. 70*, 382–424. Vol. 10 of *The Cambridge Ancient History*. London: Cambridge University Press, 1934.

The Official NBA Encyclopedia. Ed. Jan Hubbard. 3rd ed. New York: Doubleday, 2000.

Olson, Mancur. *The Rise and Decline of Nations: Economic Growth, Stagflation and Social Rigidities.* New Haven: Yale University Press, 1982.

Ornstein, Norman. "Myths and Realities About the Bipartisan Campaign Reform Act of 2002." Brookings Institution, May 7, 2002, http://www .brookings.edu/research/articles/2002/05/07campaignfinancereform-mann, accessed October 11, 2012.

Ornstein, Norman, and Thomas Mann. *It's Even Worse Than It Looks.* New York: Basic Books, 2012.

Pamuk, Sevket. "The Evolution of Financial Institutions in the Ottoman Empire, 1600–1914." *Financial History Review* 11, no. 1 (2004): 7–32.

———. "Institutional Change and the Longevity of the Ottoman Empire, 1500–1800." *Journal of Interdisciplinary History* 35, no.2 (2004): 225–47.

Pense, Alan W. "The Decline and Fall of the Roman Denarius." *Materials Characterization* 29 (September 1992): 213–22.

Peterson-Pew Commission on Budget Reform. "Tied to the Mast: Fiscal Rules and Their Uses." Washington, D.C., December 13, 2011, http://budgetreform.org /document/tied-mast-fiscal-rules-and-their-uses, accessed October 15, 2012.

Pomeranz, Kenneth. *The Great Divergence: China, Europe, and the Making of the Modern World Economy*. Princeton: Princeton University Press, 2000.

Pozen, Robert C. "Japan Can Rebuild on New Economic Foundations." Brookings Institution, March 22, 2011. http://www.brookings.edu/research /opinions/2011/03/21-japan-rebuild-pozen.

"Prisoner's Dilemma." *Stanford Encyclopedia of Philosophy*. Last modified October 22, 2007. http://plato.stanford.edu/entries/prisoner-dilemma/.

Rajan, Raguram, and Luigi Zingales. "The Persistence of Underdevelopment: Institutions, Human Capital, or Constituencies?" National Bureau of Economic Research, Working Paper No. 12093, March 2006.

Rauch, Jonathan. *Government's End: Why Washington Stopped Working*. New York: Public Affairs, 1999.

Reinhart, Carmen M., and Kenneth Rogoff. *This Time Is Different*. Princeton: Princeton University Press, 2009.

Reischauer, Edwin O. *Japan: the Story of a Nation*. New York: Alfred A. Knopf, 1970.

Ridley, Matt. *The Rational Optimist*. New York: HarperCollins, 2010.

Romer, Christina D., and David H. Romer. "Do Tax Cuts Starve the Beast? The Effect of Tax Changes on Government Spending." Brookings Papers on Economic Activity (2009): 139–214.

Rostovtzeff, Mikhail. *The Social and Economic History of the Roman Empire*. Oxford: Clarendon Press, 1957.

Rostow, W. W. "Beware of Historians Bearing False Analogies." Review of *The Rise and Fall of the Great Powers*, by Paul Kennedy. *Foreign Affairs* 66 (Spring 1988): 863–68.

Saha, Brigadier Subrata. "China's Grand Strategy: From Confucius to Contemporary." Strategy Research Project, U.S. Army War College, http://www.dtic .mil/cgi-bin/GetTRDoc?AD=ADA518303, accessed August 5, 2012.

Saxonhouse, Gary, and Robert Stern, eds. *Japan's Lost Decade: Origins, Consequences and Prospects for Recovery*. World Economy Special Issues. Oxford: Blackwell, 2004.

Shelton, Jo-Ann. *As the Romans Did: A Sourcebook in Roman Social History*. New York: Oxford University Press, 1998.

Shigenori Shiratsuka. "Asset Price Bubble in Japan in the 1980s: Lessons for Financial and Macroeconomic Stability." Institute for Monetary and Economic Studies, Bank of Japan, Discussion Paper No. 2003-E-15, December 2003. http://www.imes.boj.or.jp/english/publication/edps/2003/03-E-15.pdf, accessed July 20, 2012.

Siegel, Fred, and Joel Kotkin. "The New Authoritarianism." *City Journal* 31 (Autumn 2011).

Simmons, Bill. *The Book of Basketball: The NBA According to the Sports Guy*. New York: Ballantine Books. 2009.

Sullivan, George. *All About Basketball*. New York: G.P. Putnam and Sons, 1991.

Tax Foundation. U.S. Federal Individual Income Tax Rates History, 1913–2011 (Nominal and Inflation-Adjusted Brackets). Washington, D.C., September 9, 2011. http://taxfoundation.org/article/us-federal-individual-income-tax-rates -history-1913-2011-nominal-and-inflation-adjusted-brackets, accessed October 11, 2012.

Thurow, Lester C. *Head to Head: the Coming Economic Battle Among Japan, Europe, and America*. New York: Morrow, 1992.

Trende, Sean. "What Has Made Congress More Polarized?" RealClearPolitics, May 11, 2012. http://www.realclearpolitics.com/articles/2012/05/11/what _has_made_congress_more_polarized-3.html, accessed October 11, 2012.

Tullock, Gordon, Arthur Seldon, and Gordon L. Brady. *Government Failure: A Primer in Public Choice*. Washington, D.C.: Cato Institute, 2002.

U.S. Bureau of the Census. Population Division. "California: Population of the Counties by Decennial Census: 1900 to 1990." http://www.census.gov /population/cencounts/ca190090.txt.

Van Doren, Charles. *The History of Knowledge*. New York: Birch Lane Press, 1991.

Volcker, Paul, and Richard Ravitch. Report of the State Budget Crisis Task Force, July 17, 2012. http://www.statebudgetcrisis.org/wpcms/wp-content /images/Report-of-the-State-Budget-Crisis-Task-Force-Full.pdf, accessed October 11, 2012.

VoteView. "The Polarization of the Congressional Parties." Last modified May 10, 2012. http://voteview.com/political_polarization.asp, accessed October 3, 2012.

Ward-Perkin, Bryan. *The Fall of Rome and the End of Civilization*. Oxford: Oxford University Press, 2005.

Wennekers, Sander, André van Stel, Martin Carree, and Roy Thurik. *The Relationship Between Entrepreneurship and Economic Development: Is It U-Shaped?* Hanover, MA: Now, 2010.

West, Patrick. "The New Ireland Kicks Ass." *New Statesman*, June 17, 2002, http://www.newstatesman.com/node/143189, accessed July 17, 2012.

"Why Pay Taxes?" Identity Economics. http://identityeconomics.org/research /why-pay-taxes/, accessed July 23, 2012.

World Bank. *The East Asian Miracle: Economic Growth and Public Policy*. New York: Oxford University Pres, 1993.

Yglesias, Matt. "Licensed to Decorate," *Slate.com*. May 21, 2012. http://www .slate.com/blogs/moneybox/2012/05/21/licensed_to_decorate.html.

————. "Nobody Knows Where Economic Growth Comes From," *Slate.com*. August 6, 2012. http://www.slate.com/blogs/moneybox/2012/08/06/nobody_knows_where_economic_growth_comes_from.html.

Zakaria, Fareed. *The Post-American World: And the Rise of the Rest*. New York: Norton, 2008.

NOTES

1. INTRODUCTION

1   Angus Maddison, *The World Economy* (Paris: Organization for Economic Co-operation and Development, 2006).

2   Paul Kennedy, *The Rise and Fall of Great Powers* (New York: Vintage Books, 1987).

3   Francis Fukuyama, *The End of History and the Last Man* (New York: Free Press, 1992).

4   Carmen Reinhart and Kenneth Rogoff, *This Time Is Different* (Princeton: Princeton University Press, 2009).

5   See NFL.com History, http://statistic.nfl.com/static/content/public/image/history/pdfs/History/Chronology-2011.pdf.

6   Daron Acemoglu and James Robinson, *Why Nations Fail: The Origins of Power, Prosperity, and Poverty* (New York: Crown, 2012).

7   Congressional Budget Office, *The 2012 Long-Term Budget Outlook* (Washington, D.C.: Government Printing Office, June 5, 2012), p. 19.

8   See Dagmar Hartwig Lojsch, Marta Rodríguez-Vives, and Michal Slavík, "The Size and Composition of Debt in the Euro Area," European Central Bank, Occasional Paper Series, October 2011, http://www.ecb.europa.eu/pub/pdf/scpops/ecbocp132.pdf.

9   "CBO's 2011 Long-Term Budget Outlook," http://cbo.gov/doc.cfm?index=12212.

10 Ibid.

11 Jim Morrison, "The Early History of Football's Forward Pass," http://www.smithsonianmag.com/history-archaeology/The-Early-History-of-Footballs-Forward-Pass.html (December 8, 2011).

12 Fox News poll, June 30, 2011 (72–20 percent favoring); Mason-Dixon poll, May 2011 (65–25 percent favoring).

2. THE ECONOMICS OF GREAT POWER

1   Lester Thurow, "Money Wars: Why Europe Will 'Own' the 21st Century," *Washington Post*, April 19, 1992.

2   Robert Kagan, *The World America Made* (New York: Knopf, 2012).

3   Paul Kennedy, *The Rise and Fall of the Great Powers* (New York: Vintage Books, 1987), p. xxii.

4   Murray Rothbard, *Economic Thought Before Adam Smith: An Austrian Perspective on the History of Economic Thought*, vol. 1 (Mises Institute, 2006), http://mises.org/daily/4694, accessed June 13, 2012.

5   William Petty, *Political Arithmetik* (Nottingham: Whitehall, 1690), preface.

6   See Madisson's prologue to *The World Economy*, vol. 2, *Historical Statistics* (Paris: Organisation for Economic Co-operation and Development, 2003).

7   Simon Kuznets, *National Income, 1929–1932* (Cambridge, MA: National Bureau of Economic Research, 1934), pp. 1–12.

8   "GDP: One of the Great Inventions of the 20th Century," Bureau of Economic Analysis, http://www.bea.gov/scb/account_articles/general/0100od/maintext.htm, accessed June 11, 2012. See also "On the Difference Between GDP and GNP," A (Budding) Sociologist's Commonplace Book (blog), http://asociologist.com/2012/04/30/on-the-difference-between-gnp-and-gdp/, accessed June 13, 2012.

9   "The Bretton Woods Conference, 1944," U.S. Department of State, Office of the Historian, http://history.state.gov/milestones/1937–1945/Bretton Woods, accessed June 11, 2012.

10 Richard A. Easterlin, review of *Modern Economic Growth: Rate, Structure, and Spread*, by Simon Kuznets, last modified October 28, 2001, http://eh.net/book_reviews/modern-economic-growth-rate-structure-and-spread, accessed June 11, 2013.

11 For a discussion of national income accounting for measuring economic activity, see R. Glenn Hubbard and Anthony P. O'Brien, *Economics*, 4th ed. (Boston: Pearson, 2013).

12 Edward Glaeser, "Pick a President to Save the U.S. From Greece's Fate," Bloomberg.com, July 25, 2012, http://www.bloomberg.com/news/2012-07-25/pick-a-president-to-save-the-u-s-from-greece-s-fate.html, accessed July 26, 2012.

13 "The International Comparison of Prices Program (ICP)," Center for International Comparisons, http://pwt.econ.upenn.edu/icp.html, accessed February 5, 2013.

14 Penn World Table 7.0 describes the series "rgdpch" which is "PPP Converted GDP Per Capita (Chain Series), at 2005 constant prices."

15 Angus Maddison, *The World Economy* (Paris: Organisation for Economic Co-operation and Development, 2006).

16 This table is taken from Maddison, Table 2-30, 114, which in the original includes "Britain" in the header and "United Kingdom" in the left column. International dollars are equivalent to U.S. dollars, but applied to goods prices in any country by transforming values using purchasing power parity.

17 Daniel Gross, "Myth of Decline: U.S. Is Stronger and Faster than Anywhere Else," *Newsweek*, May 7, 2012, http://www.thedailybeast.com /newsweek/2012/04/29/myth-of-decline-u-s-is-stronger-and-faster-than -anywhere-else.html, accessed June 25, 2012.

18 Thomas Friedman, *That Used to Be Us: How America Fell Behind in the World It Invented and How We Can Come Back* (New York: Farrar, Straus & Giroux, 2011).

19 Patrick Buchanan, *Suicide of a Superpower: Will America Survive to 2025?* (New York: St. Martin's Press, 2011).

20 Science Advisory Committee, *Deterrence and Survival in the Nuclear Age* (Washington, D.C.: U.S. Government Printing Office, 1957), http://www.gwu .edu/~nsarchiv/NSAEBB/NSAEBB139/nitze02.pdf, accessed June 28, 2012.

21 George Kennan, "The Sources of Soviet Conflict," *Foreign Affairs* 25 (1947): 566–82.

22 Steven Rosefielde, "The Riddle of Post-War Russian Economic Growth: Statistics Lied and Were Misconstrued," *Europe-Asia Studies* 55 (2003): 469–81, http://www.jstor.org.library.lausys.georgetown.edu/stable/3594609, accessed June 28, 2012.

23 Lester Thurow, *Head to Head: The Coming Economic Battle Among Japan, Europe, and America* (New York: William Morrow, 1992), pp. 115–16.

24 James Fallows, "Looking at the Sun," *Atlantic*, November 1993.

25 Ibid., p. 441.

26 Matt Yglesias, "Nobody Knows Where Economic Growth Comes From," *Slate*, August 6, 2012, http://www.slate.com/blogs/moneybox/2012/08/06 /nobody_knows_where_economic_growth_comes_from.html.

27 A 1996 econometric study in the *Quarterly Journal of Economics* (vol. 111, pp. 269–73) by Magnus Blomstrom, Robert E. Lipsey, and Mario Zejan used a technique known as Granger-causality to assess which variable was leading the other. Their important result affirmed the primacy of intangible policies over tangible ingredients in the real world.

28 See Jared Diamond, "What Makes Countries Rich or Poor?" *New York Review of Books*, June 7, 2012, http://www.nybooks.com/articles

/archives/2012/jun/07/what-makes-countries-rich-or-poor/?pagination
=false.

29 Charles A. Kupchan, "Empire, Military Power, and Economic Decline,"
review of *The Rise and Fall of the Great Powers*, by Paul Kennedy, *International Security* 13 (Spring 1989): 36–53.

30 W. W. Rostow, "Beware of Historians Bearing False Analogies," review of
The Rise and Fall of the Great Powers, by Paul Kennedy, *Foreign Affairs*
66 (Spring 1988): 863–68.

31 Kennedy, *The Rise and Fall of the Great Powers*, p. 433.

32 Alan Ingham, review of *The Rise and Fall of the Great Powers*, by Paul
Kennedy, *Economic Journal* 99 (December 1989): 1221–22.

33 Anthony Giddens, Michael Mann, and Immanuel Wallerstein, review of
The Rise and Fall of the Great Powers, by Paul Kennedy, *British Journal of
Sociology* 40 (June 1989): 328–40.

34 Brink Lindsey, "Paul Krugman and the Unbearable Lameness of Partisanship," October 31, 2007, http://www.brinklindsey.com/?p=136.

35 Niall Ferguson, "Gloating China, Hidden Problems," *Real Clear Politics*,
January 9, 2012, http://www.realclearpolitics.com/articles/2012/01/09
/chinas_coming_slump__112684.html.

36 Robert Samuelson, "Is China No. 1?" *Washington Post*, March 8, 2012,
http://articles.washingtonpost.com/2012-03-07/opinions/35450320_1
_chinese-gdp-capita-income-arvind-subramanian, accessed July 28, 2012.

37 Thomas L. Friedman, "Is China the Next Enron?" *New York Times*, January 13, 2010, http://www.nytimes.com/2010/01/13/opinion/13friedman
.html.

38 Paul Krugman, "China Goes to Nixon," *New York Times*, January 20,
2011, http://www.nytimes.com/2011/01/21/opinion/21krugman.html?_r=0.

39 One of the differences is the sudden inclusion of Germany, which the PWT
does not record before East and West Germany were rejoined.

40 The equation converts the GDP growth rate so that 4 percent is treated
as 4, not 0.04. Also, the growth term is set to a minimum of 0.2, as in
Growth = Maximum (Growth, 0.2).

41 Gregg Easterbrook, *The Progress Paradox: How Life Gets Better While
People Feel Worse* (New York: Random House, 2004), p. 82.

42 Matt Ridley, *The Rational Optimist* (New York: HarperCollins, 2010),
p. 311.

3. ECONOMIC BEHAVIOR AND INSTITUTIONS

1 Gerd Gigerenzer and Reinhard Selten, *Bounded Rationality: The Adaptive
Toolbox* (Cambridge, Mass.: MIT Press, 2002), p. 37.

2   "Prisoner's Dilemma," *Stanford Encyclopedia of Philosophy*, last modified October 22, 2007, http://plato.stanford.edu/entries/prisoner-dilemma/.

3   "All Prizes in Economic Sciences," Nobelprize.org, accessed July 23, 2012, http://www.nobelprize.org/nobel_prizes/economics/laureates/.

4   R. Glenn Hubbard and Anthony O'Brien, *Economics*, 4th ed. (Boston: Pearson, 2013), p. 327.

5   Gordon Tullock, Arthur Seldon, and Gordon L. Brady, *Government Failure: A Primer in Public Choice* (Washington, D.C.: Cato Institute, 2002), pp. 6–7.

6   Patrick West, "The New Ireland Kicks Ass," *New Statesman*, June 17, 2002, http://www.newstatesman.com/node/143189, accessed July 17, 2012.

7   George Akerlof and Rachel Kranton, *Identity Economics* (Princeton: Princeton University Press, 2010), p. 6.

8   "Why Pay Taxes?," Identity Economics, http://identityeconomics.org/research/why-pay-taxes/, accessed July 23, 2012.

9   Francis Fukuyama, *The Origins of Political Order* (New York: Farrar, Straus & Giroux, 2011), p. 440.

10 Walter Mischel, Yuichi Shoda, and Philip K. Peake, "The Nature of Adolescent Competencies Predicted by Preschool Delay of Gratification," *Journal of Personality and Social Psychology* 54 (1988): 687–96

11 Daniel Kahneman, *Thinking, Fast and Slow* (New York: Farrar, Straus & Giroux, 2011), p. 5.

12 Ibid., pp. 286–87.

13 "Keynesian Economics," Library of Economics and Liberty, http://www.econlib.org/library/Enc/KeynesianEconomics.html, accessed July 23, 2012.

14 Howard Hobson, *Scientific Basketball* (New York: Prentice-Hall, 1949), pp. 104–105.

15 George Sullivan, *All About Basketball* (New York: G. P. Putnam's Sons, 1991), p. 41.

16 "Michael Jordan," *The Official NBA Encyclopedia*, ed. Jan Hubbard, 3rd ed. (New York: Doubleday, 2000), p. 100.

17 Justin Kubatko, "Keeping Score: The Story Arc of the 3-Point Shot," *New York Times*, February 10, 2011, http://offthedribble.blogs.nytimes.com/2011/02/10/keeping-score-the-story-arc-of-the-3-point-shot/, accessed July 23, 2012.

18 Hobson, *Scientific Basketball*, p. 121.

19 Douglass C. North, *Structure and Change in Economic History* (New York: Norton, 1981), p. 201.

20 Raghuram Rajan and Luigi Zingales, "The Persistence of Underdevelopment: Institutions, Human Capital, or Constituencies?" National Bureau of Economic Research, Working Paper No. 12093, March 2006.

21   Anne O. Krueger, "The Political Economy of the Rent-Seeking Society,"
     American Economic Review 64, no. 3 (June, 1974): 291–303.
22   See also R. Glenn Hubbard and William Duggan, *The Aid Trap* (New
     York: Columbia University Press, 2009).

4. THE RUIN OF ROME

1   Joel Mokyr, *The Lever of Riches: Technological Creativity and Economic
     Progress* (Oxford: Oxford University Press, 1992), p. 20.
 2   Angus Maddison, *Contours of the World Economy, 1–2020 AD: Essays
     in Macro-Economic History* (Oxford: Oxford University Press, 2007),
     pp. 43–47, 50, table 1.10; 54, table 1.12.
 3   See section 5 of Walter Scheidel, "Roman Population Size: The Logic of
     the Debate," version 2.0, July 2007, http://www.princeton.edu/~pswpc
     /pdfs/scheidel/070706.pdf, accessed August 10, 2012.
 4   Cullen Murphy, *Are We Rome? The Fall of an Empire and the Fate of
     America* (Boston: Houghton Mifflin, 2007), citing Cassius Dio, *Roman
     History,* 56. 18–24, trans. H. B. Foster.
 5   Josephus, *A History of the Jewish War* 3.71–97, 104, 105, 107, 108, quoted
     in *As the Romans Did: A Sourcebook in Roman Social History*, ed. Jo-Ann
     Shelton, 2nd ed. (New York: Oxford University Press, 1998), p. 253.
 6   Peter Garnsey and Richard Saller, *The Roman Empire: Economy, Society
     and Culture* (Berkeley: University of California Press, 1987), p. 26.
 7   Murphy, *Are We Rome?,* p. 99.
 8   Gregory Clark, *A Farewell to Alms* (Princeton: Princeton University Press,
     2007), p. 305.
 9   Murphy, *Are We Rome?,* p. 16.
10   Cicero, *An Essay About Duties* 1.42, 2.25, quoted in Shelton, ed., *As the
     Romans Did*, pp. 125–26.
11   Mokyr, *Lever of Riches*, p. 29
12   Isaacson, "The Empire in the Mirror," *New York Times*, May 13, 2007.
     http://www.nytimes.com/2007/05/13/books/review/Isaacson-t.html?_r=0.
13   Sungmin Hong, Jean-Pierre Candelone, Clair C. Patterson, and Claude
     F. Boutron, "Greenland Ice Evidence of Hemispheric Lead Pollution Two
     Millennia Ago by Greek and Roman Civilizations," *Science* 265, no. 5180
     (1994): 1841–43.
14   Bryan Ward-Perkins, *The Fall of Rome and the End of Civilization* (Ox-
     ford: Oxford University Press), 2005. p. 124.
15   Bruce Bartlett, "How Excessive Government Killed Ancient Rome," *Cato
     Journal* 14 (1994), http://www.cato.org/pubs/journal/cjv14n2-7.html.
16   See Murphy, *Are We Rome?,* pp. 78–83.

17   Mike Duncan, History of Rome podcast number 82.

18   Mikhail Rostovtzeff, 1957. *The Social and Economic History of the Roman Empire* (Oxford: Clarendon Press), p. 54.

19   Edward Gibbon, J. B. Bury, and Giovanni Battista Piranesi, *The History of the Decline & Fall of the Roman Empire* (New York: Heritage Press, 1946), chapter 5, part II.

20   Alan Pense, "The Decline and Fall of the Roman Denarius," *Materials Characterization*, 1992, p. 213–222.

21   See A. H. M. Jones, "Ancient Empires and the Economy: Rome," *Third International Conference of Economic History*, 1965 (The Hague: Mouton, 1970), pp. 81–104, reprinted in A. H. M. Jones, *The Roman Economy: Studies in Ancient Economic and Administrative History* (Totowa, N.J.: Rowman & Littlefield, 1974), pp. 114–39.

22   Will Durant and Ariel Durant, *The Lessons of History* (New York: Simon & Schuster, 1968), p. 60.

23   A good summary of Diocletian's economy is provided by Mike Duncan's *The History of Rome* podcast #127, "Commanding the Economy."

24   Murphy, *Are We Rome?*, p. 47.

25   Garnsey and Saller, *The Roman Empire*, p. 21.

5. TREASURE OF CHINA

1   Paul Kennedy, *The Rise and Fall of the Great Powers* (New York: Vintage Books, 1987), p. 7.

2   Originally cited in Joel Mokyr, *The Lever of Riches: Technological Creativity and Economic Progress* (Oxford: Oxford University Press, 1992), p. 236.

3   "Confucius," *Stanford Encyclopedia of Philosophy*, http://plato.stanford.edu/entries/confucius/.

4   William Baumol, *The Free-Market Innovation Machine* (Princeton: Princeton University Press, 2002), pp. 255–56.

5   Ibid., p. 254.

6   "Confucius," *Stanford Encyclopedia of Philosophy*, http://plato.stanford.edu/entries/confucius/.

7   "Battle for Mongolia's soul," *Economist*, December 19, 2006, http://www.economist.com/node/8401179.

8   "Genghis Khan: Law and Order," *Los Angeles Times*, December 29, 2006, http://www.latimes.com/news/la-oe-weather29dec29,0,7853812.story.

9   Joel Mokyr, *Lever of Riches*, p. 231

10   Ibid., pp. 209–10.

11   Ibid.

12   Louise Levathes, *When China Ruled the Seas: The Treasure Fleet of the Dragon Throne, 1405–1433* (Oxford: Oxford University Press, 1997), p. 43.

13   Ibid., p. 49.

14   Ibid., p. 88.

15   Matt Ridley, p. 183.

16   Levathes, p. 163.

17   Ibid., p. 175.

18   David Landes, *The Wealth and Poverty of Nations: Why Some Are So Rich and Some So Poor* (W. W. Norton & Company, 1998), p. 341.

19   Joel Mokyr, *Lever of Riches*, p. 234.

20   Francis Fukuyama, *The Origins of Political Order* (New York: Farrar, Straus & Giroux, 2011), p. 315.

6. THE SUN FADES ON SPAIN

1   Henry Kamen, "The Decline of Spain: A Historical Myth?" *Past and Present* 81 (1978): 41.

2   Kennedy, *The Rise and Fall of the Great Powers* (New York: Vintage Books, 1987), pp. 31, 45–48, 53–56.

3   Earl J. Hamilton, "Revisions in Economic History: Viii—The Decline of Spain," *Economic History Review* 8 (1938): 168–79, at 171.

4   Kennedy, *The Rise and Fall of the Great Powers*, p. 41.

5   Dennis O. Flynn, "Fiscal Crisis and the Decline of Spain (Castile)," *Journal of Economic History* 42 (1982): 139.

6   Carmen Reinhart and Kenneth Rogoff, *This Time Is Different* (Princeton: Princeton University Press, 2009), Table 12.1, p. 183.

7   Daron Acemoglu and James Robinson, *Why Nations Fail: The Origins of Power, Posterity, and Poverty* (New York: Crown, 2012), p. 219.

8   Hamilton, "Revisions in Economic History: Viii—The Decline of Spain."

9   Ibid., pp. 178–79.

10   Robin M. Grier, "Colonial Legacies and Economic Growth," *Public Choice* 98 (1999): 317–35.

11   Douglass North discusses this in *Structure and Change in Economic History* (New York: Norton, 1981), pp. 148–54.

12   Ibid., p. 151.

13   Richard Lachmann, "Elite Self-Interest and Economic Decline in Early Modern Europe," *American Sociological Review* 68, no. 3 (2003): 350.

14   Francis Fukuyama, *The Origins of Political Order* (New York: Farrar, Straus & Giroux, 2011), p. 358.

7. RULE OF SLAVES: THE OTTOMAN PARADOX

1   Charles Van Doren, *A History of Knowledge* (New York: Birch Lane Press, 1991), p. 4.
2   Paul Kennedy, *The Rise and Fall of the Great Powers* (New York: Vintage Books, 1987), p. 11.
3   Sevket Pamuk, "Institutional Change and the Longevity of the Ottoman Empire, 1500–1800," *Journal of Interdisciplinary History* 35, no. 2 (2004): 225–47.
4   Amy Chua, *Day of Empire: How Hyperpowers Rise to Global Dominance— and Why They Fall* (New York: Doubleday, 2007), pp. 170–71.
5   Ibid., p. 175.
6   Francis Fukuyama, *The Origins of Political Order* (New York: Farrar, Straus & Giroux, 2011), p. 227.
7   Niccolò Machiavelli, *The Prince*, chapter 4. This passage is cited in Fukuyama's *The Origins of Political Order*, p. 214.
8   Sevket Pamuk, *Institutional Change*, p. 234.
9   Ibid.
10   This paragraph owes much to the research of Sevket Pamuk's published papers.
11   L. Moore and J. Kaluzny, "Regime Change and Debt Default: The Case of Russia, Austro-Hungary, and the Ottoman Empire Following World War One," *Explorations in Economic History* 42 (2005): 237–58.

8. JAPANESE OPENING

1   Edwin O. Reischauer, *Japan: The Story of a Nation* (Tokyo: Tuttle, 1995), p. 7.
2   Ibid., pp. 74–86.
3   Ibid., p. 79.
4   Angus Maddison, *The World Economy: A Millennial Perspective* (Paris: Organisation for Economic Co-operation and Development, 2001), p. 140.
5   Ibid., p. 118.
6   Daron Acemoglu and James Robinson, *Why Nations Fail: The Origins of Power, Posterity, and Poverty* (New York: Crown, 2012), p. 297.
7   Angus Maddison, *The World Economy: A Millennial Perspective* (Paris: Organisation for Economic Co-operation and Development, 2001), p. 140.
8   See Francis Fukuyama, *Trust: The Social Virtues and the Creation of Prosperity* (New York: Free Press, 1995), p. 162, which cites data from Masaru Yoshimori, "Sources of Japanese Competitiveness, Part I," *Management Japan* 25 (1992): 18–23.

9   See Paul Krugman, "The Myth of Asia's Miracle," *Foreign Affairs* (November/
     December 1994), http://www.foreignaffairs.com/articles/50550/paul-krugman
     /the-myth-of-asias-miracle.

10   Michael Hirsh and E. Keith Henry, "The Unraveling of Japan Inc.: Mul-
     tinationals as Agents of Change," *Foreign Affairs*, March 1, 1997, http://
     www.foreignaffairs.com/articles/52857/michael-hirsh-and-e-keith-henry
     /the-unraveling-of-japan-inc-multinationals-as-agents-of-change, accessed
     November 10, 2012.

11   Brian Bremner, William Glasgall, and Peter Galuszka, "Two Japans,"
     BusinessWeek, January 27, 1997, http://www.businessweek.com/1997/04
     /970127.htm.

12   Martin Feldstein, "Japan's Saving Crisis," *Project Syndicate*, September 24,
     2010,   http://www.project-syndicate.org/commentary/japan-s-savings
     -crisis.

13   Martin Fackler, "Japan Goes from Dynamic to Disheartened," *New York
     Times*, October 16, 2010, p. A1.

9. BRITISH DECIMATION

1   Niall Ferguson, *Empire: The Rise and Demise of the British World Order
     and the Lessons for Global Power* (London: Allen Lane, 2002), p. 248.

2   Deirdre McCloskey, *Bourgeois Dignity: Why Economics Can't Explain
     the Modern World* (Chicago: University of Chicago Press, 2011).

3   Daron Acemoglu and James Robinson, *Why Nations Fail: The Origins of
     Power, Posterity, and Poverty* (New York: Crown, 2012), p. 210.

4   Aaron Friedberg, *The Weary Titan: Britain and the Experience of Relative
     Decline, 1895–1905* (Princeton: Princeton University Press, 1988), p. 79.

5   Linda Colley, "Britishness and Otherness: An Argument," *Journal of Brit-
     ish Studies* 31 (1992): 324.

6   William Pitt, "On an Address to the Throne, in Which the Right of Taxing
     America is Discussed" (speech, House of Commons, London, England,
     January 14, 1766), Classic Persuasion, http://www.classicpersuasion.org
     /cbo/chatham/chat08.htm.

7   William Pitt, *Correspondence of William Pitt, Earl of Chatham* (London:
     John Murray, 1838), p. 433.

8   Basil Williams, "Chatham and the Representation of the Colonies in the
     Imperial Parliament," *English Historical Review* 22 (1907): 756–58.

9   Mancur Olson, *The Rise and Decline of Nations: Economic Growth,
     Stagflation and Social Rigidities* (New Haven: Yale University Press,
     1982), p. 78.

10. EUROPA: UNITY AND DIVERSITY

1 See Bryan Caplan's online "Museum of Communism," http://econfaculty .gmu.edu/bcaplan/museum/musframe.htm, accessed September 7, 2012.

2 All of this analysis is documented in David M. Levy and Sandra J. Peart, "Soviet Growth and American Textbooks," *Journal of Economic Behavior and Organization* 78 (April 2011): 110–25, http://papers.ssrn.com/sol3 /papers.cfm?abstract_id=1517983.

3 Stephen Parente and Edward Prescott, *Barriers to Riches* (Cambridge, Mass.: MIT Press, 2000), p. 2.

4 See Paul Krugman's remarks at the 2012 National Bureau of Economic Research Macroeconomics annual conference, April 20–21, 2012, http://krugman.blogs.nytimes.com/2012/06/24/revenge-of-the-optimum -currency-area/, accessed October 5, 2012.

5 See David Turner and Francesca Spinelli, "Explaining the Interest Rate-Growth Differential Underlying Government Debt Dynamics," Organisation for Economic Co-operation and Development Economics Department, Working Papers No. 919, p. 6 of http://www.oecd-ilibrary .org/docserver/download/fulltext/5kg0k706v2f3.pdf?expires=135152141 7&id=id&accname=guest&checksum=3069930AEBA5851BEB90BC2C1 E5591E1, accessed October 23, 2012.

6 See Paul Belkin, Martin A. Weiss, Rebecca M. Nelson, and Derek E. Mix, "The Eurozone Crisis: Overview and Issues for Congress," Congressional Research Service Report R42377, February 29, 2012.

7 BBC, "Eurozone Crisis Explained," November 27, 2012, http://www.bbc .co.uk/news/business-13798000, accessed December 15, 2012.

8 Martin Wolf, "A Permanent Precedent," *Financial Times*, May 17, 2012. http://www.ft.com/intl/cms/s/0/614df5de-9ffe-11e1-94ba-00144feabdc0 .html#axzz2Kd2oCnAj.

9 See "Acropolis Now," *Economist*, April 29, 2010, http://www.economist .com/node/16009099.

10 J. Bradford DeLong and Lawrence H. Summers, "Fiscal Policy in a Depressed Economy," *Brookings Papers on Economic Activity* (2012).

11 Rebecca M. Nelson, Paul Belkin, Derek E. Mix, Martin A. Weiss, "The Eurozone Crisis: Overview and Issues for Congress," Congressional Research Service, R42377, August 29, 2012.

12 See http://www.doingbusiness.org/~/media/GIAWB/Doing%20Business /Documents/Annual-Reports/English/DB13-Chapters/About-Doing-Business .pdf, p.16.

11. CALIFORNIA DREAMING

1   Benjamin H. Johnson, "Gold Rush, California," *Dictionary of American History*, ed. Stanley I. Kutler, 3rd ed., vol. 4 (New York: Charles Scribner's Sons, 2003), pp. 12–14, *Gale Virtual Reference Library*, August 2012.

2   http://www.dof.ca.gov/html/fs_data/historycaeconomy/20th_century_1900.htm, accessed August 14, 2012, and http://eh.net/encyclopedia/article/bakker.film accessed August 14, 2012.

3   See Adam Nagourney, "Republican Party in California Is Caught in Cycle of Decline," *New York Times*, July 22, 2012, http://www.nytimes.com/2012/07/23/us/politics/california-republicans-seek-a-turnaround.html.

4   See the Pacific Research Institute's Economic Freedom report for details. Regarding the minimum wage, California set its state minimum above the federal level starting in 1988.

5   http://www.governing.com/gov-data/economy-finance/state-debt-per-capita-figures.html.

6   http://www.bea.gov/newsreleases/regional/gdp_state/2012/pdf/gsp0612.pdf.

7   Mike Anton, "O.C. Bounces Back, Frayed at the Edges," *Los Angeles Times*, December 5, 2004, http://articles.latimes.com/2004/dec/05/local/me-ocbust5, accessed July 26, 2012.

8   Michael Lewis, "California *and* Bust," *Vanity Fair,* November 2011, http://www.vanityfair.com/business/features/2011/11/michael-lewis-201111.

9   Hannah Dreier, "Vallejo Bankruptcy: California City Emerges From Financial Disaster," *Huffington Post*, July 22, 2012, http://www.huffingtonpost.com/2012/07/23/vallejo-bankruptcy_n_1693863.html, accessed July 27, 2012.

10 CBS transcript at http://www.cbsnews.com/stories/2010/12/19/60minutes/main7166220.shtml?tag=currentVideoInfo;segmentTitle.

11 Lewis, "California *and* Bust."

12 John Seiler, "Special Series: Local Governments Face Bankruptcy Quandary," Cal Watchdog, March 16, 2012, http://www.calwatchdog.com/2012/03/16/special-series-local-governments-face-bankruptcy-quandary/, accessed July 27, 2012.

13 Autumn Carter, "Making Sense of the Mathematics of California's Pension Liability," Hoover Institution, August 21, 2012, http://www.advancingafreesociety.org/eureka/making-sense-of-the-mathematics-of-californias-pension-liability/.

14 Originally quoted by John Seiler, March 16, 2012, Calwatchdog.com Special Series: Local Governments Face Bankruptcy Quandary, http://

www.calwatchdog.com/2012/03/16/special-series-local-governments-face
-bankruptcy-quandary/.

15 See the Employment Cost Index at http://www.bls.gov/news.release/pdf
/eci.pdf, accessed August 30, 2012.

16 Chris Megerian and Anthony York, "State Deficit Estimate Hits $16 Bil-
lion," *Los Angeles Times*, May 13, 2012, http://articles.latimes.com/2012
/may/13/local/la-me-0513-state-deficit-20120513.

17 "Beyond California: States in Fiscal Peril," Pew Center on the States,
November 11, 2009, http://www.pewstates.org/uploadedFiles/PCS_Assets
/2009/BeyondCalifornia.pdf.

18 Tax Foundation, 2012, http://taxfoundation.org/sites/taxfoundation.org
/files/docs/2012_tax_foundation_index_bp62.pdf.

19 Michael J. Boskin, "California Bad Dreaming," July 25, 2012, http://www
.project-syndicate.org/commentary/california-bad-dreaming.

20 Holman Jenkins, "Our Big Fat Greek Habits," *Wall Street Journal*, August 7, 2012, http://online.wsj.com/article/SB100008723963904436592O
4577575002944563574.html.

21 Jeff Tyler, "California Prison Costs Prompt Reform," *Marketplace*, American Public Media, June 6, 2011, http://www.marketplace.org/topics/life
/california-prison-costs-prompt-reform.

22 Don Thompson, "Gov's Deal Lifts Vacation Cap for CA Prison Guards,"
Bloomberg Businessweek, August 19, 2011, http://www.businessweek
.com/ap/financialnews/D9MMU7S00.htm.

23 Kevin Drum, "California's Ridiculous High Speed Rail Plan," Mother
Jones.com, January 17, 2012, http://www.motherjones.com/kevin-drum
/2012/01/california-hsr-now-even-more-ridiculous.

24 Charles Van Doren, *A History of Knowledge* (New York: Birch Lane Press,
1991), p. 85.

25 Allysia Finley, "The Trials of a Democratic Reformer," *Wall Street Journal*,
September 1–2, 2012, p. A11.

26 See http://www.opensecrets.org/bigpicture/reelect.php, accessed September 18, 2012.

27 See http://www.rasmussenreports.com/public_content/politics/general
_politics/september_2011/71_favor_term_limits_for_congress.

28 An excellent resource on term limits is provided the National Conference
of State Legislatures at http://www.ncsl.org/legislatures-elections/legisdata
/legislative-term-limits-overview.aspx, accessed September 7, 2012.

29 See Marisa Lagos, "Term Limits Measure—Prop. 28-Wins Big," *San Francisco Chronicle*, June 6, 2012 http://www.sfgate.com/politics/article/Term
-limits-measure-Prop-28-wins-big-3612146.php.

30   See Jean Merl, "State's Redrawn Congressional Districts Protect Incumbents," *Los Angeles Times*, February 9, 2002, http://articles.latimes.com /2002/feb/09/local/me-cong9.

31   Judy Lin, "Analyst Agrees Brown's Calif. Budget In Balance," Associated Press, http://bigstory.ap.org/article/analyst-agrees-browns-calif-budget -balance, accessed February 12, 2013.

32   See Jennifer Steinhauer, "Coffers Empty, California Pays with I.O.U.'s," *New York Times*, July 2, 2009, http://www.nytimes.com/2009/07/03/us/03 calif.html?pagewanted=all.

33   Allan Meltzer, a professor of economics at Carnegie Mellon University, wrote these words in an essay explaining the subprime lending crisis in early 2008. See http://american.com/archive/2008/february-02-08/why-the -crisis, accessed September 16, 2012.

12. UNITED STATES BEHIND THE CONSEQUENCE HORIZON

1   See Clive Crook, "Paralysis in Congress Better Than Self-Destruction," Bloomberg.com, November 22, 2011, http://www.bloomberg.com/news /2011-11-23/paralyzed-congress-better-than-self-destruction-commentary -by-clive-crook.html.

2   Catherine Drinker Bowen, *Miracle at Philadelphia* (Boston: Little, Brown, 1986), p. 41.

3   See Tax Foundation, http://taxfoundation.org/article/us-federal-individual -income-tax-rates-history-1913-2011-nominal-and-inflation-adjusted -brackets.

4   The Thomas Jefferson Heritage Society asked a dozen scholars to carefully examine allegations that Thomas Jefferson fathered one or more children by Sally Hemings, one of his slaves. The resulting Scholars Commission issued a detailed report in early 2001 on the issue, updated with new evidence in 2011. All but one member of the commission expressed skepticism of the claim, with some declaring it to be "almost certainly false." See Robert F. Turner, *The Jefferson-Hemings Controversy: Report of the Scholars Commission* (Durham, N.C.: Carolina Academic Press, 2011)

5   See http://voteview.com/political_polarization.asp, accessed October 3, 2012.

6   Royce Carroll, Jeff Lewis, James Lo, Nolan McCarty, Keith Poole, and Howard Rosenthal, "Who Is More Liberal, Senator Obama or Senator Clinton?" working paper, http://voteview.com/Clinton_and_Obama.htm, April 18, 2008.

7   See http://www.theatlanticwire.com/national/2012/03/us-senate-now -completely-polarized/49641/.

8   See http://www.tnr.com/article/the-vital-center/103394/polarization-norm
    -ornstein-republicans-democrats#.

9   See Sean Trende, "What Has Made Congress More Polarized?," May 11,
    2012, http://www.realclearpolitics.com/articles/2012/05/11/what_has_made
    _congress_more_polarized-3.html.

10 See "Are the Republicans Mad?," *Economist*, April 28, 2012, http://www
    .economist.com/node/21553449.

11 David Broder and Haynes Johnson, *The System: The American Way of
    Politics at the Breaking Point* (New York: Little, Brown, 1996), p. 623.

12 See supplemental data table for Figure A-3 in CBO's 2012 Long-Term
    Budget Outlook, available at http://www.cbo.gov/publication/43288.

13 Ibid.

14 See Congressional Budget Office, *Federal Debt and the Risk of a Fiscal
    Crisis*, July 27, 2010, http://www.cbo.gov/publication/21625.

15 See Amy Belasco, *The Cost of Iraq, Afghanistan, and Other Global
    War on Terror Operation Since 9/11*, Congressional Research Service,
    RL33110, March 29, 2011.

16 See Kevin Murphy and Robert Topel, "The Value of Health and Longev-
    ity," *Journal of Political Economy* 114, no. 5 (October 2006), http://www
    .dartmouth.edu/~jskinner/documents/MurphyTopelJPE.pdf.

17 See http://www.imf.org/external/pubs/ft/gfsr/2012/01/pdf/c4.pdf.

18 See John F. Cogan, R. Glenn Hubbard, and Daniel P. Kessler, *Healthy,
    Wealthy, and Wise: Five Steps to a Better Health Care System*, 2nd ed.
    (Stanford, Calif.: Hoover Institution Press, 2011).

19 Cowen spoke these words at the opening of a Mercatus Center sympo-
    sium on January 23, 2012. See http://mercatus.org/publication/us-sovereign
    -debt-crisis-tipping-point-scenarios-and-crash-dynamics/introduction.

20 David Broder, "The Party's Over," *Atlantic*, March 1972, http://www.the
    atlantic.com/past/politics/policamp/partysov.htm.

21 Ibid.

22 Ibid.

23 See, for example, Norman Ornstein, "Myths and Realities About the Bi-
    partisan Campaign Reform Act of 2002," Brookings Institution, May 7,
    2002, http://www.brookings.edu/research/articles/2002/05/07campaign
    financereform-mann.

24 Case No. 08-205. *Citizens United v. Federal Election Committee*. Alderson
    Reporting Company (Supreme Court of the U.S.A., 2009), http://www
    .supremecourt.gov/oral_arguments/argument_transcripts/08-205.pdf, ac-
    cessed June 4, 2012.

13. AMENDING AMERICA

1 See Johnny Munkhammar, "The Swedish Model: It's the Free-Market Reforms, Stupid," *Wall Street Journal*, January 26, 2011, http://online.wsj.com/article/SB10001424052748704698004576104023432243468.html.

2 Robert Solow, "Technical Change and the Aggregate Production Function," *Review of Economic and Statistics* 39 (August 1957): 312–20.

3 See Tyler Cowen, http://marginalrevolution.com/marginalrevolution/2012/10/multiple-equilibria.html.

4 The countries included in the South America region are Argentina, Brazil, and Chile. Europe includes seventeen countries: Belgium, Denmark, Finland, France, Germany, Greece, Iceland, Ireland, Italy, Luxembourg, Netherlands, Norway, Portugal, Spain, Sweden, Switzerland, and the United Kingdom.

5 We assume a convergence growth rate of GDP per capita equal to a base rate of 2 percent per year, multiplied by a natural logarithm of (2.5 times the ratio of U.S. per capita GDP to country per capita GDP). Another ingredient in this forecast is to population growth, because the rate of population growth has declined much faster than expected over the last half century. We assume current population growth rate through 2030 for each individual country.

6 See Kevin Hassett's testimony to the House Ways and Means Committee on January 20, 2011, at http://waysandmeans.house.gov/uploadedfiles/hassett.pdf.

7 See Duanjie Chen and Jack Mintz, "Corporate Tax Competitiveness Rankings for 2012," Cato Institute, September 2012, http://www.cato.org/pubs/tbb/tbb_65.pdf.

8 Sander Wennekers, André van Stel, Martin Carree, and Roy Thurik, "The Relationship Between Entrepreneurship and Economic Development: Is It U-shaped?" *SCALES*, vol. 6, no. 3, July 2009 (Hanover: Now Publishers, 2010). http://www.ices-study.org/WhatIsEnterpreneurship/Research/(knowledge%20web)%20the%20relationship%20between%20enteprenurship%20and%20economic%20development.pdf, accessed February 10, 2013.

9 Matt Yglesias, "Licensed to Decorate," Slate.com, May 20, 2012, 2013, http://hive.slate.com/hive/10-rules-starting-small-business/article/licensed-to-decorate, accessed January 7, 2013.

10 Niki Kitsantonis and Rachel Donadio, "Athens Shaken by Riots after Vote for Austerity," *New York Times*, February 13, 2012, http://www.nytimes.com/2012/02/14/world/europe/athens-shaken-by-riots-after-vote-for-greek-austerity-plan.html.

11   Megan Suzanne Lynch, *Budget Process Reform: Proposals and Legislative Actions in 2012*, Congressional Research Service, R42383, March 2, 2012.

12   Alison Acosta Fraser, "The Broken Budget Process: Legislative Proposals," Testimony before the Committee on the Budget, United States House of Representatives, May 31, 2012.

13   Originally cited in the Peterson-Pew report *Tied to the Mast*, p. 16, quoting Ben S. Bernanke, Remarks at the Annual Meeting of the Rhode Island Public Expenditure Council, Providence, R.I., October 4, 2010.

14   Letter to John Taylor, 1789, in *The Writings of Thomas Jefferson*, Memorial Edition (Lipscomb and Bergh, editors), 20 vols. (Washington, D.C., 1903–04), vol. 10, p. 78.

15   Scott Rogers. "Active Article V BBA Application," Balanced Budget Amendment Task Force. January 11, 2013, http://bba4usa.org/uploads/Active_Article_V_BBA_Applications_as_of_01112013.pdf, accessed February 10, 2013.

16   Bruce Bartlett, "Balanced Budget Amendment a 'Phony' Deficit Solution," *Fiscal Times*, August 27, 2010, http://www.thefiscaltimes.com/Columns/2010/08/27/Balanced-Budget-Amendment-a-Bad-Approach.aspx.

17   Bruce Bartlett, "A Balanced Budget Amendment," *Fiscal Times*, August 27, 2010, http://www.thefiscaltimes.com/Blogs/Bartletts-Notations/2010/08/27/Bartletts-Notations-A-Balanced-Budget-Amendment.aspx.

18   See its "Special Report" at http://www.cbpp.org/archiveSite/bba.htm.

19   Edward Glaeser, "Balanced Budget Suddenly Looks More Appealing," Bloomberg, August 1, 2011, http://www.bloomberg.com/news/2011-08-02/balanced-budget-suddenly-looks-more-appealing-edward-glaeser.html.

INDEX

Page numbers in *italics* refer to illustrations.